M000034771

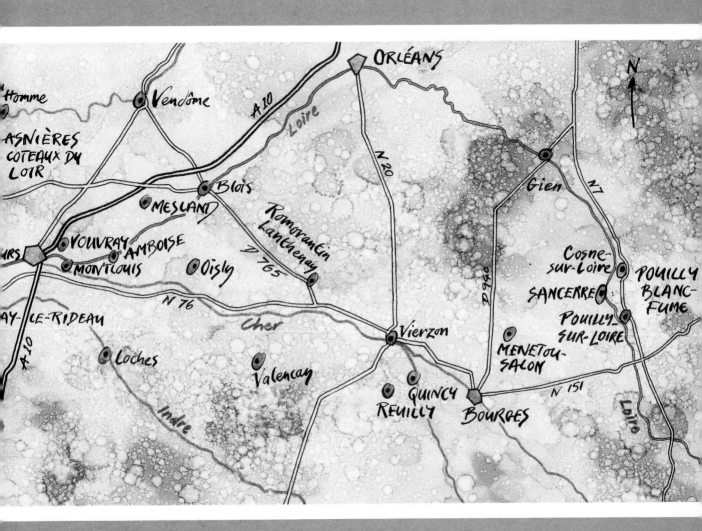

N

Homme

Vendôme

A 10

Loire

ORLÉANS

N 20

Gien

N 7

ASNIÈRES
COTEAUX DU
LOIR

Blois

MESLAND

Romorantin
Lanthenay

D 765

D 940

Cosne-
sur-Loire

POUILLY
BLANC-
FUMÉ

URS

VOUVRAY

MONTLOUIS

AMBOISE

Oisly

SANCERRE

POUILLY-
SUR-LOIRE

N 76

Cher

Vierzon

MENETOU-
SALON

AY-LE-RIDEAU

A 10

Loches

Valençay

Indre

QUINCY

REUILLY

BOURGES

N 151

Loire

THE LOIRE VALLEY
AND ITS WINES

THE
LOIRE VALLEY
AND ITS
WINES

JAMES SEELY

Lennard Publishing
1989

Lennard Publishing
a division of Lennard Books Ltd
Musterlin House, Jordan Hill Road, Oxford OX2 8DP

British Library Cataloguing in Publication Data
Seely, James, 1940–
The Loire valley and its wines.
1. Loire wines
641.2′2′09445

ISBN 1 85291 053 4

First published 1989
© James Seely 1989

This book is copyright under the Berne Convention.
No reproduction without permission. All rights reserved.

Editor Michael Leitch
Designed by Cooper · Wilson
Jacket design by Pocknell & Co
Typesetting by Goodfellow & Egan Ltd
Photographs by Christian Seely, Jonathan Sibley, CIVAS and CIVT
Reproduced, printed and bound in Great Britain by
Butler and Tanner Limited, Frome

Acknowledgement
The author would like to acknowledge
the work of Suzanne Blanchet and
Hubrecht Duijker to which he has
referred in his research for this book.

CONTENTS

The author (centre) enjoys the hospitality of Alphonse Mellot (left) in his cave privée

INTRODUCTION

I must start this book with a shameful confession; during the 30 years that I have spent in the wine trade, I have taken the wines of the Loire for granted. Sandwiched between white Burgundy and the Rhône, they form part of every restaurant and merchant's list. It is a shameful admission, but I am sure that there are other merchants like me, who tend to think of these wines in generic terms – a Sancerre is a Sancerre, likewise Pouilly Fumé, Vouvray, Saumur, Chinon, Muscadet and the rest. As long as the wine is of acceptable quality, little further thought is given to it.

I am not trying to saddle the whole of the wine trade with my own shortcomings. There are a few merchants, whose names cropped up with consistent regularity throughout my travels, especially in the many corners where I found wines of really outstanding quality being made. Men like Robin Yapp of Yapp Brothers in Mere, Wiltshire, Ronnie Hicks of Hicks and Don, and Jeremy Hunt of Thorman-Hunt, all had clearly trodden my path before me. Like me, they have been rewarded, as have their customers, by the astonishing variety, quality and, above all, value that can be obtained from this vast and beautiful vineyard.

Eight months of research have passed like a flash. It has been a voyage of discovery for me, a joy and a privilege. I have learnt much, but am still humbled by my own ignorance and by the enormous knowledge, skill and dedication of the winemakers of this, so rightly named, the Garden of France. My gratitude to these growers cannot be expressed in mere words, but I hope that this record of my travels will serve as a token of my heart-felt appreciation, not only of their expertise and ability, but also of their unstinting generosity and never-failing welcome.

At this point it is fitting that, in addition to my expression of thanks, I should also make my apologies. These are due to the many fine wine-makers whom lack of time and space have prevented me from visiting or including in this book. If you will consider that, in the relatively small *appellation* of Sancerre alone, there are in excess of 500 growers and more than double that number in Touraine, you, and I trust they also, will understand the physical impossibility of visiting them all.

Each section concludes with notes and recommendations on certain hotels and restaurants. Here again I apologise to the undoubtedly numerous restaurateurs and hoteliers who are just as worthy of mention. This book does not set out to be a guide to hostelries, and these are simply my own recommendations based on personal experience.

The same comment applies to places of particular beauty or historic interest that are given mention in my text. The whole area is so rich in châteaux great and small, battlefields, medieval towns and villages and great tracts of lovely country and forest, that whole volumes have been written for the interested visitor. My book is first and foremost for the wine-lover, but he or she, like me, cannot but fall under the magic spell of this incomparably lovely part of France. If you have not already spent some time here, do so soon: if you have, come again.

There are certain people in each region to whom special thanks are due, whose ready assistance and hospitality helped especially to make my task not just possible, but a positive joy. I hope that I can call them friends, and to let this opportunity pass without mentioning their names would be nothing short of churlish.

Starting in the east, my thanks to Patrick, Baron de Ladoucette of Château du Nozet in Pouilly; he allowed me to stay in the château, and gave me invaluable help and many introductions, not least of which was to Jean-Jacques Renaud of St Andelain. This kind and knowledgeable grower and *courtier* (wine broker) took me under his wing, and with him I visited countless growers in both Pouilly and Sancerre.

This leads me naturally on to a special friend, Alphonse Mellot, the uncrowned King of Sancerre. For days I was propelled at breakneck speed in Alphonse's Porsche, Jeep or occasionally the little Peugeot of his wife, Marie-France, around the winding, hilly lanes of Sancerre. We would visit anything up to a dozen growers in a day, sampling white, rosé and red, and sometimes more than one vintage. Alphonse never spits, and there were moments of sheer terror when my British *sang-froid* was sorely tried. I ask Marie-France's pardon for detaching the grab-handle from the roof of her car by its roots. I could not admit the crime at the time for fear of losing my macho image. I hope she forgives me.

In Vouvray I am deeply indebted to Michel Sébéo, the erstwhile general manager of the ancient house of Marc Brédif, now the property of Patrick de Ladoucette. Michel ran Marc Bredif from 1980, when de Ladoucette acquired the company, up to the vintage of 1986, when he left to seek pastures new. In that relatively short time he gained a remarkable knowledge of and love for this much undervalued *appellation*, a knowledge and love that he willingly and convincingly passed on not only to me, but to the many visitors to the cellars in Rochecorbon. He has done much to promote the wines of Vouvray; I hope that success will attend him, and thank him for his friendship and generosity.

Three more growers in Touraine merit a thank-you. Firstly Joel Taluau and Pierre-Jacques Druet in St Nicholas de Bourgueil and Benais, who gave me much of their time and patience; Pierre-Jacques, whose love and enthusiasm for his wines are both fanatic and infectious, was especially kind and taught me much. I am grateful, too, to Gérard Chauveau and his wife, who received me kindly and fed me well in their lovely house near Panzoult in the commune of Chinon.

Extraordinary kindness was also shown to me in Touraine by the Pasquier family, owners of the new Château-Hotel, Château de Rochecotte at St Patrice, near Langeais. I stayed with them for many weeks, and without their friendship and generosity my researches would have been far less enjoyable and infinitely more difficult. Their hotel is perfection, the welcome warm and the cooking superb. I wish them all the success that their venture so richly deserves, and thank them from the bottom of my heart. I would also like to thank a wonderful old lady, Madame Untersteller, owner of the historic Château de Cinq-Mars in the village of that name, also near Langeais. She offers excellent *chambre d'hôte* accommodation to the traveller, and generously put me up for a few nights. She is a talented artist in ceramics, and a kind and gallant lady.

I cannot pass on from Touraine without a special word of gratitude to James de Lestang and his beautiful wife Olivia. James was the *chargé de tourisme* for the Touraine region, and introduced me to many people, hotels and restaurants, and generally smoothed my path to the most extraordinary degree. They are lovely people, and I hope to see them often in the future.

In Saumur I was greatly helped by Philippe Treutenaere of Ackerman Laurance, Alain Seydoux of Gratien & Meyer and Monsieur Leroux of Langlois-Chateau. I thank them all for their kindness and help.

The wines of the Coteaux de l'Aubance were revealed to me in all their glory by Monsieur Daviau of Brissac. Not only did he give me a magnificent tasting of old vintages of his remarkable wines, but he also provided me with one of my most memorable days, shooting and feasting with his friends in the forest of the Duc de Brissac.

I apologise for sounding like the Academy Awards, but I have to go on a little longer. Madame Michèle Bretault of Faye d'Anjou gave up much of her valuable time, and, in spite of her protestations to the contrary, she is a good cook. This large family concern produces excellent Coteaux du Layon, as well as the whole gamut of Anjou wines from Blanc Sec to Cabernet d'Anjou, and even a little sparkling wine. Thank you to them; I hope to see more of them and their wines.

The Pays Nantais, my last area of research and birthplace of Muscadet and Gros Plant, was made more accessible to me by the kindness of Antoine Subileau, Pascal Guilbaud, André Vinet, Louis Metaireau and by the encyclopaedic knowledge of the *courtier* André Luveau.

A general acknowledgment for all their assistance is due to the following officers of the various professional bodies of each *appellation*: Messrs Figeat and Masson of the Syndicat Viticole de Pouilly les Loges, M. Laporte of the Union Viticole Sancerroise, M. Cariou of the Conseil Interprofessionnel des Vins d'Anjou et Saumur, M. Thevenet of the Comité Interprofessionnel des Vins de Touraine and M. Dessaigne of the Comité Interprofessionnel des Vins d'Origine du Pays Nantais.

My son, Christian Seely, has been a major contributor to this work. Not only did he give up a great deal of his valuable time to produce the splendid photographs, he also gave me countless enjoyable and recuperative week-ends at his house near Fontainebleau, the exotic sounding Villa Zaza. I thank him profoundly. I am also most grateful to his friend, Jonathan Sibley, a fellow alumnus of INSEAD, who shared the photographic work.

Finally, how can I ever begin to thank or repay my beloved Wendy, the poor writer's widow? For the best part of eight months she has been alone in England, running a home and two companies with great efficiency and never a complaint. She has had little reward and deserves much; as the saying goes, she is the one without whom this book would not have been possible.

THE RIVER AND ITS VINEYARDS

The Loire rises undramatically in the mountains of the Cevennes in the Massif Central, and winds its way some 500 kilometres to the north as far as Orléans; thence it veers south-east through Blois to Tours, finally following a more or less easterly course through Saumur, passing to the south of Angers, through the city of Nantes, meeting the Atlantic at St Nazaire. The total distance from the source to ocean is some 1000 kilometres, making this the longest of all France's mighty rivers.

The vineyards of the Loire are vast, and the variety of grapes grown and wines produced are almost infinite.

From the vinous point of view, there is nothing much along the banks of the Loire to interest us from the source near Le Puy for about 450 kilometres, when we reach the vineyards of Pouilly and Sancerre, with Menetou-Salon, Reuilly and Quincy to the west. Interestingly enough, some of the best red wines of France are made only 70 kilometres from the source, for Tain l'Hermitage on the Rhône is only this distance away, but that is all part of another book.

Before setting off on our voyage of discovery, it may be interesting to set out an itinerary, showing the course we shall follow, *appellation* by *appellation*, including the more important VDQS wines, showing what grapes are grown in each *appellation*, and what types of wine are made.

Appellation/VDQS	Grape varieties	Type of wine
EASTERN LOIRE		
Pouilly-sur-Loire	*Chasselas*	*Dry white, still, plus some* méthode champenoise
Pouilly Blanc Fumé	*Sauvignon*	*Dry white, still*
Sancerre	*Sauvignon* *Pinot Noir*	*Dry white, still* *Red and rosé, still*
Menetou-Salon	*Sauvignon* *Pinot Noir*	*Dry white, still* *Red and rosé, still*
Reuilly	*Sauvignon* *Pinot Noir* *Pinot Gris*	*Dry white, still* *Red and rosé, still* *Red and rosé, still*
Quincy	*Sauvignon*	*Dry white, still*

TOURAINE

Touraine, Generic	Sauvignon, Chenin Blanc, Chardonnay	Dry, medium dry and sweet white, still and dry, medium dry and sweet, sparkling
	Gamay, Cabernets, Malbec, Groslot, Pineau d'Aunis	Red and rosé, still and sparkling
Touraine-Mesland	Chenin Blanc	Dry, medium dry and sweet white, still
	Gamay, Cabernet Franc, Malbec	Red and rosé, still
Touraine-Amboise	Chenin Blanc	Dry, medium dry and sweet wine, still
	Cabernet Franc, Malbec, Gamay, Cabernet Sauvignon, Groslot	Red and rosé, still
Montlouis	Chenin Blanc	Dry, medium dry and sweet white, still and sparkling
Vouvray	Chenin Blanc	Dry, medium dry and sweet white, still and sparkling
Touraine Azay-le-Rideau	Chenin Blanc	Dry, medium dry and sweet white, still
	Groslot, Gamay, Malbec and Cabernets	Dry and medium dry rosé, still
Chinon	Chenin Blanc (very little)	Dry, medium dry white, still
	Cabernet Franc, and very little Cabernet Sauvignon	Red and rosé, still
Bourgueil	Cabernet Franc, and very little Cabernet Sauvignon	Red and rosé, still
St Nicolas de Bourgueil	Cabernet Franc, and very little Cabernet Sauvignon	Red and rosé, still
Cheverny VDQS	Sauvignon, Chenin Blanc, Chardonnay, Pineau Menu, Romorantin	Dry white, still and sparkling
	Gamay, Cabernets, Pinot Noir, Malbec	Red, still

Valençay VDQS	Pineau Menu, Chardonnay, with Romorantin, Chenin Blanc	Dry white, still
	Gamay, Cabernets, Malbec and Pinot Noir	Red and rosé, still
Jasnières	Chenin Blanc	Dry white, still
Coteaux du Loir	Chenin Blanc	Dry white, still
	Pineau d'Aunis, plus Gamay, Cabernet, Malbec and up to 25% Groslot for rosé	Red and rosé, still

ANJOU & SAUMUR

Anjou	Groslot, Malbec, Pineau d'Aunis	Rosé d'Anjou – medium dry rosé, still
	Cabernet Franc	Cabernet d'Anjou – medium dry and sweet rosé, still
	Cabernet Franc, Gamay, Malbec, Groslot and Pineau d'Aunis	Rosé d'Anjou – dry rosé, still
	Cabernet Franc, Cabernet Sauvignon, Pineau d'Aunis	Anjou Rouge – red, still
	Gamay	Gamay Rouge – red, still
	Chenin Blanc (80%), Sauvignon, Chardonnay	Anjou Blanc – dry and medium-dry white, still
Saumur-Champigny	Cabernet Franc (90%), plus Cabernet Sauvignon, Pineau d'Aunis	Red, still
Saumur	Chenin Blanc, Sauvignon, Chardonnay, Cabernets, Gamay, Malbec, Pineau d'Aunis, Groslot and Pinot Noir	Dry, medium dry and sweet white and rosé méthode champenoise, under AC Saumur d'Origine and the new, stricter, Crémant de Loire
	Chenin Blanc plus 20% of Sauvignon or Chardonnay	Saumur Blanc, dry white, still
	Chenin Blanc	Coteaux de Saumur medium-dry to sweet white, still
	Cabernet Franc, plus a little Cabernet Sauvignon and Pineau d'Aunis	Saumur Rouge – red, still

Coteaux de l'Aubance	Chenin Blanc	Medium dry to sweet white, still
Coteaux du Layon	Chenin Blanc	Medium dry to sweet white, still
Quarts de Chaume	Chenin Blanc	Sweet white, still
Bonnezeaux	Chenin Blanc	Sweet white, still
Savennières, Clos de la Coulée de Serrant	Chenin Blanc	Dry white, still
Savennières, La Roche aux Moines	Chenin Blanc	Dry white, still
Savennières	Chenin Blanc	Dry white, still

THE PAYS NANTAIS

Coteaux d'Ancenis VDQS	Chenin Blanc	Dry white, still
	Malvoisie	Dry, medium dry and sweet white, still
	Gamay	Red and rosé, still
Gros Plant du Pays Nantais VDQS	Folle Blanche	Dry white, still
Muscadet Coteaux de la Loire	Melon de Bourgogne	Dry white, still
Muscadet	Melon de Bourgogne	Dry white, still
Muscadet de Sèvre et Maine	Melon de Bourgogne	Dry white, still

EASTERN LOIRE
CONTENTS

COMMUNES AND GROWERS VISITED

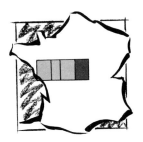

EASTERN LOIRE

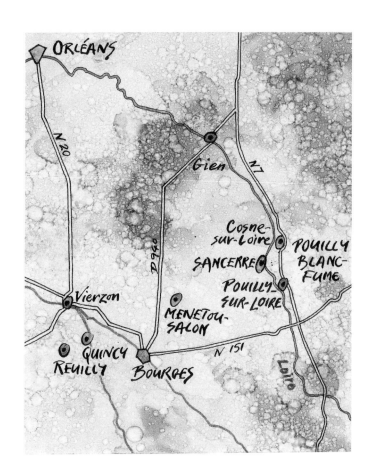

APPELLATIONS: POUILLY-SUR-LOIRE & POUILLY BLANC FUMÉ

Sauvignon grapes – the only type of grape used in the making of white Sancerre and Pouilly Blanc Fumé

Pouilly-sur-Loire, the village in the Nièvre *département* from which Pouilly Blanc Fumé and Pouilly-sur-Loire come, is about 200 kilometres south of Paris, between Cosne and Nevers. Probably due to its having been by-passed by the once-important Route Nationale 7, which has in turn been superseded by the Autoroute 6, Pouilly has a slightly sad and neglected air. Little seems to be going on there, apart from market-days, when the influx of locals from the surrounding villages and hamlets gives one an idea of the place's past importance. In the days when the N7 was the *Route Bleue*, the main road from Paris to the South of France, Pouilly must have been a welcome watering-place for tired, hungry and thirsty travellers; now they whirl swiftly southward on the *autoroute*, stopping only for minutes in the service areas to grab a sandwich on their impetuous non-stop dash for the sun.

There have been vines grown here since the fifth century AD, though the vineyards were laid waste in a great battle in 840 between Charles le Chauve and Lothaire at Fontenaye-en-Puisaye. The name of Pouilly is derived from the Latin name Paulius, and suggests that in Gallo-Roman times the vineyards may have been part of the estate of a Roman of that name.

Following the devastation of the vineyards, the cultivation of the vine was re-started, as elsewhere, by monastic foundations, principally Benedictine monasteries. There is to this day a four hectare parcel of vines called Loge aux Moines, from which we may deduce that there was nearby a resting-place for passing pilgrims, who were no doubt refreshed and fortified by the local wine. Here in Pouilly, as elsewhere, monastic communities cultivated the vine and made wine for sacramental use, and doubtless for the table of the good friars. Any surplus that may have been available would have been sold locally to supplement the finances of the monastery.

From the writings of Guy Coquille, we have evidence of active viticulture in the Nivernais during the sixteenth century. He tells us that even then the vignerons would not work the soil in the vineyards when the north wind blew in April, since this was often the herald of the deadly spring frosts. It was the lord of the manor who set the date for the vintage to start, and he had the right to start picking first, and he also tells us that boatmen and carriers who transported wine were legally obliged to insure their cargo, since it had a curious habit of diminishing in volume during its passage.

Until nearly the end of the nineteenth century, the grape grown in this part of France was the Chasselas, and the market was Paris where it was sold as a table grape; transport to the capital was relatively easy by water, along the Loire as far as Briare and thence by the Canal de Briare and the River Loing up to Moret-sur-Loing, where the Loing flows in to the Seine. The advent of the railways provided easy access to Paris and the rest of northern France for the cheaper and more abundant table grapes from the south, and the growers were then forced into concentrating more of their efforts on the making of wine.

When one door closes, it is not unusual for another one to slam in your face, and the good vignerons of Pouilly, like those of the rest of Europe, were crippled in the 1880s and 1890s by the twin scourges of, firstly, mildew and secondly the dreaded root-eating beetle *Phylloxera vastatrix*. The latter pest caused unimaginable hardships for grape-growers throughout Europe; no cure or treatment could be found, and not until the mid-Nineties was it discovered that grafting the native varieties on to phylloxera-resistant American root-stocks was the sole road to survival.

In the early part of this century, with the answer to phylloxera and mildew treatment discovered, the growers re-planted their vineyards with an eye to wine production, and the Chasselas began to disappear in favour of the Sauvignon, or 'Blanc Fumé de Pouilly', as it became known locally. It is widely believed that the name 'Blanc Fumé' derives from the characteristic gunflint or smoky flavour of the wine, but it comes in fact from the grey, smoke-coloured bloom that grows on the skin of the Sauvignon grape.

Each year less and less Chasselas is planted; it produces a coarser, cheaper wine than the Sauvignon, sold under the name Pouilly-sur-Loire, and it is moreover a tricky variety to grow. The eventual total disappearance of this variety from the Pouilly vineyard is not unlikely, and all that will remain to remind us of the Chasselas' former glory will be the little huts, or *cabanes*, that dot the vineyards; these were used to store the picked bunches, destined for the dinner tables of nineteenth-century Paris.

In a survey dated 1829 the total area of vines in Pouilly was recorded as 1,890 hectares, the vast majority of which were Chasselas, grown for the table. Today there are only 520 hectares of vineyard, spread over half a dozen communes. The best of these are Pouilly-sur-Loire, including Les Berthiers and Tracy-sur-Loire; the best vineyards are to be found on the high ground in a crescent-shaped area to the north and north-west of Pouilly, bounded by Tracy-sur-Loire on the banks of the river, following a line eastward to St Andelain and back to Pouilly itself.

Within each commune there are many well-known *lieux-dits*, or vineyard names, such as La Loge aux Moines in Pouilly, Le Champ du Clou in St Andelain and Les Champs de la Croix in Tracy. These names are occasionally seen on the label of a bottle of Blanc Fumé de Pouilly; more often a vigneron, who will probably have only a small parcel of one such vineyard, as well as vines elsewhere, will blend his wines together to produce a consistent and harmonious style and sell it simply as Blanc Fumé de Pouilly.

A good Pouilly Blanc Fumé will have a light golden colour, 12° of alcohol and around 5 grammes per litre of acidity. It is a wine that requires a year to eighteen months in bottle to give of its best, and, generally speaking, ages better than its neighbour, the white wine of Sancerre. For me, a good bottle of Blanc Fumé is one of the great dry white wines of France, and shows beautifully with all fish, shell-fish and white meats. The proof of quality, if any is needed, can be readily deduced from the increasing world sales of Pouilly over the past few years, when prices of white Burgundies have been escalating at such a ludicrous rate. This is just one of many instances I shall quote, showing not only the quality but the amazing value that is to be had from the wines of the Loire.

POUILLY-SUR-LOIRE

BARON PATRICK DE LADOUCETTE, Château du Nozet. I sat alone at the head of a huge dining-table in the Château du Nozet. An excellent dinner was served by the kindly housekeeper – four courses, each accompanied by a bottle of wine, a Chablis from Albert Pic, Blanc Fumé de Ladoucette, Baron de L, and Saumur Champigny from Baron Briare. A perfect end to a perfect day, and an auspicious beginning to my researches in the Valley of the Loire, I thought, though whether my liver could stand such Strasbourg treatment for the whole seven months was doubtful.

Patrick, Baron de Ladoucette, had kindly invited me to spend a few days at du Nozet, and I am grateful to him for his hospitable and sybaritic welcome to the area. The château is Victorian, Gothic and enormous. For the greater part of the year it is empty, except for the reception of visitors and occasional visits by Patrick and members of his family. Built around 1850 on the site of an earlier castle, the Château du Nozet is hidden in a vine-clad valley to the left of the N7 as you drive southward towards Nevers; the driveway to the château is immediately opposite the turning to the town of Pouilly-sur-Loire.

Du Nozet is a Walt Disney castle, complete with moat (dry), towers, turrets, pinnacles, a chapel, acres of steep, slate roofs and gargoyles, set in a lovely park with formal gardens and a man-made lake. The dining-room, a drawing room and a study are furnished, as are the family rooms upstairs. Patrick is refurbishing bedrooms for lucky guests like myself, but it is a job which could last a lifetime. There must be dozens and dozens of rooms, some empty, some filled with the collected lumber of a hundred years. I am not by nature of a nervous disposition, but I confess that the very vastness of uninhabited space surrounding the comfortable and well-lit oasis of my bedroom did, on occasions, get to me. Each evening the good housekeeper would serve coffee, clatter about with the washing-up in some nether region and depart; I would then dash up the spiral staircase to my room, slam the door and lock it – against whom or what, I know not, but it seemed a wise precaution.

To the rear of the château are the wine-making buildings, and here fancies flee away. Château du Nozet is a highly efficient 'winery', where every advantage is taken of modern technology and oenological know-how. Administration is in the very capable hands of Joel André, de Ladoucette's general manager, who lives in a wing of the château. He gave me a great deal of his time, and taught me much.

The scale of the operation here is impressive. In terms of volume, de Ladoucette produces and sells about a third of all the Pouilly Fumé made. The estate's own vines cover 56 hectares, the biggest vineyard by far in the *appellation*, where the average vineyard is only about 6 hectares; over and above the production of their own wines, de Ladoucette buys grape-must and finished wine from many growers to meet world demand.

Three wines are produced at Château du Nozet. Blanc Fumé de Ladoucette accounts for the majority of the 1,200,000 bottles average annual output. The balance is made up of Sancerre, sold under the Comte Lafond name, and the prestige Pouilly Blanc Fumé, Baron de L. The latter is Patrick de Ladoucette's brainchild, and was first made in 1973; it is made exclusively from grapes from five parcels of the Château du Nozet vineyards, where the average vine age is high – Le Désert, La Fontaine, La Belle Vue, La Croix and Les Bleus. The wine from each of these parcels is vinified separately, and Baron de L is a carefully chosen *assemblage* of these *cuves*. Vinification for Baron de L is similar to that employed for the standard de Ladoucette wine, apart from the meticulous selection process described above, and the fact that the wine is kept on its lees for twelve months, and undergoes but one light filtration before bottling. Only made in good years – there was no Baron de L produced in '74, '77, '80 or '84 – production is limited to about 100,000 bottles; the wine is of exceptional quality, and is commensurately expensive. The price proves no barrier to sales, however; Baron de L is found on the wine lists of the best hotels and restaurants all over the world, and connoisseurs, restaurateurs and wine-merchants alike have difficulty in obtaining stocks to meet their requirements.

Blanc Fumé de Ladoucette is made from a carefully selected blend of du Nozet's own grapes, wine bought in from other growers, as well as wine made from the unfermented grape-juice also purchased from the growers. The finished wine and must bought in this way are treated and vinified exclusively at the château, with the same meticulous care and attention that is given to the estate's own produce. For the wine vinified on the premises, the juice of only the first three light pressings is used, representing about 70% of the total. *Débourbage*, the clarification of the wine by allowing the lees to settle, is effected by lowering the temperature to 4° Celsius for 48 hours; Joel André prefers this method to the use of a centrifuge or the addition of sulphur, since it preserves the aromas of the wine, and at the same time eliminates any possible trace of pesticide and is less fatiguing for the delicate young wine.

Fermentation takes place at 15° Celsius, and can last anywhere between three and eight weeks. Long, cool fermentation is now favoured almost universally for the making of white wine, since it has been proved most beneficial for the conservation of bouquet and aromas. The wine then rests on its lees until the June following the year of vintage, when it

Château du Nozet

is racked off the lees and transferred to another vat to await bottling.

Sancerre, Comte Lafond, is made entirely from finished wine or grape-must bought in from various growers across the river in the Sancerre *appellation*, since de Ladoucette owns no vineyards there, though this could change in the not-too-distant future. The name is taken from Patrick de Ladoucette's ancestor, Comte Lafond, who purchased the du Nozet domaine at the time of the French Revolution. Quality is assured by the purchase of only the best wine and grape-must, through the medium of Jean-Jacques Renaud, the knowledgeable *courtier* and *vigneron* of St Andelain; Renaud also handles the buying of wine and grape-must from the Pouilly growers for de Ladoucette.

The platform on which Patrick bases his whole approach to wine-making and the marketing of his wines is one of quality above all else. His wines are by no means cheap, and one could be forgiven for thinking that in an operation of this scale, the standard of the wine might suffer. Not so, for de Ladoucette's wines are always impeccably made, and always show well in blind tastings against other Blanc Fumés and Sancerres. Patrick drives and flies his business all over the world, and his acumen and dedication are unquestionable. In addition to Château du Nozet, the family also owns the old-established house of Marc Bredif in Vouvray, Albert Pic in Chablis and has interests in the Touraine business of Baron Briare; Patrick also runs a successful wine-merchant business, the *maison* Bristol, in Paris, which among other things holds the agency for the prestigious house of Louis Latour in Burgundy.

Raised in Argentina, where the family still owns a large *estancia* near Buenos Aires, Patrick now lives in Paris, running the de Ladoucette business and his merchant company. He started his active involvement in the family business after leaving Swiss business school in the early Seventies, taking over much of the workload from his mother, who ran things very capably for some fifteen years.

During my stay in the Château du Nozet I was well looked after, and spent some time with Joel André; with him, as well as with Patrick, I tasted many of their wines at different stages of their lives. Most of the 1985 vintage was still in vats at the time, and I was able to taste Blanc Fumé and Sancerre both before and after their pre-bottling filtration; it was an excellent year for this region, and the wines promise well. I was also lucky enough to try the lovely 1983 Baron de L, once at dinner at the château and on another occasion at a memorable lunch with Patrick at the Hôtel Château d'Artigny near Tours.

I am indebted to de Ladoucette for all his help and hospitality; his dynamic efforts on behalf of his own wines must also be of great benefit to every *appellation* wherein his interests lie, as he is a courteous and persuasive ambassador in the many countries that he visits, indeed wherever fine wine is drunk and enjoyed.

Before leaving the luxury of Château du Nozet for the more meagre comforts of *chambre d'hôte* accommodation, I was introduced to Jean-Jacques Renaud, the *courtier*, from St Andelain, who knows just about everybody who has a row of vines from Pouilly to Reuilly. He also makes excellent wine.

Jean-Jacques took me on many expeditions in Pouilly and Sancerre to meet the growers. To say that he broke the ice for me would be to do an injustice to the warm welcome and friendliness that I encountered wherever I went, but I am more than grateful to him for his friendship and help.

PAUL FIGEAT, Les Loges. Paul Figeat lives in the attractive hamlet of Les Loges, a cluster of houses on a narrow street running down to the river from the vineyards, about two kilometres to the north-west of Pouilly. Figeat is currently President of the Union Viticole de Pouilly-sur-Loire.

Sound wines are made here, sold on the home and export markets. Paul Figeat is something of a

traditionalist, and I tasted a good Pouilly-sur-Loire and his Pouilly Blanc Fumé, both from the vat and both of the 1985 vintage. The style was somewhat austere, and both will benefit from some time in bottle.

JEAN-MICHEL MASSON-BLONDELET, Pouilly-sur-Loire. M. Masson is Director of the Union Viticole, and gave me a good measure of help and information about the *appellation*, as well as an excellent dinner, for which, as he kindly assured me was not at all uncommon in the area, I was unpardonably late.

Jean-Michel and his wife, *née* Blondelet, a large family of wine-makers in Pouilly, work hard together in their wine business. They have an attractive and welcoming shop in the main street of Pouilly-sur-Loire, next door to the restaurant La Bouteille d'Or, opposite the hotel.

The Masson-Blondelet vinification and bottling plant is housed in a modern building some 50 metres up the street, on the same side. All of the building work and the installation of equipment has been done by Jean-Michel and his wife, and is a sparkling monument to their industry and capability.

The vineyards of this hard-working couple are somewhat scattered, due to the amalgamation of parts of the Blondelet family vines. Everything is vinified here, and I tasted excellent Pouilly-sur-Loire and Pouilly Blanc Fumé of 1983, 1984 and 1985 vintages. The 1984 was particularly good, which indicates the quality of the winemaker, since it was not an easy vintage.

MICHEL REDDE, 'La Moynerie', Pouilly-sur-Loire. You cannot miss Michel Redde's property 'La Moynerie'; it stands on the right of the N7 as you drive south from Paris, about 1 kilometre before the turning off to Pouilly-sur-Loire. A huge old wine-press sits in front of his house, and there are flowers everywhere; signs invite the passing motorist to taste and buy, and the shop/tasting room, which takes up the entire ground floor, has been carefully decorated with rustic furniture and old vineyard tools and equipment. One feels more as if this were a cosy bar or restaurant than a shop. Once inside there is much to tempt the traveller; Redde is a wine-maker first, and his excellent special Cuvée Majorum and standard Pouilly Fumé, all attractively presented and packaged, are obviously what he is really selling. Other local produce is also on sale, however, such as the local goat's cheeses 'Crottins de Chavignol', walnut oil, honey, etc.

Michel Redde's son Thierry, who works with him, represents the seventh generation in a father-to-son line who have made wine here. They have currently some 27 hectares in production, split about equally between the *vignoble* of St Andelain and that of Pouilly-sur-Loire. No Chasselas are grown. The soils of St Andelain are clay-silex, and those of Pouilly clay-limestone, and the production of the two is blended.

Since 1973, Michel Redde has made a special blend called Cuvée Majorum, which he only makes in very good years, and then only from the produce of the older vines. It usually has greater ageing potential than the normal Pouilly Fumé, and for optimum enjoyment should be drunk when at least three, four or even five years old. He has chosen a distinctive bottle, reminiscent of the Baron de L, and offers the wine for sale in wooden boxes of varying capacity. Seventy per cent of Redde's production is exported world-wide.

The vinification, stocking and bottling installations are impressive in their size, modernity and cleanliness. Recent extensions to his buildings have resulted in an unfortunate concrete blockhouse appearance when viewed from the back across the vines from the hill above Les Loges. No doubt this will all be properly rendered in due course, and will blend in more harmoniously with the landscape. All vinification takes place in an impressive array of stainless steel *cuves*, and there is an extremely modern Italian-made bottling line on the lower ground floor, near which further tanks are being installed for keeping and bottling. Two giant, square oak presses still stand in the basement, mute reminders of a bygone age.

I tasted both the straight Pouilly Blanc Fumé 1985, La Moynerie and a bottle of Cuvée Majorum. The La Moynerie had a light greeny-gold colour, nose and taste were fresh and clean. The wine had the expected hints of gun-flint. The Cuvée Majorum was good too, but did not seem to me to be worth the extra money, though it may need more time to develop its full potential.

CAVES CO-OPÉRATIVES DE POUILLY-SUR-LOIRE The co-operative vinifies and sells some 5–6,000 hectolitres a year. It buys its wine from 120 members, who sell the co-op anything from 100% of their crop down to nothing in some years.

All wine comes in to the *cave* as must and is vinified here in the efficient and modern winery. *Cuves* are of all sizes and types, so that the produce from small growers can be vinified separately before being blended. Pouilly Fumé and Pouilly-sur-Loire are both made here, plus about 10% from the Coteaux du Giennois, red, white and rosé. The Pouilly wines are marketed under the label Cave du Moulin à Vent, and anywhere between 60% and 80% goes for export worldwide, the rest being sold to private customers, restaurants and wholesalers.

M. Bouchié, the director, is keen, energetic and seems very capable. I tasted a range of wines, including the 1985 Pouilly-sur-Loire, Blanc Fumé and the red Coteaux du Giennois, and found the standard extremely high for a co-operative.

ST ANDELAIN

PATRICK COULBOIS, Les Berthiers. Patrick Coulbois has split away from his family firm, and operates from a neat, modern bungalow, built in 1979, which is one of the last houses on the right as you drive up the hill from the N7 through the hamlet of Les Berthiers towards the dominating church of St Andelain. The wine-making buildings are all underneath the house, well insulated and purpose-built. Somehow Patrick Coulbois' operation encapsulates for me the way most Pouilly Fumé is made; here we have a name that I have known – and indeed shipped – for many years, as I am sure it is known to other merchants and wine-lovers worldwide, and yet the scale is so small. It is perhaps the limited size of their operations which allows the good wine-makers of the area to give proper attention to the quality of their wines.

Patrick has some 6 hectares under vines, of which 15% is still devoted to the Chasselas; not all of this goes in to the making of Pouilly-sur-Loire, however, for Patrick's father, Gérard, has for many years made a *Méthode champenoise* from this variety, and quite good it is too. Each year Patrick sends some of his Chasselas down the road to his father for this purpose. This is one property on which Chasselas wines will continue to be replanted.

Some 80% of Patrick's production is sold on the export market. The vines are principally around Les Berthiers and St Andelain, but he also has some across the N7 in Les Loges. This is a fairly common situation in Pouilly and Coulbois says that he follows the local practice of making an *assemblage* of all his vineyards to produce a consistent style from year to year, though of course the wine will vary with the vagaries of succeeding vintages.

In spite of the extremely up-to-date appearance of Patrick's house and equipment, I think there is a strong element of the traditionalist in his make-up, for he still uses the same team of hand-pickers, a gang of railway workers who have made his vintage their annual holiday for many years.

Tasted: *Blanc Fumé 1985*. Lovely light gold, fresh Sauvignon nose, with hints of *pierre-à-fusil* (gunflint). Well-made Pouilly from a good year. Will be even better with a year in bottle.
Méthode Champenoise 1984. The first sparkling wine from Pouilly that I have tasted. Made from the Chasselas grape, and *champagnisé* by Patrick's father, Gérard. Pale gold, with a fine mousse. Good, clean flavour, with just a hint of *goût de terroir* (tang of its soil). Surprisingly good, especially considering the vintage.

BERNARD BLANCHET, Les Berthiers.

The first house that you come to, having turned off for St Andelain from the N7, is on your right-hand side, and bears the placard of M. Blanchet. I went there on a sunny June morning with Jean-Jacques Renaud. Bernard Blanchet was out, but we were enthusiastically received by his son, who was in the middle of revising for exams, and seemed to welcome the natural break.

We were ushered in to the Blanchets' newly constructed, or excavated, underground cellar; from the outside it had more the appearance of a Second World War air-raid shelter, but inside all was cool, organised and very functional. M. Blanchet *fils* lost no time in offering us a *dégustation*, and opened first a bottle of his father's 1984 Pouilly Blanc Fumé; I found this to be an extremely well-made wine, drinking perfectly after some fifteen months in bottle, fresh, light and crisp. Jean-Jacques said that it was 'très marqué '84', but I could find little fault with the wine. This was followed by the 1985, which had a lower acidity and more fruit and length, and, looked at side by side, I could then see which of the two was the better vintage.

A vineyard in Pouilly-sur-Loire with a typical cabane *in the background*

As we were savouring the '85, we were joined by the Mayor of St Andelain, another wine-maker of Les Berthiers. His entrance signalled another tasting of the '84, and long discussions of the relative merits of the two years, punctuated by much sniffing and tasting. I hope young M. Blanchet passed his exams.

ROBERT PESSON, Les Caissiers.

Following the visit to M. Blanchet, Jean-Jacques drove me up through St Andelain, out along the country lanes, past the vineyards of Château du Nozet, to the little hamlet of Les Caissiers, where we visited the old stone-built farm of Robert Pesson. Again the boss was out, but his son, who works with him, showed us round and gave us a tasting of their wines.

The buildings were old and somewhat delapidated, the main wine-making room reminding me more of a granary than a *cuverie*. White-bleached oak timbers abounded everywhere, and, apart from the fibre-glass vats, little seemed to have changed for the past two or three hundred years. I half expected to see Athos, Porthos or Aramis emerge from the hayloft, brandishing a goblet of wine in one hand, with the other arm around a buxom wench.

In spite of this timeless atmosphere, there was clearly nothing wrong with the Pessons' wines, as witnessed by two pallets of immaculately cartoned, shrink-wrapped Pouilly Fumé, awaiting collection for shipment to one of the foremost wine importers of the United States.

If further evidence were needed of the quality of the wines made here, it was quickly provided by a tasting of Pesson's 1985 Pouilly-sur-Loire and Blanc Fumé. The former was an excellent example of the clean, refreshing and uncomplicated style of the Chasselas, whilst the Blanc Fumé had all the class and flinty appeal that one expects of this *appellation*, with that delicious light sparkle of CO_2 that the vignerons of Pouilly strive to capture in their wine.

MARCEL LANGOUX, Le Petit Soumard.

Our next port of call was in the tiny hamlet of Le Petit Soumard. Jean-Jacques warned me that I was in for a surprise here, since few people realised that Jean-Marie Le Pen, head of France's National Front party, was a wine-maker here in Pouilly in his spare time.

I was introduced to the stocky, bull-like figure, and was singularly impressed by his powerful personality. Le Pen was clearly an anglophile, and asked tenderly after our glorious *Dame de Fer*, whom, he assured me, he knew well and admired greatly.

We soon got down to the serious business of tasting, comparing the '83, '84 and '85 Pouilly Blanc Fumé. It was not an easy tasting, since, for some unexplained reason, none of his glasses had feet; if one wanted to keep a little of each vintage in order to compare one with another, the solution was to find an open bottle and stick the stem of the glass in it. The only drawback to this wheeze was that Le Pen would suddenly decide he wanted to re-taste the wine in which my glass was balanced, and remove the glass to the neck of another bottle. This happened so many times that it became increasingly difficult to remember which glass was where, and which contained which vintage. Before the whole *dégustation* collapsed into total confusion, I was able to establish that the quality of all three was excellent, even the talked-down '84; the '83 was certainly the readiest of them, but the '85 would clearly be the best after a little time in bottle.

All bottles tasted were unlabelled, and it was only as I was leaving that I saw some cases of wine, clearly marked with the name of Marcel Langoux. I asked M. Le Pen, as tactfully as my French would allow, if he used this name in order not to offend his more liberally inclined customers, and intercepted a giant wink passing between him and Jean-Jacques Renaud. I had been made the victim of a *grande carotte*, as Mr Harrap informs me the French would say. I am not alone; it is a big local joke, and many have been fooled as I was. Marcel Langoux is that rare thing, a perfect double; he is also a great fellow, and on later occasions we had many a laugh over my gullibility.

JEAN-CLAUDE CHATELAIN, Les Berthiers.

The Chatelains' offices are on your right as you drive up the hill to St Andelain from the N7, through Les Berthiers, and their buildings are opposite with the vineyards behind. As with many families in the region, there is a long history of succession here; the Chatelains have made wine in Les Berthiers, father-to-son, since 1683.

Pretty, vivacious and super-efficient, Madame Chatelain is actively involved in the business, mainly on the sales side. I was struck here, as elsewhere in Pouilly, by the evident prosperity yielded by a comparatively small holding. Ten hectares of vines appears to justify an astonishing array of software and hardware in the office, and Mercedes, large Citroëns, Renaults and Range Rovers abound.

Jean-Claude Chatelain has 10 hectares, mostly in Les Berthiers and a little parcel in St Laurent de l'Abbaye. Production is mainly Pouilly Blanc Fumé, but he keeps one hectare of Chasselas to satisfy local demand. This was said to me here, as at other wine-makers, with an almost apologetic shrug, as though the making of Pouilly-sur-Loire was some kind of anarchic, feudal obligation rather than a matter of business.

An amazing 92% of Chatelain's wine, including his special *cuvée*, Chatelain Prestige, which is made only in good years from the first pressing of grapes from the oldest vines, is sold on the export market. Over half goes to the United States, and 17% to Great Britain, where Joseph Berkmann is their main customer; various labels, using names of members of the family, are employed to give *soi-disant* exclusivity to different customers.

I did not have the opportunity of tasting the Chatelain Prestige, with its rather flashy black and gold label, but the Pouilly Fumé 1985 was well made, crisp and clean, with a comparatively low acidity.

Before leaving, we crossed the road to look at the vines, where I met Jean-Claude Chatelain. It was the hottest day of my whole trip, with the temperature in the vineyard nudging up to the high thirties Celsius. The flowering had just begun, and at this stage quantities looked as if they could be above average for the 1986 crop. Relative to average years, the flowering was late – it was the 24th June – but Chatelain explained that this was due to the long winter and late spring. Everything was about two to three weeks behind, but the current heatwave, which was to continue for several weeks, soon helped the vines to catch up, and 1986 looks promising.

JEAN-CLAUDE DAGUENEAU, Les

Berthiers. One of the large tribe of Dagueneaus in Les Berthiers, Jean-Claude is probably the largest. A bearded giant of a man, he carries before him a stomach of noble proportions, of which both he and his very attractive wife seem inordinately proud. His dedication to the gastronomic arts is further witnessed by a framed certificate on the tasting-room wall, proclaiming him to be a member of the august Confrérie des Andouillettes, a local delicacy closely resembling the English faggot.

The Dagueneaus' wine-buildings and house are the first ones on your left as you drive up through Les Berthiers towards St Andelain from the N7. An old well stands in front of the virginia creeper clad house,

Jean-Claude Dagueneau with his wife in their tasting-room

and when I first visited them in June, the overall impression was of flowers everywhere; in addition to a pretty garden, every window was ablaze with geraniums.

Jean-Claude's property, some 15 hectares of vines, rejoices in the name of Domaine des Berthiers; only about half of his vineyard, however, is in the commune of St Andelain, the other half being across the N7, near Les Loges. The clay-silex soil of St Andelain gives a finer wine, with a tendency to slower maturation, whilst the clay-limestone mix of Les Loges produces wine with more instant appeal and a shade less finesse; the two types, when blended, yield a Pouilly Blanc Fumé of excellent quality.

Approximately half of the Domaine des Berthiers production goes for export, mainly to the United Kingdom, Germany, Belgium, Holland and the United States. Jean-Claude no longer produces Pouilly-sur-Loire, although he still grows a little Chasselas for making *méthode champenoise*. He also makes a special *cuvée*, which is sold under the name of Cuvée d'Eve. It comes from the produce of the oldest vines and is very fine; Jean-Claude told me that this wine is enjoying great success with the Paris restaurant trade.

The family have been rooted in Les Berthiers since the 1830s. Serge, who has the next property on the same side of the street, is a cousin, and Didier is Jean-Claude's son, and makes his own wine.

My photographic team and I tasted two bottlings of the very good 1985 Pouilly Blanc Fumé, as well as the outstanding – for the year – 1984, a wine which won the Gold Medal in the INAO tasting .

GILLES MAUDRY, Maltaverne. Maltaverne is a straggling village, the first that you come to as you approach the Pouilly *appellation* along the N7 from the Paris direction. The Maudry establishment is on your left as you leave the village; it reminded me somewhat of a film-set for one of those westerns in which the goodies fight off the baddies in defence of the cruelly subjugated Mexican peasants, even down to the ruined chapel. Any *mañana* impression created by their square of derelict-looking farm buildings is soon dispelled when you enter the *cuverie*. Housed in an old barn, an impressive array of vast stainless-steel fermentation vats greets the eye; all is immaculately clean, and the huge expanse of roof is in the process of total renovation and insulation.

Madame Maudry, a very jolly lady and every inch the farmer's wife, made me welcome and gave me a tasting of their 1984 Pouilly Fumé. This surprised me, since, almost without exception, I had been given 1985 to taste first with every other proprietor. It was certainly a very good wine, and I now looked forward to tasting the unquestionably better vintage of 1985. Sadly this was not forthcoming. Madame Maudry told me that they had suffered huge frost damage in 1985, had made less than one vat of wine and would have virtually none to sell.

All twelve hectares of the Maudry vines are situated around the farm on the Maltaverne plateau, which is very prone to frost damage. Only Pouilly Fumé is made here; very little of their wine is sold on the export market, and this, surprisingly, goes to Germany. The vast majority of sales is to passing motorists, and the Maudrys are certainly in one of the best sites for this type of trade.

TRACY-SUR-LOIRE

ROGER PABIOT, Boisgibault. A neat, white-painted house, with vinification, stock and bottling-line buildings behind. There is a courtyard in the centre, with an old well-head, and vines for table-grapes (Chasselas) trained up the walls. Outside the entrance to M. Pabiot's small tasting room, there are some amazing fossils on display, all found in the local vineyards. Inside there are more, including enormous snails and mammoths' tusks, as well as an interesting assortment of old cooperage and vineyard tools.

The Pabiots are a Les Loges family, and have a long tradition of wine-making. Roger is the mayor of Boisgibault, and is also a *courtier-en-vin*, both of which activities keep him fairly busy so that most of the work falls upon the shoulders of his two sons and one employee. Both his sons have studied oenology and ampelology, and are duly qualified.

The vineyard is currently 10 hectares, but will be expanded to 15 within two years. All the vines are on *cailloté*, or pebbly soil, giving a wine of good finesse. Half a hectare is under Chasselas, producing Pouilly-sur-Loire. All the wine is from their own vines, and they have their own picking machine – Roger told me that 10 hectares is the minimum area on which this is an economic proposition. He also said that the Chasselas is dying out for two reasons; first Pouilly-sur-Loire sells much more cheaply than Blanc-Fumé, and secondly it is a more tricky variety to grow – the flowering lasts much longer than the Sauvignon, eight days instead of three, and therefore is much more prone to *coulure*, the failure of the infant berries, due to bad weather, at the time of the flowering in June.

He exports a large proportion of his production – 85% for the 1985 vintage – under two labels, Les Champs de la Croix for the UK, Les Girannes to Holland, Belgium and Germany. The major part of his home market is through wholesalers, though there is some direct selling to passers-by.

Tasted: Pouilly-sur-Loire 1985. Light greeny gold. Clean nose – strong acid-drops on nose and in mouth. A good Chasselas.

Blanc Fumé 1985. Colour similar, nose and taste finer with some steel. Touch of CO_2, deliberately sought and kept in *cuve* and in bottle.

HENRI D'ESTUTT D'ASSAY, Château de Tracy, Tracy-sur-Loire. In 1419 four Scottish brothers, Stutts of Laggan, came to France to fight for Charles VII against the English; they served as archers in the Garde Ecossaise. They must have served the King well, for he granted the eldest brother, Gauthier, the Seigneurie of Assay in the Berry. Gauthier died, childless, in 1474, but Louis XI assured continuity by giving Gauthier's brother Thomas *lettres de naturalité*, making him head of the d'Estutt d'Assay family, as it had now become called. It was one of his descendants, François, who in 1586 acquired the Tracy estate by marrying Françoise de Bar, in whose dowry the property was included.

The château sits well on a rocky spur, not far from the eastern bank of the Loire. The oldest parts date from the thirteenth and fourteenth centuries, though the major part of the present structure is from the seventeenth. Built of a rather crumbly stone, Château de Tracy is a harmonious blend of varying styles and periods. The main façade is pierced by a fine Renaissance gateway giving on to a spacious courtyard which is dominated by a tall, narrow fourteenth-century donjon or keep. Various dates appear in haphazard fashion here and there; above the family coat-of-arms over the gateway – motto *'Don Bien Acquis'* or 'We got it by fair means' – is carved the date '1507', and in two separate places on the tower to the left of the gate can be seen '1421' and '1231'.

Wine has certainly been made here since the fourteenth century, since a deed of sale exists in the château's archives dated 1396 for a parcel of land called 'le Champ de Crix' mentioning that it is planted with vines, and that there is a 'pressing

The escutcheon over the gateway of the Château de Tracy

place'. Le Champ de Crix is still part of Château de Tracy's vineyard today.

At the end of the last century there were about 40 hectares under vines, but, in common with most of the area at the time, the variety grown was the Chasselas, sold as dessert grapes on the Parisian market. With the coming of the phylloxera beetle, the Château de Tracy vineyards were abandoned, and it was not until after the last war that Comte Alain d'Estutt d'Assay began the re-planting programme that has resulted in today's 23 hectare vineyard.

Sauvignon is the only variety grown, all being made into Pouilly Fumé. The vines are all grafted on to American phylloxera-resistant SO4 or 3309 rootstocks. The soil around the château is a clay-silex mixture, whilst that of the famous Champ de Crix vineyard is of clay and limestone. The proprietors of Château de Tracy are pure *'viticulteurs'*, and do not buy wine from elsewhere.

The current generation of this ancient family is represented by Henri d'Estutt d'Assay, son of Comte Alain, who is not in the best of health. Henri has studied oenology in Beaune, and is keen to restore Château de Tracy's wine to its former glory. Much needed modernisation of the cellars and *'cuverie'* is already underway, and much work is also being done to bring the vineyards back into top condition. Certainly when I first joined the wine trade, Château de Tracy was the Rolls Royce of Pouilly Fumés, but in recent years the quality has not been up to par. Judging by the excellent 1985 which I tasted, and by the visible results of the investment and effort that are being put into the running of this fine old property, it will not be too long in regaining its rightful place in Pouilly's roll of honour.

As well as enjoying a healthy share of the domestic market, Château de Tracy's Pouilly Fumé sells widely in the export market, going to all the major European countries, as well as the USA, Venezuela, Singapore and Australia.

DENIS GAUDRY, Boisgibault. My last visit in the commune of Tracy was to Denis Gaudry in the village of Boisgibault. The Gaudry family have made wine here for many generations, and their business is spread all over the village, with a vat or two in one building, a press in another; in the centre of Boisgibault, they have a lovely old house which used to be a convent, with a 500-year-old plane-tree in the courtyard; it is currently unoccupied and somewhat derelict, but Denis plans to restore it and turn it into a showplace.

Only Pouilly Fumé is commercialised, though they grow a little Chasselas for *méthode champenoise* for themselves and their friends. They have a comparatively large area of vines – some 21 hectares, all in the commune of Tracy-sur-Loire. It is an area very prone to frost damage, and they suffered major losses in the icy January of 1985. Despite this and the countless other risks and difficulties of the winemaker's life, Denis Gaudry clearly has great confidence in the future. He is currently adding about 1 hectare per year to his vineyard – the maximum permitted by the INAO, and last year he bought his first picking-machine. There are many old-timers who condemn these machines as if they were the antichrist, but Gaudry has made a careful study, and has total confidence that, with good drivers and proper care and attention, they can do as good a job as the traditional *vendangeurs*, and more quickly.

Approximately 55% of Gaudry's production is exported, mainly to the USA, the UK, Belgium and Holland; on the home market he sells some to the restaurant trade, some in bulk to the *négociants* and the rest – probably around 10,000 bottles – is sold to passing private customers.

Before leaving Boisgibault, I repaired with Denis Gaudry to the neat tasting-room beside his house. We tasted a recent bottling of his 1985 Pouilly Fumé, which had a delicious bouquet of white peaches; the wine was light, nervous and fine, with excellent fruit and length. To ensure that his wines leave the cellars with the maximum of freshness and fruit, Gaudry bottles regularly every two months, starting in the December following the vintage.

APPELLATION: SANCERRE

The small mediaeval hilltop village of Sancerre is about 200 kilometres south of Paris, just off the N7 near Cosne and the west side of the Loire (the other side from Pouilly). The wine sold under the name of this village comes from fourteen communes; the most important of these lie in the fan-shaped area to the north, south and west of Sancerre, and the best wines are made in the commune of Sancerre itself and in the villages that nestle in the folds of the hills to the west of the town – Bué, Crézancy, Verdigny, Chavignol, Maimbray and Sury-en-Vaux.

Before phylloxera devastated the Sancerre vineyards, this area produced red wine for the most part and the grape grown was the Pinot Noir. Perhaps for once, we may give thanks to the dreaded beetle, for post-phylloxera growers have found the soil and climate better suited to the production of white wine from the Sauvignon grape, which now accounts for some 80% of the 1,600 hectares currently planted. It is true that the rest of the Sancerre vineyard is planted with Pinot Noir, and that from it both red and rosé are produced, but there is no doubt in my mind that, with a very few exceptions, the white is of a far superior quality. Red Sancerre is a *vin de mode* among Paris restaurateurs and their clients, and Sancerre Rouge they must have, regardless, almost, of the quality of the wine. By osmosis, this fashion is gradually spreading throughout France and to Sancerre's export market. The result is that almost every grower is producing a red wine to meet the ever increasing demand, and all too often their undoubted knowledge and skills are rooted in the making of white wine rather than red. Often, as well, a grower will plant his Pinots Noirs in a section of his vineyard where the soil and exposure have proved unsatisfactory for the Sauvignon, with the vague – and disastrously wrong – idea that anything will be good enough for the red. The Pinot Noir is every bit as 'noble' a grape as the Sauvignon – if not more so – and demands proper treatment and its proper place, just as the making of red wine is every bit as skilled a process as the making of white, and must be duly studied and understood. Out of some sixty properties that I visited, almost all of which boasted a red wine, I can only recall tasting half a dozen really well-made red wines. This is an unhappy situation; a fashion can disappear as quickly as it starts – even more quickly if the goods are sub-standard.

Before moving on to my personal adventures and impressions of each commune, it is interesting to look at a survey of the 1985 vintage in Sancerre, which gives some idea of the structure of the *appellation*. Of 1,550 hectares of AOC planted vines, 1,224 were Sauvignon and 326 Pinot Noir. The total area was divided between 442 growers, 342 of whom had less than 5 hectares of vines, a large proportion of these having less than 1.5 hectares; of the remaining 100 growers, 50 had between 5 and 7 hectares, 22 between 7 and 10 and 17 had between 10 and 15 hectares; only 7 growers had between 15 and 20 hectares, 2 between 20 and 25, and only 2 had over 25. To summarize, 72% of the entire *appellation* belonged to 414 growers with less than 10 hectares of vines each, of whom well over half had less than 3 hectares.

This is very much the general picture throughout the Loire Valley, where as much as half the huge volume of wine produced comes from small growers who grow vines as one of several crops. This is an assumption, based on the Dutch writer Hubrecht Duijker's calculation that the smallest area of vines that can support an average family is between 3½ and 4 hectares. Such a structure means that more than half the wine made in the Loire valley is sold either to various *négociants*, or wine merchants, or through the co-operatives that exist in every *appellation*, since the small grower has neither the time, the expertise nor the will to bottle and market his own produce.

Wine that passes through the *négociants* or through the co-operatives comes to their cellars from the growers in one of three ways; it is either in the form of grapes, unfermented grape must or finished wine in bulk. Obviously, as in all businesses, there are good and bad merchants, well run and less well run co-operatives. On the whole the good outweigh the bad, but much harm is certainly done to the image of small-grower *appellations* such as exist in the Loire by a few of the large *négociant* firms. In order to secure markets with large distributors, both in the home and export trade, these firms find it necessary to offer a total range of wines from all over France. Many of their clients, such as the vast supermarket chains, do not concern themselves so much with the quality and regional characteristics of the wines they buy, as with the price. This means that the *négociant* knows exactly how much he can afford to pay per litre for each *appellation*, with the result that, so long as the grower can live off this price, everybody is happy, except perhaps the eventual consumer, who may frequently get a totally wrong – and bad – impression of what Sancerre, Vouvray, Muscadet, etc., should be like.

There is no simple answer to this problem. Various people have suggested that compulsory bottling in the *appellation* could be enforced by the INAO; this would certainly eliminate some of the sub-standard wines that reach the public, but it would also close off an enormous sector of the market to thousands of small wine-makers, who could surely be encouraged to make better wine by some other form of control.

The soil around Sancerre, clay and limestone on the high hills, known as *terres blanches*, fine pebbly limestone on the middle slopes, and stony silex soil to the east of the *appellation*, are all healthy, well-drained, heat-retaining and ideally suited to the cultivation of vines.

Street scene, Les Loges, Pouilly-sur-Loire

Sancerre vineyards and the viaduct in St Satur

Clos de la Poussie, Cordier's vineyard in Bué, Sancerre

A village in Sancerre among the Sauvignon vines

Château de Tracy, Tracy-sur-Loire

As with other vineyards, the stony soil gives finesse and elegance to the wine, whilst the clay produces a wine with roundness, weight and body.

Although the white wines of Sancerre are basically made to be drunk and enjoyed in the year after the vintage, I have been lucky enough to taste one or two excellent wines from earlier years, kept for the amusement of the growers and their friends. 1978 and 1974 from Alphonse Mellot were exceptional, while 1978 and 1969 from François Milon in Chavignol were veritable milestones in my tasting experience.

The people of Sancerre are among the kindest and most welcoming of all the wine-makers I have met. I was seduced by them, and stayed much longer than I had planned, but I regret not one minute or one glass.

SANCERRE

Armed with lists of the growers in each commune, my head full of sound advice and my stomach not quite full of his delicious wine, I left the house of René Laporte, President of the Syndicat Viticole Sancerrois, to discover Sancerre. I decided, logically enough, to start my visits in the commune of Sancerre itself, and what better way to introduce myself, I thought, than to go and have lunch in the place. With the blazing June sun burning the top of my head through the open car roof, I roared merrily up the hill into the village, turned left at the top and parked in the Place de la Halle.

This is the true centre of Sancerre. Cafés, bars and restaurants abound, and all the winding, cobbled streets of this mediaeval town seem to lead here. There is a strangely Italian atmosphere about the square, for during the lunch period and in the evenings the locals tend to drift around, seeing who is drinking or eating where, and stopping to exchange gossip or take a glass with friends. It is also a very popular place with tourists, for Sancerre is undoubtedly one of the most picturesque spots in central France; just off the square, beneath the walls of the château, there is a fabulous view of the Loire and the vine-clad hills in whose bosom lie the lovely villages of Bué, Chavignol, Amigny and Verdigny.

ALPHONSE MELLOT, Sancerre. Comfortably installed at a pavement table outside one of the square's many restaurants, I had lunched lightly and well on the local goat's cheese delicacy, hot Crottin de Chavignol with green salad, and was finishing my half-bottle of Sancerre rosé with a cup of coffee. I asked the bearded man at the next table for a light, and we fell into conversation; he turned out to be a painter, whose family owned the pink-painted gift shop at the top of the square. When I told him I was writing a book about the Loire, he said that I must meet a friend of his at once. As good as his word, he leapt from his seat, sprinted across to a café on the opposite side of the square and came back in no time at all with a man whom he introduced as Alphonse Mellot.

The name was already familiar, since it is plastered liberally about the square and streets of Sancerre, on wine shops, over cellar doors and on the *auberge* in the corner of the square by the château. The Mellots have been wine makers and merchants in Sancerre from father to son since 1513; they have, for Sancerre, an enormous area of vines, nearly forty hectares, and are also *négociants* in quite a big way not only for the wines of Sancerre but for Pouilly Fumé, Menetou-Salon, Reuilly, Quincy and other *appellations* as well. Their best wine, Domaine de la Moussière, comes from what must be the largest single vineyard in the *appellation* at just over 33 hectares. They also produce a prestige *cuvée* of la Moussière called Cuvée EAM (Alphonse's initials) which is chosen very carefully from the best vats each year. La Moussière and Cuvée EAM are fine Sancerres, clean and delicate with a hint of gunflint. All in all, the firm of Alphonse Mellot is the most important organisation in Sancerre, and its owner and general manager now stood before me.

Alphonse the Umpteenth – the rather old-fashioned Christian name is passed from father to eldest son – shook me by the hand and invited me to the first of many congenial lunches, with a party of giants from South Africa. Useless to protest that I had already eaten, 'So what? Can you not eat two lunches? Besides, you can always drink the wine!'

This encounter set the pattern of my adoption by Alphonse. A man of tremendous energy, appetite and humour, he became in a few weeks a real friend,

Place de la Halle – the main square in Sancerre

and I hope he will always remain so. He is a dangerous man to know, but the greatest fun. A typical day with Mellot starts with *le petit déjeuner anglais* at the pizzeria beside his office – bacon and eggs, bread, beer or red wine and coffee; we then spring into whichever family vehicle is nearest, Porsche, Jeep, wife's Peugeot 205 or, once only, a vast eight-wheeled lorry, and set off on a round of visits.

I once drove round Oulton Park with a racing driver in his Lister-Jaguar and learnt what fear is, or at least I thought that's what it was until I journeyed the blind corners and precipitous lanes around Sancerre with Alphonse as charioteer. On my first day with him we visited perhaps a dozen growers, with each of whom we tasted, never spitting, at least one and often more vintages of red, white and rosé; according to my calculations, this adds up to a minimum of 36 glasses of wine per person, or six bottles, and takes no account of the numerous stops for beer when Alphonse felt thirsty, nor the wine consumed at lunch and dinner. In all the time I spent with the Emperor of Sancerre, as he is known locally, I never noticed any alteration in his race-precision driving, nor in his faultless judgment of wine. On the first day, however, I did not know my Jehu's capability; as we approached some blind corner at totally impossible speed, to my eternal shame I pulled the grab handle out of Madame Mellot's Peugeot 205 by its roots in a paroxysm of sheer terror. I stuffed it

back as best I could and never mentioned it to anybody. English *sang-froid* was at stake – 'il faut rester cool', as the French are currently wont to say.

In the commune of Sancerre itself I made several visits, mostly with Alphonse. His own operation is run from his office at the château end of the square. There is also another wine business and restaurant, which is run from the Auberge Alphonse Mellot in the opposite corner of the same end of the square. Confusingly, this does not belong to our Alphonse, but to a cousin of the same name. The Emperor's wine-making buildings and cellars occupy two sides of the square behind his office, which also contains the post office and the war memorial; the latter, as is customary in France, is lovingly cared for, and contains many familiar names of wine-making families.

The Mellot vat-house, half cement and half wood, is a model of efficiency and cleanliness, and the capacity is sufficient to cope with even the most abundant vintages.

Up a flight of steps from the *cuverie* lies Alphonse's personal Aladdin's cave, his private cellar where he keeps his own collection of wine, and where lucky visitors are entertained. The outer room of this cellar contains only past vintages of Sancerre, and if you are as fortunate as I, you may get a chance to taste some of the older wines. The 1974 was still amazingly fresh and not at all oxidised though I found with this wine, as with other old Sauvignons I had tasted, that age has given it more of a Chardonnay taste. In the inner sanctum, Alphonse has a dazzling collection of Bordeaux, Burgundies (including many bottles of Romanée-Conti), a huge variety of Loire wines and even some vintage port.

Like the generations before him, Alphonse is not content to be a large fish in a small pond. He spends much time visiting his Paris restaurant clientèle – an easy run for dinner in the Porsche – and jets happily about the world promoting the name of Sancerre in general and Mellot in particular.

He is blessed with yet another Alphonse to follow him, as well as three impossibly beautiful daughters. Some people are born with a silver spoon – or is it a *tastevin*?

MARNIER-LAPOSTOLLE, Château de Sancerre.

The rambling sprawl of the Château de Sancerre crowns the hill on which the town is built. Its very height and situation have singled out this hill for centuries as a natural defensive and strategic position, but this has also meant that it has been involved in many battles, wars and sieges. The last siege was in 1621, when the castle was virtually razed to the ground. The present dwelling was built in 1874, and was bought at the end of the First World War by the Marnier-Lapostolle family of Grand Marnier renown. The family still own it today, though they only use it for weekends and holidays. As well as the château, the Marniers own 19 hectares of vineyards, all in the commune of Sancerre, two-thirds of which is on silex and a third on clay-limestone.

The very able and friendly *régisseur* is Gérard Cherrier, who gave me a splendid tasting of the 1982, 1984 and 1985 whites and 1984 and 1985 reds. The style of both red and white I found to be acceptable, but a little on the bland side. The 1985 red was the best wine tasted, with a lovely, sweet fruitiness and tremendous length.

With a brand-leader like Grand Marnier as owner, it came as no surprise to discover that of the 60% of the château's output that is sold on the French market, 80% goes to the restaurant trade.

JEAN-LOUIS VACHERON, Sancerre.

When I first arrived in Sancerre, Jean Vacheron, a leading light among the wine-makers of the *appellation*, had just died. Apart from being one of the best producers of Sancerre, particularly of the red variety, Vacheron was a much loved and respected member of the community. Everywhere I went, his peers spoke well of him and deeply regretted his passing, and I am very sad to have missed him.

The business is carried on with the same skill and dedication by Jean's two sons, Jean-Louis and Denis, whose premises are in one of the tiny cobbled streets, the Rue du Puit Partton. The cellars and *cuverie* are all beneath the house, and are a veritable rabbit warren. All the Vacheron Sancerre Rouge spends a period, which varies according to the vintage, in wooden casks here in the cellars; I noticed a considerable number of new casks among the 1985 wine, and Jean-Louis told me that he considers the use of new oak vital to the production of a good red Sancerre; the proportion of new casks used is varied according to the style of each vintage.

We tasted many vintages in Vacheron's private cellar, and I found the quality uniformly excellent, especially the reds, which certainly benefited from their sojourn in oak; the 1982 was particularly fine. The Vacheron wines enjoy a wide distribution both in France and on the world market.

The Vacherons also run the bar called Le Grenier du Sel in the square, where their wines can be drunk by the glass or bottle.

CAVE CO-OPÉRATIVE DE SANCERRE

The Sancerre Co-operative handles about 6% of the entire production of the region. Its premises are a modern complex of buildings to be found on your right as you leave the village of Sancerre in the direction of Bourges.

There are about 180 *adhérents*, or members of the Co-opérative who must supply it with a minimum of 20% of their crop each year, which may be in the form of grapes, unfermented must or finished wine. Monsieur Renaud is the manager (no relation to my friend from St Andelain) and he runs a very efficient and well-equipped operation.

Produce from the Sancerre Co-operative is widely distributed under several different labels on the export market, and they also supply the huge French wine chain Nicolas.

CAVES DE LA MIGNONNE, Sancerre.

During my visit in Sancerre, I had been much intrigued by the signs pointing to this emporium, and decided to investigate. The Caves de la Mignonne is an extensive series of natural caves cut into the limestone rock of the hill of Sancerre. They are to be found on the right as you drive up the hill into the town from St Satur.

This is basically a PR outfit, owned and run by an association of some 40 growers – Association pour la Propagande et le Développement Touristique du Sancerrois – which has offices in the Hôtel de Ville in Sancerre (tel: 48.54.00.26).

Open to the public from the 15th March to 15th November, from 10.00 to 12.00 and 14.00 to 19.00, you may taste and buy the wines of Sancerre and the goat's cheese, Crottins de Chavignol, for which the area is famous, as well as sundry souvenirs like plates, vine corkscrews, maps etc. Prices for tasting and drinking on site are F5.50 per glass or F50.00 per bottle for red, rosé or white.

The day of my visit was scorchingly hot, and the damp cool of the *caves* was most welcome, as was the glass or two of chilled rosé that I took with the local gendarmes, who seemed to know a good hidey-hole when they saw one. Their little white Renault vans kept driving straight into the *caves* and doing a sharp left turn, parking where they were safely hidden from the eyes of any passing superior officers. Much politics, weather, football and local gossip is discussed here.

The manager is Paul Raimbault, an old Sancerre wine-making name. Four major promotional events are held in the *caves* annually.

1 *Nearest weekend to 1st May*
Fête du Crottin de Chavignol (and other cheeses) – taste and take-away of cheeses
Saturday 20.30, Dîner-Dansant (au fromage)!!

2 *Saturday, Sunday and Monday of Pentecost*
Foire aux Vins de Sancerre
Sunday 20.30, Dîner-Dansant

3 *Last weekend of August*
Foire aux Vins de France – 40 *crus* presented by the growers
Sunday 20.30, Dîner-Dansant

4 *Last week-end of October*
Foire aux Huîtres – presented by oyster farmers of the Marennes basin
Sunday 20.30, Dîner-Dansant

THE SANCERROIS DE PARIS AND LA SABOTÉE SANCERROISE. The Sancerrois de Paris was originally an 'expatriate' association of exiles, who were driven to seek employment in the metropolis at the time of the phylloxera. With the return of the vine, they became active promoters of the region and its wines, persuading cafés, bars and restaurants of the merits of Sancerre, white, rosé and red. In their early days they were especially active in the area around Les Halles.

To this day there is still a great annual celebration given by the Sancerrois de Paris at the feast of St Vincent, patron saint of the vignerons. There is a mass in the Church of St Germain l'Auxerrois on the last Sunday in January, followed by much eating and drinking to the music of La Sabotée Sancerroise. This is a group of musicians, all from Sancerre and its satellite villages, who perform folk songs and dances to the music of the hurdy-gurdy and the bagpipes. They are led by M. Dubois, the leading producer of goat's cheese in Chavignol, and the musicians, singers and dancers are largely drawn from the wine-making families of the area.

ST SATUR

St Satur might be said to be the cradle of Sancerre, for there was a monastery here in the Middle Ages, and it was the monks, as elsewhere in France, who started the cultivation of the vine.

The village is situated between the riverside village and erstwhile port of St Thibault and Sancerre itself, and is spanned by a huge stone viaduct. The vineyards of the commune are mostly on the slopes between St Satur and Verdigny, and the soil is predominantly silex on a marl subsoil. In terms of area, it is one of the smallest of the Sancerre *vignobles*, with about 50 hectares of Sauvignon and 9 of Pinot Noir.

DOMAINES LAPORTE, St Satur. Kindly, courteous and endlessly helpful, René Laporte, currently President of the Syndicat Viticole Sancerrois, runs Domaines Laporte, the largest concern in St Satur, with the help of his three sons.

He lives in a house above his old cellars, where he still vinifies his red wine in large oak *fûts* (vats), and also holds tastings from time to time. They have now built an impressive new winery on the hill as you drive from Sancerre towards Verdigny, which stands amid part of their 20 hectares of vines.

Laporte owns vines in several different parts of the Sancerre *vignoble*, and is a strong believer in keeping the wines from each *lieu-dit* separate. To blend everything together, losing the individual character of the different soils and micro-climates in search of a standardised wine vintage after vintage, seems to him to risk ultimately losing the individuality of Sancerre's wines. He has vines in the vineyard of La Cresle (an old French word for slopes), on the Clos de la Terre des Anges – which he sells to Grants of St James in England – and also at Le Rochoy, a south-west facing slope and the nearest vineyard in Sancerre to the River Loire, as well as Laporte du Clos, another vineyard which used to be a church property (Clos de l'Abbaye). Most of his vines are planted in silex on marl subsoil, though La Cresle is more clay-limestone: Le Rochoy also has an individual soil which he calls *pierre à fusil*, which presumably is flint.

Laporte make about 80% white wine and 20% mixed red and rosé. As a *négociant* he buys in a certain amount of wine to meet market demands, but the greater part of his production is from his own vines.

Laporte exports about 45% of his production to England, Holland, Belgium, Germany, Canada and the United States. He has exhibited his wines regularly for 20 years at the various Concours Agricoles, and he has a wall covered in gold, silver and bronze medal certificates to show his success. A new departure for the family was the acquisition some four years ago by René's youngest son of six hectares of vines in Pouilly across the river. The 1985, as their first vintage, was a great success.

Tasted: Domaine du Rochoy 1985. Good pale straw. Nose good, not overpowering. Quite fat, long in the mouth with some richness and quite low in acidity. A distinctive and fine wine, quite different from other Sancerres, which derives from the unusual soil.
Cave la Cresle 1985. Paler colour, more finesse and fruit in bouquet and taste.
Rosé 1985. Lovely light pink. Good Pinot nose. Good, soft tannins with fruit and some ageing potential.
Clos la Comtesse 1984, Chavignol. Light straw colour with a fine nose. Nice clean wine, crisp with good fruit, excellent for the year. No discernible faults. (This vineyard belonged to a M. Cautin at the turn of the century, and he fought phylloxera with his own methods of treatment. The vines remained ungrafted until just before the Second World War.)

VERDIGNY

The village of Verdigny, which also embraces the hamlet of Chaudoux, is one of the biggest communes of the Sancerre *vignoble*, with some 250 hectares of vines, and boasts some really good wine-makers.

The principal vineyards of Verdigny, which are mostly shared by several owners, include most of La Perrière, Les Renardières, La Crêle, the Côte de Chaudoux and the Côte de Verdigny, as well as a small part of the famous Montdamné, most of which is in Chavignol.

PIERRE AND JEAN-PAUL FLEURIET, Cave de la Petite Fontaine, Verdigny.

My first visit in Verdigny was made to the Fleuriet brothers in the company of Alphonse Mellot and a party of Parisian restaurant-owners. The Fleuriets have about nine hectares of vines, all around Verdigny, and the quality and capacity of their vinification, bottling and storage facilities is most impressive. All their red wine is vinified and aged in large wooden *fûts*, whilst the white wine is made in stainless-steel *cuves*. Before leaving the cellars, we were shown the tiny freshwater spring bubbling up from the ground, from which the property takes its name.

The tasting and reception room was hung about with old cooperage and vineyard tools, and a great old stone fireplace was laid with vine twigs. We tasted a 1984 red, which was light in colour, with a nice nose of summer fruits. In the mouth, the fruit was excellent, with nice, supple tannin and some length – all in all a very good 1984. The 1985 white had a strong *bon-bon anglais*, or pear-drop, nose, together with a hint of banana. Initially mouthfilling, the flavour fades disappointingly fast. A curious wine, which I did not altogether like.

PIERRE AND ETIENNE RIFFAULT, Chaudoux.

My memorable visit to the brothers Riffault was made in the company of my friend Alphonse and his banker. The Riffaults are dedicated wine-makers, and are active promoters of the *appellation*, Pierre being a member of the Sabotée Sancerroise.

They have 10 hectares of vines, all grouped around the hamlet of Chaudoux, 95% of which is planted with Sauvignon and 5% with Pinot Noir. This small percentage does not mean that the Riffaults do not take their red wine seriously, rather the reverse; their red wine is all aged in new oak casks, and is not bottled until the September following the vintage. I tasted the 1985, which was all contained in half a dozen brand new oak casks in a special cellar. The wine had a nice deep colour and a good fruity bouquet, with the vanilla hints of new oak. The wine was well made, with bags of fruit, good tannin and ageing potential. New wood was certainly evident, but did not dominate the whole.

After tasting the red, we adjourned to the small reception-cum-tasting room and were seated at a table with a checked cloth, at the centre of which was a huge plate of Tartines aux Fromages de Chèvres, sprinkled with chopped chives. These make the perfect accompaniment to the white wines of Sancerre, whether you are conducting a serious tasting or drinking them for pure pleasure.

We tasted four vintages of their white wine :

1985. Pale greeny gold. Nose of *bon-bon anglais* or pear drops. Lovely, clean wine with lots of good fruit and just the right level of acidity.

1978. (Very late harvest.) Only a shade darker than the '85. A distinct whiff of asparagus on the nose, which can also be detected in the mouth; good fruit and balance – acidity on the low side.

1976. Colour still good, nose quite subdued. I found this one a slight disappointment, as it had lost the freshness that is Sancerre's appeal. A hot vintage white wine, way past its best.

1974. Still has lovely, youthful greeny colour and a fresh, fruity bouquet. Fruit still good, definite taste of fresh limes. Marvellous for a Sancerre 12 years of age.

One of the most enjoyable visits in Sancerre was made perfect by the parting gift of a splendid magnum of the Riffaults' 1985 white. I drank it in December of 1986, and it was even better.

FOURNIER, Père et Fils, Chaudoux.

Paul and Claude Fournier run an active wine-making and *négociant* business in Chaudoux. Their own vineyards amount to about 15 hectares, spread over Verdigny, Sancerre, Bué and Chavignol; they also buy in some Sancerre as well as the wines of Pouilly-sur-Loire, Pouilly Fumé, Menetou-Salon and other Loire wines for their merchant business. Of their own wines, 75% is white and 25% rosé and red; the red spends no time in wood, but has a four-week maceration period in vat.

Apart from their straightforward white Sancerre, they also make a prestige *cuvée* white wine called La Chaudouillonne; 1984 was their first effort with this wine, and they plan to limit production to 3,000 bottles, and will only produce it in good years. 1984 was not, strictly speaking, a great year for Sancerre, but the wine was of an acceptable quality, as was their ordinary 1985 white, though I did not find either particularly exciting. The 1985 was of better quality, but did not have a great deal of ageing potential.

Fournier Père et Fils sell about 60% of their entire production, both their own wine and others, on the home market; they sell both directly and through commission agents to restaurants, *épiceries fines*, and wholesalers, as well as doing a considerable mail-order business to private customers. Of the 40% that is exported, a large volume goes to the United Kingdom where they use a wide variety of labels, all bearing names of past and present relations, in order to give a *soi disant* exclusivity to their various importers.

PAUL PRIEUR ET FILS, Route des Monts Damnés, Verdigny.

I was welcomed by Madame (Paul) Prieur. Her husband works the 12-hectare property with his two sons, Didier and Philippe. They make mainly white, plus some red and rosé from four hectares of Pinot Noir. Their sales are split equally between the home and export market, the latter being chiefly represented by a 20-year association with John Harvey and Sons Limited of Bristol, though they also export to Holland, Belgium and the USA. All the wine that they sell comes from their own vines, which are mainly in Verdigny, though they also have a small plot at Les Garennes in the Sancerre commune.

Madame Prieur told me that they used to do more general farming – some corn, cattle, etc. – but now the only way to economic survival was to concentrate on wine or on general farming. Obviously to make and commercialise good wine one must have sufficient land under vines to merit the purchase of good vinification equipment, a modern bottling line and vineyard equipment such as tractors, a harvesting machine, etc.

After visiting the *cave* with Madame, where all was a model of cleanliness, with *cuves* of concrete-lined steel and stainless steel, I tasted the 1985 white; it had the bright greeny gold colour of Sancerre and a clean, fresh Sauvignon nose, and the taste was crisp and fresh with good fruit and fairly low acidity. The low level of acidity stems partly from the peculiarity of 1985 as a vintage, and partly from the fact that the Paul Prieur vines are entirely on clay-limestone soil, with no gravel.

Returning from the cellar, I met one of the sons, Didier, and talked for a while about the making of red wine in Sancerre. In answer to my question about the danger of Sancerre Rouge being a 'fashionable wine', he reminded me that before phylloxera, Sancerre was devoted almost entirely to the production of red wine from the Pinot Noir. He had seen records of English importers, showing that only red Sancerre was imported during the nineteenth century. In the early 1900s, when people began to drift back to wine-making from vines grafted on the phylloxera-resistant American stocks, they tended to go for the white Sauvignon, since it was – and is – a prolific and reliable variety, and constant supplies of good quantity and quality were what were needed to get the area back on its feet. It was only 10 years ago that they planted Pinor Noir, but Didier is optimistic about the future of red Sancerre.

We then returned to the cellar and tasted the red wines of 1983, 1984 and 1985. The colour of all three was light, though the '85 was very much the darker of the three. The wines were all light, fruity and nicely perfumed, though did not, in my opinion, have much ageing potential. No wood is used at any stage of vinfication here, and it shows. The 1985 will be bottled either just before or just after the 1986 vintage.

ANDRÉ DEZAT, Les Celliers de St Romble, Chaudoux.

André Dezat is Mayor of Verdigny; he came here in 1949 from Sury-en-Vaux, a village only two or three miles to the north. His family have a long history of wine making in Sury, and indeed brother Pierre and nephew Alain still make excellent Sancerre in the hamlet of Maimbray next door to Sury.

This is very much a family business; André's two sons, Simon and Louis both work with him, and the daughters-in-law run the office. They have 13 hectares of Sancerre vineyards, which are spread over the communes of Sancerre, Verdigny, Sury-en-Vaux and Menetou-Ratel; they also have five hectares across the river in Tracy-sur-Loire, one of the very few proprietors I came across who make both Pouilly Fumé and Sancerre. Of the Sancerre vineyards, eight hectares are given over to the production of white

wine, and five are planted with Pinot Noir for rosé and red.

By far the greater part of André's production is sold on the home market, as much as 80%, and most of that is sold to the restaurant trade, with the balance going to regular private customers. The 20% that is exported goes mainly to the United Kingdom, where it is imported by the Wine Society and Thorman Hunt. A little is also sold to Denmark, Holland and Belgium.

I tasted the 1985 white, which was excellent, and everything a fresh, young Sancerre should be. I was then treated to a red and a rosé of the 1979 vintage, which were both delicious. Reds are fermented in vat, and then aged in wood for a period which varies according to the vintage; the 1979 was beautifully smooth, but still had some nice tannins, good body and lots of life.

Dezat knew much of the history of the region, and believes strongly in the ability of the area to produce good red wine; like Didier Prieur, he reminded me that before phylloxera, there were 2,000 hectares of Sancerre planted with Pinot Noir, which was made into red and rosé, and only a tiny amount of white grapes were grown, mostly Chasselas for the table.

Among the many other excellent wine-makers in the Verdigny commune, whom I sadly did not have the time to visit properly, are the multitudinous Reverdy family, Pierre Archambault, who owns a large chunk of the famous La Perrière vineyard, Roger Neveu and Jean Vatan. I have tasted their wines both here in England and in France, and their quality increases my regret at not having got to know them better.

AMIGNY

Amigny is one of the smallest wine villages of the *appellation*, and is in fact part of the commune of Sancerre itself. A handful of vignerons, only one of whom has more than seven hectares of vines, exploit about 53 hectares. The best-known of these are Raymond Berneau-Carroger, Dominique Mellot, a cousin of Alphonse, and Cherrier, Père et Fils.

RAYMOND BERNEAU-CARROGER, Amigny.

My only visit in Amigny was to Raymond Berneau-Carroger. I found the Berneau establishment up a narrow little side street in Amigny, and was greeted by Raymond's wife and his mother-in-law, who turned out to be yet another Mellot. The whole region is run by about half a dozen families; they are all inter-married, and you soon learn to be most careful what you say about whom to whom. The names that crop up frequently are Mellot, Reverdy, Vatan, Riffault, Raimbault, Millerioux and Laporte.

Raymond Berneau is a stocky, powerfully-built man of 47, with an open and friendly manner that would charm the most reluctant bird from the tallest tree. He carries on a family tradition of wine-making that goes back to the end of the last century. He has two children, but they are as yet too young for him to know if succession will be assured. Although he did not say so, it was very clear that he wished for nothing more than that his son should follow him; he is a great traditionalist, and he knows that what he does is right and that the way that he lives is the right way – and he convinced me.

Berneau has just 3½ hectares of vines and the major part of his wine is sold to private customers, who return to him year after year. He is a great believer in making wine naturally and as well as he possibly can. It would be boring, he says, if his wine tasted the same in every vintage; each year the wine should reflect the properties of that particular vintage, otherwise, if one strives by blending and other artificial means to achieve a constant taste, one may as well be making Coca-cola!

All Berneau's vines are around Amigny, and all are planted on clay-limestone soil, which tends to make the wines a little slower to mature and to give them good ageing potential. He makes a little red wine, and it always spends two years in the wood. He believes, however, that the Sancerrois should concentrate more on their white wines, because that is their speciality, and what they do best.

Berneau's conservative approach to wine-making is reflected in his attitude to picking by machine, to which he is quite violently opposed. For optimum efficiency, growers are changing the height at which their vines grow. This is wrong for it must change the speed of ripening; machines should be adapted to conform with the best methods of production rather than vice-versa. All is done by hand here.

Tasted:Red 1982. This had a good deep colour and a nice, flowery Pinot nose. Nice soft tannins and plenty of fruit. Will keep well, though good to drink now.
Rosé 1984. Typical light delicate pink colour with a fresh bouquet. Light and dry with

pleasing fruit. A tiny prickle of fermentation, which R.B. says is normal when the vine is in flower, and this is always more noticeable in rosé than white.
White 1984. Only bottled in May this year, because R.B. believes in keeping stock and bottling at optimum state, rather than selling quick and grabbing the money. Good light colour, fresh bouquet.
White 1985. Tasted two samples from two separate *cuves*. Both were excellent, but quite different in character. R.B. said one had far better ageing potential, with a higher acidity than the other. He would *not* make a blend, but bottle the lighter wine first and keep the other *en cuve* until it was more ready.

A very nice and genuine man with very definite ideas about the integrity that should be applied to wine-making, he strongly believes, for instance, that red Sancerre should only be made when the vintage suits it, since in a poor year it is almost impossible to make a decent red wine.

CHAVIGNOL

Again part of the commune of Sancerre, Chavignol is one of the most important of the wine villages in terms of size, quality and certainly atmosphere. Almost the entire population is engaged in making either wine or goat's cheese, for this is the home of the world famous Crottins de Chavignol, the little, round, white cheeses of goat-milk, which can be either hard or soft and go so well with the wines of Sancerre, red, rosé or white. They are delicious served hot on a crouton of French bread, with a simple green salad, dressed with oil and wine-vinegar as only the French know how. They also make a delicious *fromage blanc*, or cream cheese, from goat's milk: marvellous on tartines cut from freshly baked baguettes with a glass or two of Sancerre.

Before leaving the subject of cheese and Chavignol, I would relate to you a tale that shows both my woeful ignorance of matters gastronomic as well as, I like to think, a certain measure of courage. I would like to say that this happened many years ago in my green and callow youth, as it would excuse my gaucheness, but it was, in truth, all too recent. The occasion was a magical *dîner à deux*, with my wife – of course – in my favourite restaurant in the Loire

Valley, the Auberge du XIIème Siècle at Saché, near Azay-le-Rideau. Glancing through the mouth-watering hand-written menu, I noted that, as an alternative to the *plateau de fromage*, we were being offered Crottin Chaud de Chavignol et sa Petite Salade. There was a party of sophisticated and glamorous Parisians at the next table who had reached that stage of the meal, and they were exclaiming loudly about the perfection of the Crottins. By now I was intrigued and my intellectual and gastronomic curiosity aroused. Darling – and sensible – wife that she is, Wendy always carries a dictionary in her bag when we are abroad; I, an arrogant Chauvinist, scorn such a studious admission of non-fluency, and never stop to ask the way when I am lost. The consequence of the former sin of pride is that I learn nothing, while Wendy's French improves, and of the latter that we are frequently late and sometimes never arrive at all.

I palmed Mr Harrap's pocket edition under the tablecloth and riffled through the pages to the Cs; here it was – 'Crottin, n.m. (horse) dung; (sheep's) dropping'. I could scarcely believe my eyes, as I glanced to my right and watched the bronzed and bejewelled beauty on the next table munching away with such obvious relish. I have always known that the French are mad. They dig for fungus with pigs, do revolting things to geese, eat frogs and even snails; I have eaten all these things – truffles, foie gras, frogs and snails, and must admit that what may seem like lunacy is usually justified by the end product, but this – surely they had overstepped the culinary mark? I summoned Madame Niqueux, wife of the chef/proprietor; 'Madame,' I demanded, 'has there, perhaps, been a spelling mistake? Are these truly *crottins* you are offering us?' 'But, yes, Monsieur. They are a delicacy of the Loire Valley!' 'Of course,' I replied, not wishing to appear in any way a tourist, 'sheep or horse?' 'Goat's, Monsieur. They are delivered to us fresh twice a week from Chavignol in Sancerre. You will try them, yes?'

Of course I would. There was no backing down now. I was fighting, or eating, for my country, and my courage must not fail in face of the enemy. The thin red line would hold, and at least they were fresh goat's droppings. I suppose a chap must feel like this when he orders up his first 'snort' of cocaine, I was set on the path of addiction, and was soon to become a coprophiliac. Where would it all end?

My enjoyment of the Sandre au Beurre Blanc was only slightly marred by what I knew was to follow,

The goats' cheese of Chavignol

but no human emotion can compare with the relief I experienced with that delicious first forkful of melting goat's cheese. It only goes to show that courage pays, and you don't have to believe everything you read in a dictionary.

It was of Chavignol that King Henri IV said, 'If everyone drank the wine from this village, there would be an end to religious wars.' The people certainly seem happy, and belligerence is not one of their characteristics. There is, however, a dark side to Chavignol, as I learnt during one of my cellar visits. I was cornered by a relentless cheese-maker in short trousers who had, let's face it, had too much Sancerre that day. He was anxious that I should know everything about him and about the cheese business and about Chavignol. Communication was tricky, not only due to my ignorance of the curious *patois* he spoke, but mainly due to the fact that he kept going to sleep in the middle of his sentences. I gathered that he was an extremely important figure in the goat-cheese world, and was especially well-known in Wales, to which country he was the sole exporter of goat's cheese. I also understood him to say that Sancerre in general, and Chavignol in particular, were the centre of French witchcraft; what is more, he whispered, there was a witch here tonight. I think he must have meant a warlock, for there were no women present, but I never found out who it was.

I do not entirely dismiss these tales of *sorcellerie*; I have heard the same from more sober sources. There is something else which leads me to believe that there are strange goings-on around Sancerre; I have never met so many men in such a small area who have the index finger of their right hand missing, and who have been so universally reluctant to explain how it happened. Months after my visit to Sancerre, I was at a dinner-party in Villandry; the girl on my right had worked for a PR company some years before, and had been involved in compiling an *annuaire* of all the growers in Sancerre. Naturally we fell to talking about the places and people we both knew, and I launched merrily forth in to my theories about witchcraft and missing fingers; my companion went rather quiet and something made me glance down at her hand, which was resting on the table beside her place – the index finger was missing.

But let us talk a little of the growers of Chavignol, who surely weave their own spells. The ingredients that make up their potions are the soils and micro-climate of this magic corner of Sancerre, the juices of the Sauvignon and Pinot Noir grapes, and the love, care and knowledge acquired by generations of the same families.

JEAN-MARIE BOURGEOIS, Chavignol.

A complex maze of cellars, vat-houses, stock rooms and offices on both sides of the road at the top of the village house the Bourgeois wine business. Jean-Marie, who was kind and helpful in the extreme, took over from his father, the late Henri Bourgeois, on his death in 1985.

This is the biggest firm in Chavignol, indeed one of the biggest in the *appellation* of Sancerre. The Bourgeois vineyards extend to some 37 hectares, and are situated not only here in Chavignol but are spread over just about every commune of the district. Bourgeois believes in keeping the characteristics of the different soils in different vineyards apart, rather than making a homogeneous blend, with the result that you may come across various different labels bearing the H. Bourgeois et Fils name. In England the one most commonly encountered is Les Princesses, shipped exclusively by the excellent and traditional firm of Walter S. Siegel, and sold widely by them throughout the wine trade in the proper and

all too rarely found manner of a true wine shipper. The grapes for this wine are grown on south-west facing slopes of clay and limestone, and it is for me one of the most consistently pleasing and reliable wines of Sancerre.

Bourgeois' other labels include his own Côtes des Monts Damnés, that impossibly steep and erosion-prone vineyard of Chavignol which has broken many hearts. Jean-Marie believes the effort is worthwhile – it is so steep that every operation must be done by hand, including dragging back the topsoil washed down by the rain; having tasted the 1985, I have to agree with him. Working the Mont Damné vineyard is not for the faint-hearted; it was virtually washed away in the great storm of 1921, and since then the older generation have not had the courage to start again, while the majority of the young have better things to do with their time. Only about one third was ever replanted, and the Bourgeois vines figure largely on these slopes.

As well as selling the wine from his own vineyards, Jean-Marie is a *négociant*, and therefore buys in wine from other growers. He is a careful and selective buyer, and purchases only wines that come from the same soil types and the same communes as his own vineyards, so that they will marry readily with his own wines. He shed some interesting light on the operation of co-operatives in general, and the Sancerre one in particular. If, as is the case in Sancerre, a co-operative only insists that its members supply a very low percentage, such as 15%, of their crop to the co-operative, it follows that good professional buyers like Jean-Marie and Alphonse Mellot will always pay the best price and get the best wines, thus the quality of the co-operative's wines will only be suitable for the supermarket giants.

Before retiring to the tasting-room, we were shown the impressive new *Cathédrale des Vins* that the Bourgeois firm are building. This stands at the very top of the village, and will replace the widespread buildings already in use. This is the plan, but I got the distinct impression that, following Parkinson's Law, the production of wine will expand to more than fill the space available, and all those little *caves*, *cuveries* and *salles de dégustation* will still be used.

In company with a Paris restaurateur and his wife we tasted the following wines:

White:Standard Blend 1984. This was very fine, clean and fresh with a nice degree of astringency.
Duc Etienne de Louvy 1984. This wine had

more body than the standard blend, and came from a clay/limestone soil.

La Bourgeoise 1984. A large proportion of Mont Damné wine. Very fine and elegant, coming from the silex of the vineyard.

Standard Blend 1978. This wine had held its freshness and youth well. The fruit was still excellent, and the degree of acidity just right.

Standard Blend 1981. This was a most extraordinary Sancerre; the nose was very perfumed, and smelt almost like a Muscat. Very fine and complex wine.

Mont Damné 1985. Very big on bouquet and masses of fruit and complexity in the mouth. A lovely wine that still needs a little time in bottle.

Red: 1984. Excellent colour for this year. Nose very typical Pinot Noir. Really good for this vintage, with lots of nice fruit. Good for drinking now.

Jean-Marie made the point here that the Pinot Noir seems to do better in the reddish clay/limestone soils, and the white in the lighter coloured ground, and he plants accordingly.

VINCENT DELAPORTE, Chavignol. Like meeting Jean-Marie Bourgeois, it was a special pleasure to make Vincent Delaporte's acquaintance. As a wine-merchant I have shipped, sold and enjoyed Sancerre from both these fine growers for over 10 years, and it was good to put faces to the labels at last.

The Delaporte family live in a substantial house on the left as you drive uphill through Chavignol just before the village square. I visited them on a sunny June evening, and we sat in the courtyard beneath a shady tree, sipping delicious cool glasses of Sancerre.

From 13 hectares, of which only two are planted with Pinot Noir, this old-established Sancerre family produces wine of very high quality, half of which is exported world-wide. One can gauge the quality of Vincent Delaporte's wine by his customers; in England, for example, it is served in the Roux brothers' restaurants and at The Manoir aux Quat' Saisons near Oxford. The half of their production that is sold on the French market goes almost entirely to the restaurant trade.

As with all good wine-makers, the secret of Delaporte's formula is the correct mixture of respect for tradition and modern wine technology. Vincent's son has studied oenology in Beaune, whilst he

himself is much in demand in the Californian vineyards where he advises and, no doubt, learns a little as well.

Picking is done by hand; apart from other reasons, the vineyards around Chavignol are far too steep for machines. Once picking has begun, it is one of Delaporte's first principles to encourage all possible speed between vine and vat; this eliminates the possibility of oxidation at this early stage. Fermentation is started in vat with their own yeast strains; whites complete a slow, cool fermentation in vat at around 16°, never more than 18°, while the reds start the process in vat at around 25°, and are transferred into new wood to finish their fermentation.

We drank the excellent fresh 1985 white, but this was followed by the '83, which, for me, was the better wine, having a higher level of acidity and a lot more finesse. The conversation, as always, drifted on to the history of the region; apparently, in the early days of wine production in this area, St Satur was the quality wine producer, closely followed by Chavignol, and both were well-known before the name of Sancerre was even heard of in connection with wine.

By the smells from the house and that very slightly over-emphasised banging of pots and pans, I knew that the Delaportes' dinner was ready and took my leave, amid protestations that there was plenty of time for another bottle. I preferred to remain in Madame Delaporte's good books.

FRANÇOIS MILON, Chavignol. During a whirlwind tour with Jean-Jacques Renaud of St Andelain, we called in on François Milon, an elderly and courteous man, of whom I later heard nothing but good spoken among his peers; apart from making some truly remarkable Sancerre, he is a pillar of the local church, acting as bell-ringer and sacristan.

He took us to his small and rather shabby cellar, where he produced a bottle of his 1969 white Sancerre, the oldest I have ever tasted; the wine was amazingly fresh still, with a tremendous concentration of fruit and a good level of acidity – the acidity is the key to old Sancerre, apparently. This wine started its life with a very high acidity and 14° of alcohol. Before leaving, Monsieur Milon gave me two bottles of this nectar, and two bottles of the 1978, which was also very fine. I would like to thank this remarkable man for offering me an entirely new wine experience.

EDOUARD VATAN, Chavignol. Edouard Vatan is a member of one of the endless dynastic Sancerre families. He is very short, and has shoulders like a bull; his extraordinary physique comes from years of tending his – and other people's – near vertical vineyards around Chavignol. The most arduous task, he told me, is spraying the vines by hand, which involves climbing up and down the precipitous rows with a 40-litre tank on his back.

He makes wine of his own, and if the lovely 1985 white was anything to go by, he makes it very well. We tasted this in the slate-floored cellar beneath his house in Chavignol. All his wine spends time in wood, and he has the most unusual array of casks, some of which are from Bordeaux and some from Oporto.

PASCAL THOMAS, Chavignol. Pascal and his wife, as well as making wine, keep the café and bar on the left-hand side of the street as you wind up the hill in Chavignol.

BUÉ-EN-SANCERROIS

Largest of the wine-producing communes of the Sancerrois, Bué is situated about five kilometres to the south-west of Sancerre, to the right of the Bourges road. There are some 60 proprietors here, working just over 270 hectares of vines, nearly 26% of which are Pinot Noir. The most famous vineyards of Bué are the Chêne Marchand, Le Grand Chemarin and La Poussie, the latter being the sole property of the firm of Cordier in Bordeaux.

Bué is an attractive village, which meanders on either side of the street up the hill towards the Clos de la Poussie and the plateau above the Côte d'Amigny. In the square in front of the church there is a bar run by one of the jolliest French ladies I have met; one gets the distinct feeling that, if one had been on the run during the war, Danielle would have been working for the Resistance, and would have hidden you until it was safe to move on. Up the hill to the right of the street is the Caveau des Vignerons, a simple but excellent restaurant which is owned by a consortium of Bué wine-makers.

DOMAINES CORDIER, Clos de la Poussie, Bué-en-Sancerrois. Situated on the hilly road to Menetou-Ratel out of Bué, the offices, bottling line and vinification plant of Clos de la Poussie are housed in an ivy-clad cluster of buildings with the faint appearance of a Swiss chalet. There are a total of 32 hectares under vines, 10 of which are represented by the spectacular amphitheatre of a vineyard just up the hill from Bué. The name of Clos de la Poussie is picked out in huge white letters on the hill, *à la* Hollywood. There are a further 13 hectares in the Sancerre *vignoble* and another nine which are split between Ménétréol and Thauvenay. The Bué vineyard gives the best wine from its clay-limestone soil, having a good deal of finesse and fruit.

Of the total vineyard, 10 hectares of the Sancerre vineyard are planted with Pinot Noir, and the rest with Sauvignon Blanc. Following the emerging taste for red Sancerre, Pinots Noirs were planted first in 1966, and the first vintage was in 1969. Cordier obtained a Gold Medal for their red wine in 1970 at the Paris Fair. I learned from M. Schall, general manager at Clos de la Poussie since Jean Cordier acquired it in 1961, that red-wine vinification here is slightly less well understood and therefore more expensive mistakes tend to be made, and the revenue is therefore inclined to be lower.

Of the production at Clos de la Poussie, 25% of the total output is bought in in the form of unfermented must or finished wine, while the other 75% all comes from the company's own vines, and as such bears a Domaine label, while the bought-in wine is sold as, for example, Sancerre 1985, Cordier. Around 50% of the whole is exported; the home market is largely sold direct to the restaurant trade.

Historically, Clos de la Poussie used to belong to a religious foundation, and was acquired by the Crochet family; the devastation of phylloxera in the late nineteenth century caused the owner to sell up and go to Paris, where he ran a successful *crémerie* business, selling cheese, cream, butter and milk. After the war, Octave Crochet returned to Bué and set about the reconstruction of the property, which involved no less than 150 purchases of small parcels of land. Much of the labour in the replanting of the war-neglected vineyard was done by German POWs.

The Crochets are an old Bué family, and the name is still seen on many wine-growers' signboards in the village today. Octave, however, sold out to Jean Cordier in 1961. Schall, who came with the Cordiers, had already worked for the company in Bordeaux, running the Premières Côtes de Bordeaux Châteaux Lauretan, Tanesse and Le Gardera. He is of Alsatian origin.

Tasted:Clos de la Poussie 1985. Fresh and clean with good fruit, and a touch of CO_2, kept deliberately *en cuve* to preserve aromas. In bottle too.

Red 1985. From the silex soil of the Orme au Loup vineyard near Sancerre, which gives wine good ageing potential. Good fruit, long aftertaste. Good drunk young and cool. (No wood is used at Clos de la Poussie.)

JEAN-FRANÇOIS BAILLY, Bué-en-Sancerrois.

My visit to the Bailly-Reverdy establishment was made on the day of the Grand Tour with Alphonse Mellot and his banker. It was one of the hottest June afternoons I have ever experienced in France, and the tenebrous cool of Jean-François' cellar was like a blessing.

Jean-François, who is married to one of the Reverdy family, has 12 hectares of vines, two-thirds of which are Sauvignon, and one-third Pinot Noir. This is a relatively high proportion of red and rosé for the *appellation*, but Jean-François is one of the few wine-makers in Sancerre who really understand red wine techniques and produce consistently good results.

They commercialise all their own wine in bottle, of which approximately half is exported, the United Kingdom being a major market.

Tasted:Rosé 1985. Pleasing, light pink, with a nice fresh bouquet. Dry, clean and delicate with good fruit. Ideal picnic wine.

White 1985. Brilliant, greeny gold, with quite a perfumed nose. Fine, aromatic and mouthfilling. Alphonse remarked that it was typical *terres blanches* wine, and would age well.

White 1985. This was from a more pebbly soil. Quite different – more finesse, with less assertive bouquet and aroma – more my style of Sancerre.

Red 1984. Very pale, almost rosé. I thought it a bit maderised, and was not over-impressed.

Red 1985. The first cask was in the midst of its malo-lactic fermentation and was therefore not tasteable. Good deep red, with a gentle Pinot nose and a hint of oak. Nice fruit and the right amount of soft tannin. Will be a really good red Sancerre.

All then retired to Jean-François' private cellar, armed with a basket of bread, a copious supply of Crottins de Chavignol and a corkscrew. A detailed inspection and discussion of several older vintages, both red and white, then ensued. I remember being particularly impressed by the 1979 white, and a 1982 red of nuclear proportions.

OTHER IMPORTANT GROWERS IN BUÉ.

It was sadly impossible to visit more than a handful of growers in each *appellation*, but there are so many really able *viticulteurs* in Bué that it would be churlish not to name a few of them. I visited Joseph Balland very briefly on one of my lightning and somewhat hazy trips with the Emperor of Sancerre. We tasted an excellent Sancerre called Comte Thibault of the 1985 vintage, as well as a good 1985 Coteaux Giennois, which Balland buys in and vinifies.

Among the other major Bué producers are Jean-Max and Dominique Roger, the Millet brothers, Lucien Crochet and Lucien Picard.

CRÉSANCY-EN-SANCERRE

This commune, with over 140 hectares of AC vineyards is about three kilometres to the west of Bué, and the main vineyard area is in fact nearer to Bué than Cresancy, all around the little hamlet of Champtin, on the south and south-west facing slopes of the Côte de Champtin and the south facing Clos du Ray, which butts onto the Clos du Chêne Marchand in Bué. The soil type is *caillotté*, a combination of gravel and porous tuff, producing Sancerre of freshness and elegance which drinks well in extreme youth.

Among the best growers are Roger Champeau, President of the local Syndicat, Paul Millerioux, Ray Tassin, René Malleron and Jack Pinson. Champeau's red is one of the best I tasted; it is aged in wood and undergoes no filtration.

SURY-EN-VAUX

Sury-en-Vaux, after Ste Gemme, the most northerly of the Sancerre wine-producing communes, is also one of the biggest, though it has the highest number of small *vignerons*; of 73 *exploitants*, 52 work less than three hectares and there are no holdings larger than 10 hectares.

PIERRE & ALAIN DEZAT, Maimbray, Sury-en-Vaux.

Pierre, jolly, powerful and squat, with short,

grey hair *en brosse*, is brother to André, the Mayor of Verdigny. Sury-en-Vaux is where the Dezat family come from, however, and it is André who is the émigré.

Pierre showed us an excellent 1985 rosé from the vat, and three or four samples of his 1985 white, also in vat; all were of fine quality with the correct balance of fruit and astringency. We then looked at the 1985, 1984 and 1982 red, the first and last of which were very well-made wines; the 1984, like several other red Sancerres of that year, I found thin and pallid.

His Sancerre, Domaine du P'tit Roy, as the white is labelled, is to be found on the wine-lists of many great restaurants in France, including Les Troisgros at Roanne, a certain guarantee of quality, if one required further proof.

GEORGES ROBLIN, Château de Maimbray, Sury-en-Vaux.

The Château de Maimbray is a very pretty, long low house that sits on your right as you enter the hamlet of Maimbray from Sury-en-Vaux. The stone is like that used in the Cotswolds, and the general appearance has an Englishness about it, even down to the duckpond.

Monsieur Roblin, who runs the 12 hectare property with his two sons, is famous for his red wine which is reputed to be one of the best in the Sancerre *appellation*. He only has 2½ hectares planted with Pinot Noir, and is against increasing this even though he could sell five times his present production. Replanting is a long-term business, and the demand for red Sancerre may only be a short-term fashion, he reasons.

Almost all of Roblin's vines are planted around the hamlet of Maimbray, where the soil is a clay/limestone mix on a marl subsoil. Picking is still done by hand, and this is more because of the hilly terrain then any deep-rooted prejudice against machines.

He bought the property in 1983, and has built a solid reputation for quality. About half his production goes for export to England, Belgium, Holland and the United States. On the home market he sells his wine mostly in bottle, and a little goes to the Cave Co-opérative in Sancerre.

I tasted two vats of the 1985, which were both delicious; the first had a very assertive and distinct bouquet of white peaches, excellent fruit/acid balance, and a long, lingering aftertaste, the second being slightly less perfumed, which M. Roblin put down to different soils.

Finally, M. Roblin opened a bottle each of his 1982 and 1983 red. Both had a beautiful deep colour, nice Pinot Noir bouquets, and a lovely balanced combination of fruit, body and non-aggressive tannins. The 1982 was just a touch more rounded and ready to drink, but I guessed the 1983 to be '82 before I had tasted '82, so dark and generous was the younger wine.

LUCIEN LAUVERJAT, Domaine des Grosses Pierres, Les Plessis, Sury-en-Vaux.

A couple of kilometres east of Sury-en-Vaux is the small hamlet of Les Plessis, and Lucien Lauverjat farms the Domaine des Grosses Pierres. He is a cereal farmer as well as a wine maker, and used to raise beef too. He gave up beef because, he says, the bureaucracy involved was too complicated and time-consuming.

The soil around Les Grosses Pierres is clay and limestone with a little silex. It is an area very prone to frost risk, not in the winter but in the far more dangerous springtime. Lucien has 12 hectares under vines, 10 Sauvignon and two Pinot Noir, all of which he harvests by machine, and has done so now for five years. Although he pretends that wine is just another agricultural crop to him, he is a conscientious and skilled wine-maker. His red, which is extremely good, always stays in wooden cask for a full year, and is never sold or bottled until after the vintage following its own year.

He is exporting a little wine in bottle to the United Kingdom and Belgium and does a small volume of *vente directe* sales to private customers. The majority of his sales, however, are in bulk, to *négociants* like Alphonse Mellot; he is also a member of the Cave Co-opérative, to which he sends varying amounts of wine each year.

I liked Lucien Lauverjat and his wife, and we spent a jolly hour together. He has the right attitude to life and to wine, and his wines deserve much wider recognition.

I tasted three different samples of his 1985 white; the first was recently bottled, had the usual greeny golden Sancerre colour and quite a perfumed bouquet, and was well made, clean and crisp with nice length. The next two were in vat, one having been racked only once, the other twice; both were excellent, the twice-racked wine having more aroma and perfume, and a distinct touch of *bonbon anglais*.

Finally we looked at two of his reds, which he gave me to taste, blind, in a brandy balloon which he had

42

just brought back from a trip to Bordeaux and Cognac, and of which he was inordinately proud. Both wines were excellent, and I was lucky enough to get the years right; one was 1984, which is not too difficult as the pale colour gives it away, though it was the best red Sancerre from this vintage I had tasted. The other was his 1982, which was rounded, full, and perfect for drinking.

APPELLATION: MENETOU-SALON

Menetou-Salon is a small market town, lying about 30 kilometres south-west of Sancerre, and 20 north-east of Bourges. There are seven communes entitled to the *appellation*; Menetou-Salon itself and Vignoux-sous-les-Aix are at the western side of the *appellation*, while the other five – Morogues, Parassy, Aubinges, St Céols and Humbligny – are to the east. The *encepagement*, or permitted grape varieties, are the same as for Sancerre, Pinot Noir for red and rosé and Sauvignon for the white. Some extremely good wines are made here, especially around Morogues and Menetou-Salon. The whites are frequently the equals of Sancerre, and the reds and rosés often better. It is curious that the Menetou-Salon wines are so unknown when compared with those of Sancerre, particularly bearing in mind the considerable difference in price.

There are some energetic and capable wine makers in this *appellation*, and I predict that the name will become better known and more widely accepted as the growers of Sancerre continue to raise their prices. Generally speaking, the making of red wine is better understood and more painstakingly carried out than in Sancerre, and red Menetou-Salon will, I am sure, find its way on to more and more wine lists all over the world. The rosés are charming, light and unaffected, perfect for picnics, cold summer lunches or simply as refreshing quenchers. White Menetou-Salon at its best is somewhat lighter and less dry then Sancerre, and often has the most delicious bouquet of white peaches.

A vineyard tractor with its special spraying equipment

The countryside around Menetou-Salon is pretty and unspoiled, with high verdant hedgerows and old-fashioned meadows ablaze with wild flowers. For the dedicated sightseer there is the Château de Menetou-Salon, and the Château de Maupas near Morogues. The former was originally built by the legendary Jacques Coeur, minister of finance to Charles XII, who, presumably as a perquisite of his job, made himself the richest man in France – family motto *A vaillants coeurs* (pun) *rien impossible*. The château was acquired and virtually rebuilt in the last century by Prince Auguste d'Arenberg, president of the Suez Canal Company and it still belongs to his descendants. It was Prince Auguste who brought to the château the many priceless works of art that can be seen today; there is also a museum of old motor-cars. This was undoubtedly started by, or is in memory of, the father of the present Prince, who was a pioneeer of the motor-racing circuits.

The Château de Maupas, near Morogues, houses some fine works of art, including Aubusson and Gobelin tapestries from the collections of the Duchesse de Berry, the Comte de Chambord and King Charles X.

MENETOU-SALON

BERNARD ET PIERRE CLÉMENT, Domaine de Chatenoy, Menetou-Salon.

The Cléments have been involved in wine-making here in Menetou-Salon for many generations. Bernard and Pierre are father and son, and it was Bernard's grandfather, Pierre Alexandre, who first created the Chatenoy vineyard in 1884. Bernard,

Vineyard workers' cottages

who is currently president of the Union Viticole de Menetou-Salon, has done much painstaking research, and has turned up records of one Paul Clément, who was a *vigneron* here in 1750, and, even further back, a Sebastian Clément is recorded as producing *un nectar fort reputé* in 1627. I have also found evidence of a Jean Clément, who was killed while acting as a collector of *dimes*, or tithes for the Seigneur of Menetou-Salon in 1729. This may, or may not, have been a member of the family, but by all accounts there must have been quite a fracas, as one man was knocked unconscious, while another poor fellow suffered a broken arm and pitch-fork wounds in the back and groin. I suppose French people object to paying taxes as much as anybody, but we all know what this sort of behaviour led to some 50 years later.

Bernard's grandfather, Pierre Alexandre, or 'Le Lexandre', as he was affectionately known to the locals, was largely instrumental in getting the Menetou-Salon *vignoble* back on its feet after phylloxera had virtually wiped it out. There is an adage which the family quote, and of which they are probably the authors: *'Le paysan qui veut vivre de la terre doit, avant tout, vivre pour la terre.'*

Pierre, the newest representative of this ancient dynasty of wine makers, has much of the traditionalist about him, but he is at the same time very go-ahead in his approach to the business and seeking out new markets. He is more or less in charge of day-to-day running, since Bernard's time is much taken up with the affairs of the Syndicat Viticole. Pierre studied and received his Diploma of Oenology

M Clément (père) drawing a tasting sample of 1985 red Menetou-Salon from one of the experimental new casks

at Dijon; and is making herculean efforts with the red wine of Domaine de Chatenoy. Vinification for the white and most of the red is similar to Sancerre, but Pierre has been experimenting with a proportion of the Pinot Noir crop since 1982. The wine is aged in oak casks for one year, and one-third of these are new each year. It is a brave essay, and the initial results, on tasting, are most encouraging. Ultimately the success of such experiments will depend upon marketing skill, for the problem at the moment is that it is difficult to envisage any buyer willing to pay the necessarily high price for red Menetou-Salon, not an easy wine to sell, even when you are not buying new casks each year at F2,000 apiece.

I tasted the 1983 red, in which I found the tannins of the oak far too pronounced; the '84 was a much better-balanced wine, and will make a fine bottle. We then looked at two cask-samples of the 1985, one from a new barrel and the other from a cask of one year. Curiously the new oak sample was less *boisé* than that from the one-year cask, which was darker and had more fruit; the wines were, however, from different vats, and the *assemblage* had yet to be made.

The 1985 white, which we drank while talking about the property, was deliciously refreshing with good fruit and length; it had a most lovely nose of ripe white peaches.

MOROGUES

HENRY PELLÉ, Morogues. Henry Pellé lives opposite the church in the pretty village of Morogues; if you turn left as you face his house and drive down the hill, you will pass his son's house on your left and eventually come to his cellars at the bottom of the hill. The immaculate and beautiful garden of M. Pellé Junior may give you a clue to the family's second business, which is that of seedsmen. This *pépinièriste* activity concerns only vines, and they do much valuable experimental work in the field of clonal selection.

I found Henry Pellé most kind and helpful; he really believes in the wines of Menetou-Salon, and those of Morogues in particular, and is confident that the best whites of the *appellation* come from around here. As well as 20 hectares of AC Menetou-Salon vines, he also owns four hectares of Sancerre vineyard in the commune of Montigny, the furthest-flung of the Sancerre 'outposts', and the nearest to Menetou-Salon.

From the Menetou-Salon vines, Pellé produces 60% white wine, while the remaining 40% is divided between red and rosé from the Pinot Noir; the Sancerre vineyard was planted four years ago with 100% Sauvignon clonal selections. The 1985 is the

45

first vintage he has made, and it was awarded a Medaille d'Argent at Macon.

In the large man-made underground cellars, Pellé makes two different white Menetou-Salons, a red and a rosé, as well as the white Sancerre. Whites and rosés are cool-fermented and vinified entirely in vat; his reds spend a minimum of three months in wood, but he is not seeking to emulate the Burgundians or the Bordelais by making big, tannic *vins de garde*. Red Menetou-Salon has enough character of its own, and can sell without trying to be something that it is not. His standard white is an *assemblage* from all the Sauvignon vines, while his up-market *cuvée* comes from a particular vineyard and is sold slightly more expensively as Clos des Blanchais.

The total average production from Pellé's vineyards is between 1,000 and 1,500 hectolitres. Around 55% of his wines are sold on the domestic market to the restaurant trade and to private customers; the rest is exported to Belgium, Holland and the United Kingdom, where his wine is sold by The Wine Society, Jonathan Goedhuis and John Fells.

Tasted: White Menetou-Salon (assemblage) 1985. Nice bouquet with plenty of peachy fruit. Clean and nicely balanced with good fruit and lowish acidity. Shortish.

White Menetou-Salon, Clos des Blanchais 1985. Nose slightly finer and more spicy than the *assemblage* wine. Crisp, clean and with a touch more finesse and length than the first wine.

Sancerre (Selection Clonale) 1985. First vintage from four-year-old vines. Medaille d'Argent at Macon. Nice, fresh greeny colour, with slight gooseberry smell. Clean, crisp, well-made Sancerre, with good fruit and some length.

Rosé Menetou-Salon 1985. Pretty light pink colour. Nose and palate clean, straightforward with nice light summery fruit. Excellent for picnics or cold collations.

Red Menetou-Salon 1985. Good strong young Pinot nose. Colour brilliant, and somewhat darker than most Sancerre reds I have seen. Balance very good, with nice roundness and fruit. Would probably be even better with a few more months in bottle.

Red Menetou-Salon 1984. Very pale bricky red. Slight farmyard smell. Wine that needs drinking, but perfectly OK.

APPELLATION: REUILLY

REUILLY

Reuilly is a small town some 15 kilometres from Bourges. It is on the Arnon, a river that flows into the Cher, which in turn flows into the Loire. It is a very sleepy, rather depressing place, and there are no outward and visible signs that it has anything at all to do with wine. It took me some considerable time to find a wine-maker, who turned out to be one Claude Lafond, who is one of the biggest in Reuilly.

CLAUDE LAFOND, Reuilly. We met at M. Lafond's modest semi-detached bungalow, which like much else in Reuilly had no signs of wine-making around or inside it. I learnt that the wine business is in a decline, though much effort is being made at present to revitalise it. The main reason has apparently been that growing cereals is at the same time less risky and more profitable. A Syndicat d'Initiative is being built in Reuilly at the moment, which may help from the promotion angle.

At present there are just 70 hectares under vines in the *appellation*, which are in the hands of 20 growers of whom 14 own less than a hectare. M. Lafond, with six hectares, can therefore be considered an important wine-maker for Reuilly.

White, red and some rosé are made, with Sauvignon, Pinot Noir and Pinot Gris as the *cépages*. Lafond says he is fairly typical of the region, exporting only 25% of his output, the rest being supplied direct to private customers and restaurants.

PREUILLY

OLIVIER CROMWEL, Preuilly. As I mention in 'Tailpiece', I discovered very nearly at the end of my researches that I had missed, for an Englishman, an essential visit to a grower in Reuilly called Olivier Cromwel.

On my second-last day in France I tracked him down. He lives and farms at a village called Preuilly near Lury-sur-Arnon, about eight kilometres from Reuilly, and has 4½ hectares of vines, three of Sauvignon for white wine and 1½ of Pinot Gris for rosé. He also makes a sparkling wine from the Sauvignon which is surprisingly good. I say this, because it is not a grape variety which generally lends itself well to the making of *méthode champenoise*. Sadly, Olivier Cromwel's customers seem to have heard the same story, for he told me that he has a very large stock which he cannot sell. I suggested that a clever marketing man might be able to make use of his name to sell his wine to anti-monarchist organisations, but the combination of my French and his lack of knowledge of English history put something of a damper on this exciting proposition.

On the subject of his name and origins, Olivier Cromwel was a little vague, though he thought his ancestors may well have been Scottish; and even if he were a direct descendant of Oliver Cromwell and could lay some claim to the English throne, he said he was too busy with his vines to take the matter any further.

His white was a perfectly respectable clean, dry Sauvignon, which he sells partly to passing private customers, as well as to restaurants, bars and cafés, both locally and further afield. We enjoyed a happy hour's conversation and some laughs in his kitchen. Sadly he is the last Cromwel in the area, and we shall never know how he got there, but I feel sure there is good material here for some keen genealogist.

Olivier Cromwel at Preuilly

APPELLATION: QUINCY

The *appellation contrôlée* was granted to Quincy even before Sancerre, in 1936, and it applies only to white wines from the Sauvignon grape. These white wines can be of excellent quality, and it is sad that they are not better known outside France, for they are reasonably priced. Apart from one outfit, the Domaine de Maison Blanche, which is owned, run and commercialised by the large *négociant* house of Albert Besombes in Saumur, most of the vineyards are relatively small, and production is simply not big enough to justify export sales efforts. Most of the wine is sold by the growers to French restaurants and private customers, or to *négociant* houses such as Alphonse Mellot in Sancerre.

QUINCY

The village of Quincy is a few miles west of the city of Bourges and about the same distance east of Reuilly. Although Quincy has a sleepy sort of air about it, there is more a feeling of hope and confidence than in neighbouring Reuilly. This is very evidently a wine village; almost every other house bears the placard of a *viticulteur et récoltant*, and about 100 hectares are under the vine as opposed to Reuilly's 60.

The soil in the Quincy vineyard is a sandy gravel, deposited on its left bank by the River Cher at the beginning of the Quaternary Period, when mankind first appeared. The soil, exposure and reflective nature of the soil tend to result in early ripening, but frost risk is a great problem – in 1977 90% of the crop was lost in an April frost.

PIERRE DURET ET FILS, Quincy. Fairly typical of the growers of Quincy, the Duret family farming business is run by Pierre and his two sons. There are eight hectares of vines, mostly AC Sauvignon, of which six belong to Pierre, one to the eldest son Pascal and the remaining hectare is rented. Sadly I got the impression that, though they take their wine very seriously, and indeed make it very well, the sons feel that the money and the future is in the growing of cereals.

The high quality of the Duret wine – the 1985 which we drank was excellent – is mainly due to the very high proportion of old vines, many of which are 50 to 60 years old, which also means low yields. Vinification is carried out in a mixture of stainless steel and cement vats, and the Durets do their own bottling and labelling. Picking is done partly manually and partly by machine.

A small proportion of the production is sold as grape must to *négociants*, but the majority of Duret's wine goes to the restaurants of the locality – Jean Bardet of Tours is a customer –as well as Paris and the whole northern sector of France; about a third of their wine is bought by private customers.

OTHER QUINCY WINE-MAKERS. I have imported the wines of La Domaine de Maison Blanche into England, and always found them to be of good consistent quality. Amongst other growers whose wines I have tasted and enjoyed in the village café, Au Bon Vin de Quincy, and elsewhere, are Raymond Pipet, Maurice Rapin and Pierre Mardon.

EASTERN LOIRE:
GUIDE TO HOTELS & RESTAURANTS

Apart from my brief and glorious stay at Château du Nozet as Patrick de Ladoucette's guest, I spent my entire time whilst researching this area at the really comfortable *chambre d'hôte* establishment of Bernard and Babette Pasquet at Neuvy-sur-Loire. It is called L'Étang, and is about 20 kilometres north of Sancerre, well sign-posted, off to the left of the N7. It is, in fact, a working farm, and there are an ever-increasing number of rooms in the stone barns, stables and cowsheds which surround the courtyard. They have been well converted, and tastefully and comfortably furnished, each having its own shower, or bathroom and lavatory. The overnight charge, which includes breakfast, is extremely reasonable. There are three kitchens, with refrigerators and cookers, where you may prepare and eat your own food if your wish. The Pasquets will feed you *en famille* for dinner, if you let them know in advance, in their own dining room – in fact we ate barbecues in the garden almost every night during the magnificent June of 1986 that I spent there.

The Pasquets are an amusing and attractive couple. They know the area very thoroughly, speak several languages, including English, and are most welcoming and helpful. Tennis and badminton are offered in the grounds; there are lovely walks and interesting motoring trips to be made, and riding can be arranged. The atmosphere is relaxed, and you are encouraged to please yourself. All-in-all, a good place to relax for a few days, or even to spend a whole holiday (tel: 86.39.20.06).

In Pouilly-sur Loire I ate well in two restaurants: the Bouteille d'Or, in the centre of the village, had recently acquired a new chef, and things were definitely looking up. Across the road from the restaurant is the hotel part of the establishment, though I have not stayed there. In spite of its rather unprepossessing exterior, the food in the one-star rated L'Espérance is extremely good, and the wine list, as one would expect, carries a fine range of wines from the best growers in Pouilly and Sancerre. I note from my *Michelin* that the L'Espérance also has a handful of rooms.

If you drive across the Loire towards Sancerre by the new bridge, you arrive on the other side in the old river port of Saint Thibault. Immediately on your right is the hôtel L'Etoile (tel:48.54.12.15) which has a passable restaurant in a separate building on the river-bank. A little further along you will find an excellent restaurant on a boat; here you can get an excellent *friture*, a local speciality of deep-fried, whole tiny fish from the river, not dissimilar to whitebait but more delicate. The *sandre*, another Loire fish, is usually good, and goes well with Pouilly

Fumé or Sancerre. The owner of La Péniche (The Long Boat), Monsieur Daniel Banlieu, is very knowledgeable on the history of the river when it was a navigable waterway, and the most important commercial thoroughfare in France. At lunchtime on a sunny day it can be a most agreeable watering-hole, as you sit at your table, surveying the broad expanse of the Loire, glass in hand, enjoying the gentle breeze through the window. At night, during hot weather, the mosquitoes have to be seen to be believed.

Driving on towards St Satur and Sancerre, you pass a street on your left called the Rue Jacques Combes, a hundred yards along here, on your right, you will find L'Auberge (tel:48.54. 13.79), a country-style restaurant where the welcome is warm, the food delicious and the bill reasonable. In St Satur you can stay in comfort and eat very well at the Laurier (tel:48.54.17.20).

Sancerre itself has one or two restaurants. I have been very well pleased with the food, the wine list and the friendly service in the Restaurant de la Tour (tel:48.54.00.81) in the Place de la Halle. Daniel and Pascale Fournier have recently opened up an upstairs dining-room, which commands a magnificent view over the Sancerre vineyards. The same couple also run the Pizzeria, the entrance of which is to be found down the steps beside the restaurant; this has a lively bar, and tables inside and out where many of the local wine-makers gather for drinks or a simple meal.

La Tasse d'Argent on the Remparts des Augustins (tel:48.54.01.44) enjoys a good reputation, and also affords marvellous views over the vine-clad hills, as does Sancerre's principal hotel, the Panoramic (tel:48.54.22.44) which is under the same ownership.

Of the rest of the wine-making communes of Sancerre, we have already spoken of the Caveau des Vignerons in Bué; there is also a simple café/bar in Sury-en-Vaux, where you can eat good country fare and pay a fair price. There is a restaurant called the Maillet in Menetou-Ratel, which, according to Michelin, is open for lunches only, though I did not try it.

TOURAINE
CONTENTS

COMMUNES AND GROWERS VISITED

TOURAINE

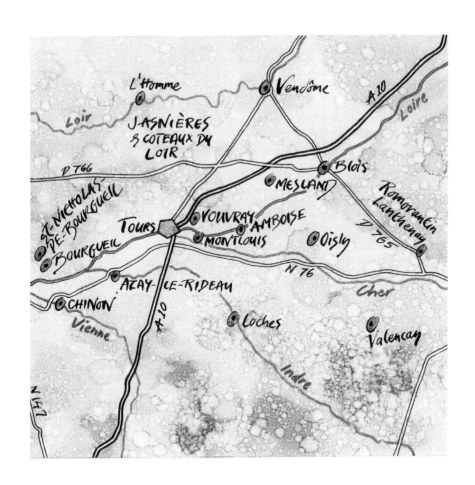

APPELLATION: TOURAINE (GENERIC)

Château de Chaumont, a popular tourist attraction on the banks of the Loire

Touraine embraces an enormous tract of country, with the city of Tours as its spiritual and commercial heart, if not its exact geographic centre. Within the limits of Touraine there are some 8,000 hectares of vineyards planted, a staggering 30 square miles, of which about 3,000 hectares produces wine which is entitled only to the simple *appellation* Touraine.

The wide variations in soil and micro-climate within such a large area, some 100 kilometres north to south and the same distance from east to west, necessarily result in a wide variety of wines. Add to the purely physical differences the range of grape varieties suited to the soil types, plus the highly individual character of the wine-makers, and you have some idea of the breadth of the canvas at which we are looking.

Still wines of the Touraine *appellation* may be red, white or rosé, and the sparkling wines, whether sold simply as Touraine Mousseux, or made under the stricter and more recently created *appellation*, Crémant de Loire, may be white or rosé, and vary from dry to sweet. Permitted grape varieties are legion, but for the red and rosé the Gamay dominates the scene, with a little Cabernet and Cot thrown in, with the Groslot and Pineau d'Aunis permitted for the rosé. Still white Touraine is most commonly made from the Sauvignon, a variety peculiarly well suited to the clay-silex soil of the vineyards on the higher ground on either side of the Cher and the Loire. The Chenin Blanc is the favoured grape for the making of sparkling wine, and the Burgundian Chardonnay is gaining ground, though its use is currently restricted by INAO regulations to 20% of the total volume of a wine.

Although AC Touraine wines are made all over the vast area of the Touraine *vignoble*, there appears to be a concentration of both effort and quality in the eastern end of the region. The large *négociant* firm of Monmousseau in Montrichard, owned by the great champagne house of Taittinger, is among the leading brands of sparkling Touraine with their Brut de Mosny, and they also market the still wines of Touraine on a world-wide basis.

SDVF, BLANC FOUSSY. Perhaps the biggest sparkling wine operator is the giant Societé des Vins de France, in the guise of Blanc Foussy, who handle approximately one quarter of all the white wine produced under the Touraine *appellation*; this vast volume of wine now passes through their giant modern winery at Bléré on the left bank of the Cher.

LES VIGNERONS DE LA VALLÉE DU CHER, St Aignan-sur-Cher. This is a recently formed SICA based in St Aignan-sur-Cher; it is composed of a number of *Vignerons* in the valley of the Cher and around Oisly who are making a concerted effort to sell their AC Touraine wines on the platform of quality.

This is an uphill task, since Touraine Sauvignon, Touraine Gamay and the various permitted mixtures of grape varieties are known more as wines of *Bon rapport qualité-prix* on the supermarket shelves. Under the extremely able direction of Michel Sébéo, however, they will surely succeed. Late of the Vouvray house of Marc Brédif, Sébéo has all the necessary marketing expertise, knowledge of both home and export markets, and, above all, the necessary enthusiasm for the project to inspire the growers and carry the day.

I can only speak for the English market, but I can definitely see a place for these wines. The traditional wines of the Sauvignon grape, such as Sancerre and Pouilly Fumé, have now moved out of the everyday drinking bracket, and wines like the excellent blends from the Vignerons de la Vallée du Cher, if properly marketed, could easily fill the vacuum thus created. Similarly, the Gamays from the Beaujolais have also become more expensive, and there too a gap in the market has opened.

Following their policy of meticulous vinification and strict selection, this brave new venture has every chance of success. Vinification of the still wines is carried out on the premises of the Confrérie des Vignerons d'Oisly et Thésée at Oisly.

In addition to Touraine Sauvignon and Touraine Gamay, they also produce a red *assemblage* wine, sold under the name Tradition; this is a blend of Cabernet Franc, Gamay and Cot Malbec, and it ages quite well, reaching its best with about three years' bottle age.

There is also some good sparkling wine made, which is vinified for the Confrérie by Celliers de Touraine in Noyers-sur-Cher, which is also part of this new SICA.

CONFRÉRIE DES VIGNERONS D'OISLY ET THÉSÉE, Oisly. By now well established as producers of some of the best wines of the Touraine *Appellation*, the Confrérie was founded in 1960 by the present director, Jacques Choquet, in association with his good friend, recently retired, who was appropriately named Monsieur Pinard. Originally called the Cave Co-opérative des Vignerons d'Oisly et Thésée, there were nine founder-growers; their ranks have now grown to around 60.

Selection of wines is by blind and scrupulously fair tasting by the growers themselves; thus it is perfectly possible for a *vigneron* to reject his own wine. The average annual production of the Confrérie is around 20,000 hectolitres, of which about 25% is sold in bulk and the rest –some 165,000 cases – in bottle. Sales are split on the rough basis of 75% on the home market and 25% export, with the majority of the home sales going to the restaurant and café business.

Obviously, by far the greater proportion of the Confrérie's production is in AC Touraine wines, some 50% of which is white, either Sauvignon or Pineau de la Loire (Chenin Blanc); about 40% is red, largely Gamay, with some *assemblage* wine of Cabernet Franc, Cot Malbec, Gamay and Pinot Noir, which is sold under the name Baronnie d'Aignan; the rest is rosé. About 3% of the total production is sold as Vin de Pays du Jardin de la France. Some sparkling wine is also produced, which is champagnised for the Confrérie by the Celliers de Touraine.

In addition to the range of wines detailed above, I also tasted an excellent experimental Touraine Blanc, which was made from 100% Chardonnay; the result was a wine of lovely medium golden colour, with a nice open bouquet of ripe fruit; in the mouth it was full and rounded, with nice length and the characteristic 'butteriness' of the Chardonnay. It was an undoubted success, but sadly not marketable, since the AOC regulations limit the permitted proportion of Chardonnay in Touraine Blanc to 20% of the total.

As a general rule, all the white wines of the Confrérie are vinified by the growers on their own premises, and delivered to the Oisly cellars as 'made wine' for ageing and blending. The reds are generally vinified at Oisly, from grapes brought in by the members.

The wine-making equipment and storage tanks at Oisly are impressive, and adequate for even the most abundant harvest, and the oenological know-how is certainly there to match. All wines are bottled within six months of the vintage, a policy deliberately followed to preserve the freshness and aromas of the wine.

Jacques Choquet, the guiding light of the Confrérie, is a great character. Of Norman origin, he spent the early part of his career in the post-war years dealing in Calvados, mostly delivered in American jerrycans to the restaurateurs and café-owners of Paris. This trade smacks more than a little of the piratical, but doubtless it gave Choquet some invaluable experience, and many useful contacts in the restaurants and cafés of the capital. He is to retire in the not too distant future, and it is to be hoped that his good work will be continued at Oisly.

CHÂTEAU DE CHENONCEAU. It was only at the very end of my researches for this book that I learnt that wine is made at Chenonceau, and made very seriously at that. Wine has in fact been made here since the castle, arguably the most beautiful in all France, was built by Thomas Bohier, controller of the Royal Treasury under François I in 1513. Bohier is reputed to be the original importer of the Chenin Blanc to Touraine. Catherine de Médicis was Châtelaine of Chenonceau from 1559, having shoved Diane de Poitiers out of the back door following the death in single combat of her husband and Diane's protector, Henri II. Catherine was also actively interested in the wine of the estate, introducing a grape variety known as the Tournon.

The interest of the proprietors of Chenonceau in their vineyards continues to this day with the Menier family, owners since 1913. The same love and care for Chenonceau as a whole can be seen in the continuous work of restoration in the château itself, and in the lovely gardens bordering the Cher.

The wine of Chenonceau, which is entitled to the *Appellation* Touraine, is made in the lovely seventeenth-century vinification buildings which, together with the *régisseur*'s house and other offices, surround a courtyard adjoining the château. The tiled roofs of these buildings extend to form a kind of cloister, which has the dual role of storage for empty casks, with the added effect of keeping the walls cool for better control of vinification.

The wine-making at this splendid property, is mainly the responsibility of Yves de la Morandière; this gentleman has been here for over twenty years, and his love of the job is clearly manifested in the

skill and care that he lavishes on every aspect of his work. Under his direction, the vinification buildings were completely re-equipped with all the latest and best in presses, *cuves* and cooling plant in the early 1980s. All may be unchanged and timeless quiet without, but immediately you enter, the ranks of Guérin vats, all with Jacques Puisais' *système de pigeage*, the Vaslin horizontal press and Kreyer temperature control system, announce that serious wine is being made here.

There are currently some 12 hectares under vines, planted with 50% Chenin Blanc, 35% Cabernet Franc, 5% Cot Malbec and 10% Grolleau. I tasted an excellent dry white and a *demi-sec* of the 1985 vintage, the *demi-sec* having some class and potential for ageing and improvement; the reds of 1985, 1986 and 1987, made almost entirely from Cabernet Franc, were respectable, with good fruit and no great pretensions – although the 1985 still has some way to go – with plenty of good tannins. The château also makes a sparkling white from the Chenin Blanc, and a sparkling rosé from the Grolleau; I tasted the latter, which was a light orangey pink in colour, with just a touch of sweetness –a very pleasing wine for an apéritif on a summer evening.

A small amount of Chenonceau wine is exported, mainly to Japan, but the bulk is sold on the home market. Presentation is excellent, the labels being commissioned each year from a known artist.

HENRY MARIONNET, Domaine de la Charmoise, Soings-en-Sologne. Some of the best Sauvignons and Gamays of the Touraine *appellation* are made around this area. Growers like Henry Marionnet of the Domaine de la Charmoise near Soings-en-Sologne, Maurice Barbou of Oisly, whose grandfather is reputed to have been the first to grow the Sauvignon in Touraine, and Jacques Delaunay of Pouillé-sur-Cher – these and many more are combining to improve the quality and market-image of the *appellation* here and abroad. I think it fair to say that much ground has been gained with the whites, especially the Touraine Sauvignons, but that the reds still have some catching up to do in terms of quality.

I spent a thoroughly enjoyable and instructive day with Henry Marionnet at the Domaine de la Charmoise. My general comments about red Touraine definitely do not apply here. Henry makes only still wines, 75% of which are red from almost

100% Gamay, and 25% white from Sauvignon. His house is completely encircled by vines, which are trained on higher than normal wires so that the bunches are between waist and shoulder level on the average person. The Domaine de la Charmoise vineyard is on some of the highest ground in all Touraine; 40 hectares of gravel and silex on a clay sub-soil are planted with about 75% Gamay and 25% Sauvignon. The soil here on the high ground is noted for the delicacy and finesse that it gives to a wine, and these qualities are paramount in the Marionnet wines; in addition to the Charmoise land, Henry also has about seven hectares of vines on the southern bank of the River Cher, where the soil tends to give wines of more weight and body. All the wine is vinified and blended here in the ultra-modern *cuverie*, where stainless steel is the material and oenological expertise the watchword.

Marionnet was one of the pioneers of the *macération carbonique* fermentation for red wines. Already widely practised in the Beaujolais, where the Gamay is also king, this was first adopted at La Charmoise in 1973. *Macération carbonique* has its advocates and its detractors; on the plus side, it produces a good result with a grape like the Gamay, which gives a fruity wine intended for drinking within a twelve-month period, whilst on the other side of the coin it tends to produce a wine of rather uniform character, regardless of grape or origin. For the kind of market in which Touraine Gamay is likely to succeed, the advantages would appear to outweigh the disadvantages.

Two types of Gamay are made here, one, by *macération carbonique*, for sale *en primeur*, the other, fermented and vinified in more traditional fashion for later bottling and sale. We tasted both at lunch; the Primeur '85, bottled in November after the vintage, had a fine deep colour and the nose of a good Beaujolais. There was plenty of fruit, but there was a curious hardness about the wine that I did not like; Henry said that this would disappear in a month or two, and that the wine would age well. The Normale '85, bottled only a month before at the end of June, had the same colour and the nose was a shade more open. The same fresh, young grapiness was there, but I found the wine softer and more pleasant for current drinking.

We had drunk the Marionnet Touraine Sauvignon with the entrée, and I found it as good an example of a young Sauvignon as I have tasted anywhere; it had a brilliant, greeny-gold colour, and lovely nose of fruit and flowers, and in the mouth it was clean, crisp and refreshing – delicious for that hot August day.

With the cheese Henry Marionnet opened a bottle of his 1978 Gamay. I have never tasted a Gamay of that age before, and was agreeably surprised. The colour was still excellent, with only a hint of brown; the nose was slightly farmyard, but not unpleasant, and the taste was more like an old Côte de Nuits than a Gamay, with good, ripe fruit and some breeding.

Henry took over the running of the estate from his father in 1967, but I gather that the changeover was not effected without some pain. Marionnet *père* was apparently something of a patriarchal martinet – Henry was not allowed to speak at mealtimes until he was nearly grown up; his father's ideas about making wine were as immutable as they were unorthodox, and Henry was faced with the task of replanting the whole vineyard, which had hitherto been filled with curious, and frequently ungrafted, hybrid varieties of doubtful origin and even more doubtful suitability. Each vine he decided to grub up provoked an argument, and it was 10 years before the task was completed.

After lunch Henry showed me the film that he has made about a year in the life of the Domaine de la Charmoise, and, like everything to which he turns his hand, it was very competently executed. We then took a tour of the Charmoise vineyards, which are immaculately maintained and a joy to behold. The only cloud on the horizon to cast a touch of gloom on an otherwise perfect day, was the sight of a large number of dead and dying Sauvignon vines. They are being attacked by a disease called *eutypiose*, which only affects this variety, and against which no treatment has been developed.

I am grateful to Henry Marionnet for all his time, trouble and hospitality, and for the generous quantity of Touraine Gamay and Touraine Sauvignon he insisted that I took 'pour la route'.

J.-M. MONMOUSSEAU SA, Montrichard.

To see how sparkling Touraine is made on a large scale, I visited J.-M. Monmousseau SA in Montrichard on the Cher. A family business, founded in 1886 by Alcide Monmousseau, the company now belongs to Taittinger champagne, though Armand still runs the firm along family lines, like his father, grandfather and great-great uncle Alcide before him. Armand's brother Patrice runs the Saumur sparkling wine firm of Bouvet-Ladubay, also the property of Taittinger.

The Monmousseaus are a Touraine family, and the name is not found outside the region; their origins are in Vouvray, where the family still own the Château de Gaudrelle and the prestigious vineyard of Clos le Vigneau. Indeed, although the majority of the two million or so bottles that are sold annually come from other parts of Touraine, I get the strong feeling that Vouvray is where Armand Monmousseau's heart and first love lie. In addition to the Vouvray family property, the company owns vineyards in varying parts of the Touraine *appellation*, notably in Montlouis and Azay-le-Rideau. In all, some 60 hectares of vines are directly owned or controlled by the company, but they also buy in grapes, must or finished wine from all around the *appellation* to supplement their own produce. They also act as *négociants* in the other wines of the Loire, from Sancerre to Muscadet.

The principal activity of J.-M. Monmousseau is the making and marketing of sparkling wine, which accounts for up to 80% of their not inconsiderable sales. This is immediately evident as you tour the 12 kilometres of their cellars at Montrichard, where they receive over 50,000 visitors a year. The seemingly endless galleries and passages of these old quarry-workings are lined with bottles in special automatic *remuage* cages designed by Patrice Monmousseau at Bouvet-Ladubay.

An excellent sparkling Vouvray is made, but their volume seller is the sparkling Touraine, which is sold under the label Brut de Mosny. The quality of the Monmousseau wines is of the highest order, especially for a *négociant* house of this size. The best wine I tasted was undoubtedly the still Château de Gaudrelle Vouvray 1985, which had a tremendous and exciting future ahead of it.

APPELLATION: TOURAINE-MESLAND

The area entitled to the Touraine-Mesland *appellation* lies to the east of that of Touraine Amboise; it covers six communes, and they are all on the north bank of the Loire. From east to west the communes are Chouzy-sur-Cissé, Molineuf, Chambon-sur-Cissé, Onzain, Mesland and Monteaux, and of these only Onzain, Mesland and Monteaux produce wine in any significant quantity. The dominant grape for reds and rosés is the Gamay, though Cabernet Franc and Cot, or Malbec, are also permitted. For the whites, the Chenin is grown, from which *sec, demi-sec* and occasionally *moelleux* wines are made. Generally speaking the reds are the most successful Touraine-Mesland wines; I tasted only one white wine of the *appellation*, a 1985 *moelleux* from the Domaine Girault-Artois; it was not very exciting, and this was from one of the best wine-makers of the *appellation*. I was very favourably impressed with the red wines of Touraine-Mesland, and am convinced that this is where the future of the *appellation* lies.

MESLAND

FRANÇOIS GIRAULT, Amboise. It was rather late when I arrived at the offices of François Girault on the Quai des Violettes in Amboise, but he was very welcoming and kindly asked me to stay on for dinner so that we would not be pushed. François is the fourth generation of the Girault family to make wine. His great-grandfather, Joseph, born in the year of Waterloo, was a cooper by trade but started a vineyard in Cangey, now in the Touraine-Amboise *appellation*; Joseph's son, another Joseph, born in 1865, kept the cooperage going, and enlarged and

improved the vineyard. He was a well-known and respected wine-taster, and won medals for his wines as early as 1894. Joseph the Second's son Robert, François's father, ran the vineyard from 1930, continually increasing the size and improving the quality until François took over in 1970.

François and his wife, Jeannine Artois, added the splendid Touraine-Mesland vineyard, Le Domaine d'Artois, to the family business. This property lies on the Plateau de la Morandière near Mesland, and amounts to some 26 hectares, most of which is on *les perruches*, a term used to describe a sandy and gravelly soil on a clay and silex subsoil.

In common with most of the *appellation*'s growers, Girault's production is predominantly in red wine. Two distinct types are made – a pure Gamay, young and fruity wine from young vines to be drunk and enjoyed in its youth, and a blend of Gamay, Cot and Cabernet Franc, a more serious wine, capable of long ageing. A rosé, called Touraine-Mesland Gris, is also made from pure Gamay; 10 years ago and before, this wine was vinified as *demi-sec* and even *moelleux* – the 1976 is still drinking well –but now that taste has moved away from sweet rosés, it is almost all vinified as *sec*. White wine is made under the Touraine-Mesland *appellation* from the Chenin Blanc, but the Domaine Girault-Artois also produces an excellent AC Touraine Sauvignon, sold under the name of Les Buttelières. There is also some sparkling *méthode champenoise* made, both white and rosé, under the recently created *appellation*, Crémant de Loire.

Vinification of the Girault-Artois wines is carried out in the ultra-modern, purpose-built winery in the middle of the vineyards, where the very latest in stainless-steel and fermentation control has been installed. Ageing in wood and in bottle takes place in the extensive rock-hewn cellars behind the Giraults' offices and house in Amboise. About 20% of their wines are exported to markets as far afield as Japan, Canada and the USA, whilst domestic sales are largely to restaurants.

The Gamay Jeunes Vignes wine is fermented at about 25°, and maceration lasts from 5 to 7 days; no wood is used. The Vieilles Vignes blend, made from three varieties – Gamay, Cot and Cabernet Franc – has a longer *cuvaison* of 15 days or more; the *assemblage* is made in January and the wine then spends six months in wood, which, in the case of the 1985 vintage, was represented by third-year casks from Château La Gaffelière in St Emilion, though larger wooden *foudres* of 75 and 30 hectolitres are also employed.

The two whites and the *gris* are fermented at a low temperature of 18° in stainless steel.

We tasted a complete range of the Girault-Artois wines, and I was especially impressed with the five vintages of the Domaine d'Artois Vieilles Vignes blend of Gamay, Cot and Cabernet. The 1985 and 1982 were superb, and the 1976 showed how a red from this part of Touraine can age when properly made and kept; it still had an amazing depth of colour and a curious but attractive 'hot vintage' bouquet. In the mouth the wine was rounded, well balanced and still had lots of fruit and a lovely long after-taste. If this is what Touraine-Mesland can produce, then I shall certainly look for it in the future.

Girault holds that there is no particular trick or secret in the making of good wine; all that is needed is the right grape on the right soil, perfect weather conditions, infinite pains at every stage of viticulture and vinification and four generations of expertise! All these elements are present in the Domaines Girault-Artois, and it certainly shows in the end product.

APPELLATION: TOURAINE-AMBOISE

Within the eight communes entitled to the Touraine-Amboise *appellation* there are some 1,700 hectares under vines, but of this area only about 210 are producing AC Touraine-Amboise; the remainder is dedicated to the less demanding production of AC Touraine, still or sparkling.

Of the eight communes, three are south of the Loire, and account for the major portion of the *appellation*'s production; these are, from west to east, Amboise itself, Chargé and Mosnes. Those north of the river are Cangey, Limeray (the largest), St Ouen-les-Vignes (the smallest), Pocé-sur-Cissé and Nazelles. These last two, at the western edge of the *appellation*, were once part of neighbouring Vouvray.

To qualify for the Touraine Amboise *appellation*, whites, which represent about 30% of production, must be made only from the Chenin Blanc. It is said that, when harvested late in good years, they can be *demi-secs* or *moelleux* the equal of Vouvray in terms of quality and longevity; my experience has only been with the younger wines, vinified dry, which are of acceptable if not exceptional quality.

The remaining 70% is red, and, to a lesser extent, rosé; the permitted varieties are Cabernet Franc and Malbec (known locally as the Cot, as elsewhere in the Loire) and Gamay; Cabernet Sauvignon is also allowed, but is rarely used and the Grolleau may be grown for making rosé.

Château d'Amboise

AMBOISE

HUBERT DENAY, Le Breuil, Amboise.
Time allowed for only one visit in Touraine-Amboise, and I chose Hubert Denay who is, apart from being a major grower, president of the Syndicat des Grands Vins de la Région d'Amboise. Hubert and his son Thierry have about 12 hectares of vines, which are mostly around Hubert's house at Le Breuil, a hamlet to the east of Amboise. They have a massive rock cellar on the Amboise-Chaumont road, and we wasted litle time in repairing thither to sample his wares.

Denay is particularly proud of his red 100% Cot wine; his father was one of the few who stuck to this variety after phylloxera ravaged the vineyards of Europe, and even to this day there are not many local growers who will make a wine from this tough, uncompromising character to the exclusion of other varieties.

We tasted an '85 Blanc Sec from 100% Chenin Blanc, which was aromatic and pleasing with a lovely

light colour. The '85 Rosé was a very pale pink wine, dry as a whisper yet with some nice fruit; a lovely picnic wine, excellent with the local pork delicacies *rillons* and *rillettes*. We then looked at an '85 red Gamay which had a nice deep colour and a pleasing Beaujolais nose; an unassuming red with a mouthful of fruit, but with enough good tannin to allow for some ageing.

The next red was Denay's Cuvée François Premier, a blend of 60% Gamay and 20% each of Cot and Cabernet Franc, also from the 1985 vintage. This had a very deep colour, and a good, but rather closed bouquet; a big mouthfilling wine, with lots of excellent fruit, but still very tannic; needs two years in bottle.

Finally M. Denay gave me his beloved Cot Pur to taste, only this time it was the 1982; the '85 would have been *trop dur* at this stage. The colour was very dark, but lighter than a Cahors of the same vintage, also made from 100% Malbec; a fat, rounded bouquet gave indications of the beautiful, full-bodied mouthful of wine that followed; excellent wine that gives much pleasure now, but will keep for years.

Denay is passionate about his wines, and as long as people of his spirit are making wine in Touraine-Amboise, the future of this tiny *appellation* must be assured.

CLOS DE LA GABILLIÈRE, Amboise. The Lycée d'Enseignement Professional Viticole, installed on an estate bought by the town of Amboise and called the Clos de la Gabillière, have done much beneficial experimental work since they started here in 1976. Their tests have been mainly concerned with clonal selection, and with the suitability of grape varieties to the local soil and micro-climate.

All their findings have come down strongly in favour of the Cot for the production of red wine of great quality and keeping power.

The enthusiasm for the Cot here and elsewhere is in fact more of a renaissance than a discovery; the Malbec originated from the Pyrenees whence it found its way to Bordeaux, across to Cahors and then northwards to central France, where it was widely grown by the end of the 19th century. After the devastation of phylloxera, the demand was for productive, disease-resistant varieties, and the coulure-prone Cot, though retained by a few diehards, was largely ousted in favour of Cabernets, Gamays and the white Sauvignon.

APPELLATION: MONTLOUIS

The wines of Montlouis have a tendency to be thought of as the forgotten, poor relations of Vouvray. There is some truth in this, but they are poor cousins because they are forgotten, not because there is anything wrong with them. Before 1936, when the *appellation* was created, all the wine of Montlouis was sold as Vouvray; when they found themselves no longer able to label their fine Chenin Blancs as Vouvray, and were obliged to use their own newly granted but hitherto unknown *appellation* of Montlouis, the growers experienced considerable resistance from the wine-buying public. The generally high quality of wine produced has ensured the survival of the *appellation*, but Montlouis still definitely suffers from the 'famous father' syndrome vis-à-vis its more illustrious counterpart across the river.

There are around 300 hectares of AC Montlouis vines, spread over the three communes of Montlouis-sur-Loire, St Martin-le-Beau and the much smaller Lussault-sur-Loire. The grape variety for Montlouis is exclusively the Chenin Blanc, and the wines produced are similar in type and range to those of Vouvray; they may be still, *pétillant* or full *méthode champenoise*, and can be dry, *demi-sec* or *moelleux*, although, as in Vouvray, the *moelleux* can only be made in years with exceptional autumn weather. The soil, on the same chalky tuff base as Vouvray, tends to be lighter, with a higher proportion of sand, silex and gravel, giving a wine of slightly less power and body. The sweet wines, made in years like '47, '59, '64, '76 and '85, however, are blessed with the same amazing ageing qualities.

As well as AC Montlouis, many growers also produce the somewhat less arduous wines entitled to the simple Touraine *appellation*. These may be red, white or rosé, and can be either still or *mousseux*; the permitted grape varieties are legion, the most common being Cabernet Franc and Gamay for the red and rosé, and Sauvignon for the white.

MONTLOUIS

Montlouis itself is a pretty little market town, about two kilometres up-river from Vouvray on the opposite bank of the Loire. Although there are a number of *vente directe* cellars, offering tastings and *visites des caves*, strung along the N751 beside the river, most of the vineyards of Montlouis are on the plateau that lies between the Loire and the Cher, some 200 feet above river level.

CHRISTIAN MARTIN, Montlouis. Take the right fork as you leave Montlouis heading east, with the Cave Co-opérative de Montlouis on your right, and you are on the road to St Martin-le-Beau. M. Martin's establishment is about 500 metres along this road on your right.

Christian Martin is a charming and interesting man. He makes extremely fine Mountlouis, as well as a whole range of AC Touraine wines, red, white and rosé, still and sparkling. He is able to talk about his wines to most visitors, since he has taught himself English, German, Spanish, some Italian, and a smattering of several other languages. He talks well and it is clearly a subject he loves.

I tasted five vintages of his Montlouis Sec, five of Demi-Sec, and the 1985 Moelleux and Doux. The latter was a new description to me, and it is apparently peculiar to Montlouis; it is only made in exceptional years, and, like Moelleux, it is made from only super-ripe grapes, often with *pourriture noble* – the difference being that it is made only from grapes from very old vines. I did not taste an old

vintage, but of the 1985s the Doux certainly had more complexity and richness than the Moelleux.

M. Martin kindly opened a bottle of his 1959 Moelleux before I left, and it was quite superb, the equal of any Vouvray of the same vintage that I have tasted. The wines from M. Martin's deep and rocky cellars were quite exceptional, and typical of the capricious wines of the Chenin Blanc; every vintage is completely different, and every wine matures in different ways and at different speeds, making them a fascinating minefield for the taster.

Christian Martin also manages the Cave Touristique in Montlouis, where a large number of growers in the *appellation* club together to promote and sell their wines.

CAVE CO-OPÉRATIVE DE MONTLOUIS. On my way back to Tours, I called in at the Montlouis Co-opérative, which is on the main road between Montlouis and Amboise, at the junction where the D40 takes you off to St Martin. The Co-opérative cellars are in the style and tradition of the area, in a

The rocky surround to the Co-opérative cellars

Château du Nozet, the home of the Baron de Ladoucette in Pouilly-sur-Loire

The Château de Chinon, seen across the Vienne river

Oak vats in the cellars of Couly-Dutheil, Chinon

The Clos de L'Écho, Chinon

The vintage in Saumur Champigny

former quarry. The entrance is impressive, set at the foot of a sheer white cliff rising 100 feet to the plateau above. There is a large car park, and the tourist and the take-away customer are actively encouraged.

More a grouping of wine-makers than a real *co-opérative*, there are 24 *adhérents*, or members, who sell virtually their entire production through the Montlouis Co-opérative. Created in 1960, the Co-opérative has sold, until two years ago, only to the private sector; they have a computerised mailing list of over 20,000 customers and about 20% of their sales are to passing motorists and coach parties. Two years ago they started exporting a little to the United Kingdom and America, but find it difficult to sell the little-known name of Montlouis.

Only 20–25% of the Co-opérative's wines are vinified as still wine, the *méthode champenoise* being easier to sell and to make. The main problem encountered with potential importers is the unpredictable nature of the Chenin Blanc. It is extremely difficult to establish a long-term relationship with an importer when, for example, a good *moelleux* can only be produced once in 10 years, and when the degree of sweetness or dryness of a wine is a matter of chance. It is small wonder that growers and *co-opératives* opt for the production of sparkling wines or, easier still, sell everything under the less stringent Touraine *appellation*.

A brief tour of the *caves* showed me that vinification is carried out with the most up-to-date equipment and know-how. The *méthode champenoise* wine benefits from *remuage* in the latest automatic Gyropalettes, a sort of huge wire basket holding 500 bottles, which turns automatically three times a day, at an angle which gradually increases from the horizontal to the near-vertical. One week on this machine saves three weeks and a great number of man hours against the manual system, and with no perceptible adverse effect on the wine.

On my way out, I joined a party of tourists for a taste of the Cave's wine. The *Sec* and *Demi-Sec* still wines of the 1985 vintage were on offer; I found both to be well-made wines, the Demi-Sec having considerable character and tremendous length. Although the Co-opérative does not as a matter of policy keep older vintages for sale, my charming guide produced from 'under the counter' a bottle of 1964 Demi-Sec; it had a beautiful mid-gold colour and a super nose of quince and apricots; a lovely mouthful of summer fruit and flower, with tremendous after-taste.

ST MARTIN-LE-BEAU

DÉLÉTANG, Père et Fils, St Martin-le-Beau. St-Martin-le-Beau, whence much of the quality wine of Montlouis comes, is some 5 kilometres south-east from Montlouis and is much nearer to the Cher than the Loire. Here I visited the cellars of Délétang, Père et Fils, situated on the left as you leave St Martin on the Amboise road. The Délétangs have about 22 hectares of vines, six of which are planted with varieties other than the Chenin Blanc for the production of AC Touraine wines. Almost all their domestic sales are to private customers, and they also export a little.

Before descending in to their extensive rock-hewn cellars, we went in to the modern vat-house and tasted the '85 Touraine red; this was a Touraine Cabernet that had spent some time in a wooden 'fût', and it had an excellent ruby colour, good fruit and tannins; I thought it would age well for two or three years.

The Délétang cellars are impressive in their size, neatness and content; labyrinthine passages are lined with rank on rank of *pupitres*, full of *méthode champenoise* Montlouis and Touraine rosé, and bins and bins of still Montlouis mature quietly around every corner.

M. Délétang gave my photographic team and myself a tasting of his Montlouis wines which demonstrated the quality and the evolution of well made wine from this *appellation*.

Tasted: Montlouis Sec 1985. Very light golden colour. Bouquet light but pleasing; agreeable wine with nice fruit, but I would describe it as medium-dry rather than dry.
Montlouis Moelleux 1985. Colour the same as the Demi-Sec, but the nose was more honeyed and giving. Terrific concentration of ripe fruit flavours in the mouth – very closed up still, will last for years and years.
Montlouis Demi-Sec 1964. Beginning to turn deep gold; lovely nose of honey and ripe fruit. Great concentration of flavour – quince, apricot and noble rot. Still lots of life, astonishingly young for a 22-year old wine.
Montlouis Demi-Sec 1959 (re-corked 1986). Deep golden syrup colour; rich, aromatic and complex nose. Tremendous quincy richness, honey and ripe fruits with long, lingering aftertaste – a star!

APPELLATION: VOUVRAY

Wine has been made around Vouvray certainly since AD 372, when the Marmoutier Monastery was founded by St Martin between Rochecorbon and Tours. There is a great feeling of age and tradition about the area, which is much enhanced by the many deep cellars and troglodyte dwellings; most of these cellars started their existence as quarries from which vast quantities of stone were hewn to build the châteaux and houses of the Loire valley in past centuries. The best examples of such quarried cellars and houses are to be seen if you take the road along the north bank of the Loire from Tours towards Amboise, through the communes of Rochecorbon and Vouvray itself. On your left you will pass a long escarpment of chalky tuff; into the base of this cliff the people of Vouvray have dug to extract the stone, which has left them with the most splendid cellars for making and storing of their wines. There are also many houses whose interiors are all or partly in the rock, sometimes rising to two or three storeys, with facades like normal houses in different styles and periods.

For dwellings, such *caves* have the advantage of saving considerably on construction costs, since materials are only needed for the front, and very often the digging out of the living space has already been done by the quarrymen of yesteryear. For wine they are perfect, since they are dark, easy to secure, and above all, the temperature usually remains at a fairly constant 52° Fahrenheit all the year round.

The vineyards are almost all on the plateau at the top of this cliff, and the slopes of the many small valleys that cut into it. The soil is a mixture of clay/limestone and clay/silex, mostly on a subsoil of clay and tuff; this soil, the exposure of the vineyards and the micro-climate are all perfectly adapted to the cultivation of the only permitted grape variety of the *appellation*, the Chenin Blanc. The Chenin is a grape of local origin, and is also called the Pineau de la Loire.

There are eight communes in the Vouvray *appellation*, though one, Ste Ragonde, has been swallowed up by the urban sprawl of Tours since the *appellation* was created in 1936. The 'active' seven are Rochecorbon, Vouvray, Vernou, Parcay-Meslay, Chancay, Reugny and Noizay; I have attempted to put these in a rough batting order of quality, but not of size. The total area of Vouvray currently under vines is in the region of 1,600 hectares, mostly divided into holdings of less than 15 hectares, and there is an enormous variety of age-groups, attitudes and aims amongst the growers.

My stay in Vouvray, which was in every way enhanced by the kind hospitality of the then general manager of Marc Bredif, Michel Sébéo, was one of the most enjoyable and stimulating periods that I spent researching this book. I say this not because the people were so kind, which they were, or the food so good, which it was, nor even because of the undoubted quality of most of the wines that I tasted. The interest came more from the many faces of Vouvray; I found here, more than anywhere else, a crystallisation of the sort of identity crisis which afflicts so many of the Loire valley *appellations*, a kind of confusion of ideas and attitudes that is emphasised and exaggerated by the many difficulties and various options that present themselves to growers in this particular corner.

To understand these problems, it is important to realise that, right up to harvest-time, the wine of Vouvray still has several possible eventual forms which are decided partly by the characteristics of the vintage and the must, but largely by the whims and economic needs of the wine maker. All Vouvray can be made into still wine, *pétillant* or slightly sparkling, or full *méthode champenoise*; within these three categories there are further options in the vinification process in that the wine may be vinified as dry, medium or sweet – *sec*, *demi-sec* or *moelleux* as they are termed in Vouvray. The *moelleux* is usually only made as a still wine, and can only be produced in really exceptional years, when the late summer and early autumn allow for the development of the *pourriture noble*, noble rot or, to give it it's Latin name, *botrytis cyneria*.

This fungus is the *sine qua non* of all great sweet wines, and it occurs also in Sauternes, the Rhine and Moselle and in the vineyards of Hungary where the great Tokays are made. The spores grow on the skin of the grape, but do not pierce it, and the result is the shrivelling of the berry and tremendous concentration of the juice, which give a wine a truly astonishing richness and complexity, and, in the case of Vouvray, quite extraordinary longevity. Yield per hectare of these *moelleux* wines is necessarily infinitesimal; harvesting has to be done by hand, and, as in the great châteaux of Sauternes, the vineyard has to be picked over two, three and sometimes even more times to ensure that only the properly rotted grapes get to the presses. All this is highly labour-intensive and therefore expensive; such wines can be made on average only once every 10 years, and 1947, 1959, 1964, 1976 and 1985 are the post-war vintages of great *vins liquoreux* from Vouvray.

Add to this the fact that the Chenin Blanc is a sensitive variety and does not respond well to the adverse weather conditions that frequently arise whilst waiting for the noble rot to appear, and it is not difficult to understand why many growers look to other and easier forms of vinification. As if all this were not enough, fashion is still against sweet white wines, although this is beginning to change; the better-known wines of Barsac, Sauternes and even the Muscats from Beaumes de Venise are hard enough to sell, without trying to persuade people to pay the necessarily high price for good *moelleux* Vouvray, wonderful though it may be, when the general conception of Vouvray is a dry or medium dry white wine of only average quality.

This general opinion of Vouvray is, sadly, not entirely unjustified, and stems from the very problems described above. There is far less risk involved for the grower if he picks as early as possible, when the sugars in the must are still low, and the wine is vinified as dry or maybe medium dry or made into sparkling wine. Many Vouvrillons opt for this safe road, and still more, particularly among the smaller growers, prefer to leave the wearisome business of commercialisation to others and sell their entire product, either as grapes, must or finished wine, to the *négociants*. Frequently the *négociant* may not be from the Loire at all, and all he needs is a wine that he can legally label and sell as Vouvray for his customers who want to buy a complete range of French wines from one source. Much of the wine that is sold to the *négociants* is bought for making into *méthode champenoise* sparkling wine, and the quality of the base wine is of lesser importance than if it is to be sold as still wine. The net result of all this is that many *négociants* are buying AC Vouvray at a price, almost regardless of quality, the unambitious *viticulteur* doesn't have to try very hard, and the standard and reputation of the *appellation* consequently suffers.

The picture is not all black, however. There are many really fine and dedicated wine-makers in Vouvray, and thanks to them the remarkable quality that can belong to great Vouvray will not be lost. The most encouraging aspect of this adherence to quality and tradition is that it is to be found not only amongst the older generation; there is a strong *coterie* of young wine-makers who believe in the potential of Vouvray. I had occasion to see at first hand how this new generation of Vouvrillons meet, exchange ideas and work together in terms of marketing and promotion in a way that their fathers and grandfathers would never have done.

ROCHECORBON

MARC BRÉDIF, Rochecorbon. My first visit in Vouvray was to the cellars of Marc Brédif on the Quai de la Loire in Rochecorbon; this is one of the oldest wine businesses in the Vouvray *appellation*, and I can thoroughly recommend a visit to anyone who wants to learn a little about the wine of Vouvray. Visitors are always welcome, and there are guided tours of the cellars, followed by a tasting, at 10.30 am and 4.00 pm every weekday; it is advisable to telephone in advance, and the number is 47.52.50.07.

Marc Brédif are pure *négociants*, having no vineyards of their own. On these premises in Rochecorbon they make, bottle, age and commercialise only Vouvray, and only Vouvray of the highest quality. They have regular contracts with some of the best growers in the *appellation*, especially in the Rochecorbon commune, from whom they buy finished wine in bulk; depending on the quality of the wine and the character of the vintage the wine is then either bottled as still wine, or destined for champagnisation. As the inventors of *pétillant*, it is hardly surprising to learn that Brédif are brand leaders at home and abroad with their *méthode champenoise* wines, but, like most people in the Vouvray wine trade, it is their old, sweet wines from the great vintages of which they are most proud.

The firm was started last century by the Brédifs, one of the oldest families in the area, and it was Marc Brédif who first discovered the technique of making *pétillant* Vouvray in 1920. On his death in 1965, the running of the company was taken over by his son-in-law, Jacques Cartier, until it was sold in 1980 to the firm of de Ladoucette of Château du Nozet fame. The arrival of Patrick de Ladoucette on the Vouvray scene has surely been of benefit to the *appellation*, for Patrick sells well, world-wide, expensively and, above all, he sells on quality. He

The circular tasting-room of Marc Brédif, showing bins of old Vouvray dating back to the last century

was fortunate in his choice of general manager in Michel Sébéo, a man of great charm and boundless enthusiasm. He arrived in Rochecorbon in 1980 with no experience or knowledge of the wine business, having worked in films and latterly in the world of computers. It speaks volumes for Michel that in six years he gained the respect and friendship of every person I met in a very hide-bound and traditional community like Vouvray. He has now left Marc Brédif, but I feel that Vouvray has not seen the last of him.

The cellars in the rock are, like most of those in the area, old quarry workings; the seemingly endless galleries are an impressive sight, with millions of bottles either binned or in the traditional *pupitres*, on which the *méthode champenoise* wine undergoes the *remuage*. The entrance to the cellar is guarded by the figures of two saints – on the left is St Vincent, patron saint of the *vignerons*, and on the right is John the Baptist in one of his lesser-known roles as patron saint of the *cavistes* or cellarmen. There is a fine collection of wine bottles dating back to the sixteenth-century, and two ancient winepresses, one from the sixteenth-and one from the seventeenth-century, the latter originating from the Château de Chenonceau.

The *pièce de résistance* of the guided tour is the circular tasting-room deep in the heart of the rock-hewn cellars, with its huge circular stone table. Around the walls are bins containing bottles of *moelleux* Vouvray going back to the last century. It is a sad reflection on contemporary behaviour that the owners have found it necessary to wire the necks of these treasures together to thwart unofficial wine collectors.

Tasted: Sparkling	*Méthode Champenoise, Brut NV (2 years in bottle)*. Mid-golden colour with good mousse, clean, uncomplicated bouquet. Clean, fresh wine with good fruit and no faults.
	Pétillant, Sec 1981. Pale gold, with small light bubbles. Nose not giving much. A light, pleasing wine with nothing assertive about it.
	Pétillant Sec 1961. Colour still very good, not browning, but quite golden. A nice, quincy nose. Fine, with good fruit and length. Mousse goes very quickly.
	Méthode Champenoise Demi-Sec 1964. Darker than the '61 *Pétillant*, almost no bubbles. On nose and in mouth less attack than the '61, but still agreeable with nice fruit.
Still:	*Sec 1985*. Good, quincy nose. already surprisingly open and approachable. Apparently typical of 1985 vintage.
	Demi-Sec 1985. Pleasing, easy wine on nose and in mouth, more sweetness and less finesse than the *Sec*.
	Moelleux 1985. Has all the flowery quince and richness on nose and mouth to make a good *moelleux*; great complexity of flavour and aromas, but still very closed. Not much *pourriture noble*, but great ripeness. Needs a lot of ageing.
	Moelleux 1955. Good deep golden colour. Very rich bouquet of dried fruits – Christmas pudding? Great, heavy, mouthfilling wine. Rich and fruity. Lacking a little in finesse.
	Moelleux 1947. A real treat, probably the greatest vintage ever for Vouvray. Lovely golden syrup colour, beginning to brown a little. Tremendous richness and quincy, flowery taste. Has great delicacy and finesse, and will probably last another 50 years.

The 17th century wine-press in the cellars of Marc Brédif which came originally from the Château de Chenonceau

CHARLES ROLIN, Château Moncontour, Rochecorbon. The vineyards of Château Moncontour were acquired in 1985 by Charles Rolin, a dynamic entrepreneur with, among other irons in the fire, one of the biggest cheese businesses in France. The château itself, an imposing edifice that sits atop the cliff between Rochecorbon and Vouvray, with sweeping views up and down the river which flows at its feet, is ideal for entertaining and tastings, quite apart from being an elegant place to live and the jewel in the crown of this estate.

Balzac spent some time at the château, and wrote in 1846, 'Moncontour est ma prédilection'. Whether he referred to his surroundings or the wine is not recorded. Ginger-haired Charles Rolin, bubbling in confidence, has no doubts about the success of his new venture into the world of wine. With 40 hectares of vines around the château, and a 70 hectare experimental spread in nearby Reugny, he has by far the biggest area under vines of any proprietor in Vouvray; he is also quite convinced that, if he is not already making the best wine, it is only a matter of time before he does so.

Before going to view the experimental Domaine de la Pilonnière at Reugny, Rolin was keen to show me a particularly choice parcel of vines he had bought on the northern limits of the Vouvray *appellation*. We left his offices in Rochecorbon in his enormous BMW; a blown silencer made the car sound as if it should be at Le Mans, and the similarity did not stop there. Rolin's theory is that travel is a waste of valuable time, and must therefore be accomplished in the minimum possible period; in this instance he decided to ignore the roads and drive across country. He was not quite sure where the vineyard was, but had a general idea of its direction. We drove through vineyards – not his – over ploughed fields, leapt ditches, tore through farmyards scattering livestock, all at a normal cruising-speed – for *autoroutes* – of around 100 kilometres per hour. After about half an hour of this exhilarating progress, we came to a halt with a grinding of tortured metal, as the damaged exhaust was finally wrenched from underneath the car by a large rock. Rolin disembarked and peered beneath the car. 'I suppose it had better be serviced,' he said, hurling the mangled remains of the exhaust-pipe into a nearby ditch. 'I don't usually bother – such a waste of time.'

We then leapt back into the car and shot off in the general direction of Reugny, where we had a whirlwind tour of the Domaine de la Pilonnière. Of the 70 hectares, 56 are AC Vouvray, whilst the remaining 14 are only entitled to the lesser *appellation* Touraine. Weedkilling and vine-spraying are all done by aeroplane. This seemed logical to me, and caused me to wonder why nobody has thought of it before.

Vouvray of all types is made at Moncontour; the *méthode champenoise* enjoyed a great success in a Champagne and Vins Mousseux blind tasting in the Belgian magazine *Test-Achats* in December 1985. Some 45 Bruts were tasted; the first 12 wines chosen were Champagnes, and Château Moncontour Sec was placed 13th. The *demi-sec* tasting was the real *succès fou*, with Moncontour Demi-Sec being placed 1st out of 18 wines, which included *demi-sec* Champagnes from Möet, Mumm, Lanson and Piper.

Rolin has great plans for expansion. He will plant blackcurrants to make a Château Moncontour Crème de Cassis, which will be put in to presentation boxes with a bottle of Moncontour Sec, still or sparkling, or both. He also plans to start a museum of Moncontour wines, putting away 1,000 bottles from every vintage.

FRÉDÉRIC BOURILLON-DORLÉANS, Rochecorbon. The Bourillon-Dorléans family live in the centre of the village of Rochecorbon. Their cellars are about half a mile from the house, and the 15 hectares of vines are all in the commune of Rochecorbon; a large part is on the clifftop, just behind the famous Lanterne, the beacon-tower set up in the Middle Ages to warn of riverborne invaders. The soil is a mixture of clay/limestone and clay/gravel; Bourillon told me that this mixture of soils is vital to obtain a balanced wine. He has planted a further three hectares this year, but it will be four years before the grapes from the new vines can be used for making Vouvray.

Tall and powerfully built, Bourillon is typical of the enthusiastic and capable younger generation of Vouvray wine-makers. He makes all types of Vouvray, but still wine is his first love; he will only make a *moelleux* when the conditions are absolutely right, and he was justly proud of his 1985. His family have made wine in Rochecorbon for over 100 years, and his approach is a blend of respect for tradition and a modern attitude to oenology and marketing.

Some of his crop is sold in bulk to good *négociants* like Marc Brédif, who are prepared to pay a proper price for well-made Vouvray. He also sells his wines in bottle to the restaurant trade as well as to private customers. When I met him, Bourillon was planning a sales trip to London with one or two of his colleagues, including his friend Monsieur Gautier from Parcay-Meslay. I hope they found some good importers – they certainly deserve them. The quality of both growers' wines was quite outstanding.

RÉNE BOUILLOT, Rochecorbon. Bouillot lives and has his cellars in the main street of Rochecorbon. He is a traditionalist, an old peasant *vigneron*, he insists, what does he know or need to know of business and export? He is a strong believer in the *négociant*'s role, which is to pay a fair price for wine and sell it at a profit; his function is to make the wine – and very well he does it. There is a certain logic in all this, but I got the impression that there was a fair old business brain working away behind that weathered, peasant face.

His cellars were large, with lots of damp mould on the walls, wooden *fûts* and casks much in evidence, and rows of *pupitres*, laden with *méthode champenoise* wines undergoing their 'twist and tilt' period.

He has seven hectares of vines, all in Rochecorbon, and sells quite a large part of his wine in bulk to good *négociants* like Marc Brédif, with whom he has dealt for over 30 years.

We tasted an exceptionally good '74 Sec still wine, a ripe and luscious 1976 Demi-Sec and finished off with his *moelleux* 1985, which showed great promise. His very jolly wife joined us at this stage, saying she didn't know why she'd married Bouillot, since she only liked dry white wine.

PARCAY-MESLAY

In terms of area under vines, Parcay-Meslay is the smallest of the communes in the Vouvray *appellation*, if you discount Ste Radegonde which has now disappeared under the urban sprawl of Tours. If not in size, then in other respects Parcay-Meslay has much to offer. The Vouvrays of this commune are particularly fine, the soil being all on high ground with a good mixture of gravel and silex on a clay base.

I visited only two wine-makers in the commune, Benoît Gautier and Michel Deniau. Like most of the dozen or so *viticulteurs* of Parcay, neither was particularly easy to find. Most are relatively small growers, often selling the bulk of their produce *en vrac* (in bulk) to the *négociants*; their vineyards tend to be split into small garden-like plots, and the cellars where they make and store their wines are often small, numerous and well-hidden.

MICHEL DENIAU, Parcay-Meslay. Michel Deniau was fairly typical. He lives in the Rue Locquets, has two cellars in the rock here in Parcay-Meslay and one in Vernou, and has eight hectares of vines scattered around this commune, and a further hectare in Vernou. He sells most of his wine in bulk, but it is all of the highest quality; for example he waited as long as he dared for the vintage in 1985, and as a result almost all of his wine was sold as still *demi-sec* or *moelleux*, and none for sparkling wine, except for the produce of younger vines. Most of his wine, especially the still wine destined for his own bottling, is vinified in wooden *fûts* of oak or chestnut. He told me that the flowering was very late, on St John's Day (24 June), and that 1986 was all set to be a fine vintage.

I tasted his 1985 *Moelleux*, which was very pale in colour, and had a fine complex, mincey-quincy nose. It was amazingly rich and concentrated in the mouth, and high enough in alcohol to make it a real stayer. His 1976 Demi-Sec followed; the colour was, obviously, darker, but still a light rather than a dark gold. It had a good rich taste of pears and quince and ripe, ripe grapes, and lots of potential still. A very genuine man, whose personality was directly reflected in his wine.

The author samples the wine of Michel Deniau at Parcay-Meslay

BENOÎT GAUTIER, La Racanderie, Parcay-Meslay. Benoît Gautier lives at a large farm called La Racauderie, on your right as you take the road to Rochecorbon from Parcay-Meslay. The family have made wine since the 17th century, and have learnt a few things along the way. Young Gautier is one of the new generation of whom I have written already. If the future of Vouvray is dependent upon the quality of wine produced and the enthusiasm, effort and applied marketing skills of Gautier and his colleagues, then Vouvray need have no fears.

LA GRANGE DE MESLAY. For music-lovers, and particularly *aficionados* of the works of Prokofiev, Parcay-Mesley has a special meaning. The converted twelfth century barn, La Grange de Meslay, was chosen as the site for an annual music festival, held in June, by none other than the great Russian piano virtuoso Svyatoslav Richter. Always a lover of Touraine, Richter wanted to repay the pleasure and hospitality he had so often derived from visits to the area, and offered to come and play here. The festival was started, but great difficulty was encountered in finding a venue with sufficiently good acoustics for the maestro. In the end it was Richter himself who discovered La Grange on one of his walks in the area. It was at that time, 25 years ago, full of pigs and manure, but Richter declared himself totally happy with the place. History relates that, for the first concert, the pigs were removed, but were put back again after the audience had gone home. They were preparing for the 26th festival at the time of my visit, and Richter was due to play.

Addicts of the French cinema will be surprised to learn that the vast and gloomy castle in Cocteau's 1947 *La Belle et la Bête* was, in fact, the very small and very cheerful château on your left as you drive from Parcay-Meslay down into Rochecorbon.

VOUVRAY

GASTON HUET, Le Haut Lieu. Le Haut Lieu is well named, for both vineyard and owner occupy high places, not only geographically but in terms of the respect in which they are held. Gaston Huet is Mayor of Vouvray and President of the Comité Interprofessionnel des Vins de Touraine. He is the third generation of Huets (the 't' is pronounced in this part of France) to have made wine here, and his wines enjoy a reputation second to none. In addition to Le Haut Lieu, he also owns two other vineyards of great renown, which, like Le Haut Lieu, he always vinifies and commercialises under their own labels – the Clos du Bourg, possibly the oldest named vineyard in Vouvray, and Le Mont. The three *premiers crus* vineyards add up to 21 hectares, and the Domaines Huet include a further 11 in scattered parcels.

The wines and the beauty of the Manoir du Haut Lieu were eulogised by Walter Scott, who wrote about the estate in 1827. Le Mont was already recognised as one of the top Vouvray vineyards as early as the fifteenth century, but both are mere newcomers when compared with the Clos du Bourg. Formerly known as the Châtellerie du Bouchet, the six-hectare walled vineyard above the parish church in Vouvray was already established and is recorded as being the property of the collegiate church of St Martin de Tours in the 8th century. This may indicate that red wine was made here at the time, since Bouchet is the name used in St Emilion for the Cabernet Franc.

Le Haut Lieu, home of M Huet

Aided by his son-in-law, Noël Pinguet, who is a recent but fervent convert to the religion of the vine, Gaston Huet combines the best elements of tradition and modern technology in his approach to making wine. The sophistication of what can only be described as his 'pressing-unit' has to be seen to be believed, and he has an impressive range of stainless-steel vats and a well-equipped laboratory. He is quick to tell you that the stainless-steel is only used in the vinification of the 'basic wine' for *méthode champenoise*. For his *vins tranquilles*, vinification takes place exclusively in the traditional wooden *demi-muids* of 600-litre capacity.

The serious nature of the Huet philosophy is also demonstrated in his attitude to *vin mousseux*, which he will only make in years when the wine is not good enough for *vin tranquille*.

He is a vigorous ambassador for Touraine, Vouvray and his own wines, despite advancing years, and thinks nothing of jetting across the Atlantic for a spot of promotion. Jet-lag does not seem to affect him, and I have heard his colleagues speak with awe of his tireless energy and indefatigable appetite for good food, when younger men are collapsing all around him at some foreign table.

All picking is done by hand, as this is the only possible method if one wishes to make proper still Vouvray from selected super-ripe bunches. Harvesting machines, says Huet, are bought by, or because of, women. Emancipated women will not labour in the kitchen to provide food for the pickers, so their husbands are forced into buying machines. He reckons himself fortunate to be where he is. The principles of making good wine have been understood far longer than people recognise, he told me; a writer on wine-making called Olivier de Sèvres wrote in the sixth century, 'L'aire, la Terre et le complant sont les fondements du vignoble.' The area and the soil are fairly obvious, but it is intriguing to note that the *complant* or variety of grape planted was understood over a thousand years ago. Given these three elements, plus a modicum of luck with the weather, M. Huet reckons a man should be ashamed of himself if he fails to produce decent wine.

Huet has, and always has had, an excellent clientèle among the top restaurants, both locally and in Paris. His export business has only expanded over the past 10 years to its present level of around 50% of total production; before that he used to sell as much as 80% of his wine to private customers, who still come back to him year after year.

Remuage à la main *in the cellars of Gaston Huet*

Before going down the hill in to Vouvray to inspect the Societé Huet's impressive cellars, we were treated to a 'proof of the pudding' tasting of three *moelleux* from classic vintages, and all many years apart. M. Huet served us these wines in the cool drawing-room of Le Haut Lieu; it was a blistering July day, and the pleasure of tasting these great Vouvrays was in some way intensified by the beauty of the garden outside.

We started with the 1985 Moelleux from Le Haut Lieu, light greeny gold in colour, with a nice rich nose of ripe fruit. Concentrated fruit was evident in the mouth, but both bouquet and flavour were still very closed in; this will develop into a great bottle.

Le Mont 1964 had a lovely medium-dark golden colour, and a superb bouquet of honey, flowers and quince. Beautiful, flowery, ripe pears and quinces in the mouth, and lovely lingering aftertaste.

The last wine was a half-bottle of Le Haut Lieu from 1937; not one of the great vintages, but still stunningly good for a wine of 49 years. The colour was dark and treacly, and the nose showed a touch of oxidation, but in the mouth the fruit was still good and fresh, and the wine had no touch of the maderisation that the nose had led me to expect. Good, medium-long aftertaste. A fine example of the ageing potential of well made Vouvray.

It is always difficult to find the ideal food with which to drink these rich and aromatic old *vins liquoreux*; Gaston Huet has spent a lifetime experimenting, and recommends a blue cheese from the Massif Central called 'Fourme d'Ambert'; I have put it on my shopping-list.

Prince Philippe Poniatowski, Clos Baudouin, Vallée de Nouys, Vouvray.

Prince Philippe Poniatowski is as Polish as he sounds; indeed, his great-great uncle was the last King Stanyslas of that warred-over, occupied, but always gallant country. Philippe's family however, have been *emigrés* since the middle of last century, when they left Poland to live on a family property in Tuscany, where they also made wine.

How the Poniatowskis came to acquire the Clos Baudouin is now almost a legend. The story goes that Philippe's grandfather, having moved to Paris, had an office in the 9th *arrondissement*, and was in the habit of lunching most days at a restaurant called the Petit Riche in the Rue Le Peletier. The restaurant was owned by a Vouvray family, and Poniatowski often drank and came to love the wine of Clos Baudouin there. One day he was told the wine was no longer available, since there were problems at Clos Baudouin and the property was up for sale. Anxious to secure a continued supply of his favourite Vouvray, the ageing Prince is reputed to have bought the house and vineyard without even going to see it.

For some time the property must have been more of a burden than an asset, since at the time of the purchase, around 1910, it was a mere four hectares. This was no more a viable unit then than it is today, but the Poniatowskis could afford their indulgence. In 1935, Clos Baudouin passed into the hands of Philippe Poniatowski's father; Philippe himself took on the responsibility in 1970. The property has now been increased to 22 hectares, and volume is sufficient to supply an ever-increasing demand.

'Ponia', as he is known amongst his friends and colleagues here in Vouvray, is, like his father and grandfather, a Parisian by nature, but he visits his beloved Clos Baudouin enough to know everything that goes on and to take all the important decisions. He has travelled widely and spoken eloquently to promote Clos Baudouin, and as a result half his production is now exported, mostly to the United States. The other 50% is sold on the home market to restaurants – the Petit Riche, of course, among them – and to private customers. Clos Baudouin also

supplies sparkling wine to the giant Nicolas chain of shops.

Like the old guard who make proper Vouvray, and the new generation of whom I have already spoken, Poniatowski imposes strict disciplines in the running of his business. In 1985, for example, *no* wine was made for champagnisation, since the degree of the must was high enough for all to be vinified as still wine, the hard but true path. Picking is still 100% by hand, for by no other method can the proper series of *tris* (picking over) be made to select the grapes affected by noble rot. Fermentation of the still wines is carried out slowly at a low temperature in the traditional wooden cask or *demi-muid* of 600 litre-capacity; no added yeasts are employed, and the process usually lasts between two and three months. The wines are bottled in March or April of the year following the vintage.

Poniatowski also produces a 'pink *mousseux*' AC Touraine Rosé from 100% Cabernet Franc; his AC Vouvray Sparkling is sold under the label Aigle d'Or and Clos Baudouin. Unusually, the wines from the Clos Baudouin estate never carry the description of sweetness, such as *brut*, *sec*, *demi-sec* or *moelleux*. Poniatowski argues that Vouvray, with age, changes from *sec* to *demi-sec*, *moelleux* back to *demi-sec*, and *demi secs* may become much sweeter; it is therefore unfair, inaccurate and muddling for the consumer. I take his point, but feel it might be less confusing if the degree of sweetness at the time of bottling were indicated, and perhaps a back label could tell of the idiosyncratic evolution of fine Vouvray in bottle.

My visit to Clos Baudouin was made in the company of Michel Sébéo from Marc Brédif, who brought with him a sample of his 1985 *Moelleux* to taste against Poniatowski's wine. We tasted three 1985s; Marc Brédif, Aigle Blanc and Clos Baudouin. All had a very pale colour, and pronounced quincy bouquets, even in such extreme youth; the Clos Baudouin had a touch more finesse on the nose, it also had more concentration of aroma and potential for future development than the other two wines. They were all fine examples of 1985 *Moelleux*, but not over-marked by the noble rot.

Later we tasted a 1982 and 1983 Clos Baudouin. I found them both excellent, but the '83 had in my opinion more finesse, character, concentration of flavours and a greater potential for longevity than the 1982.

Finally 'Ponia' produced for us a glass of liquid gold, and asked me to guess the vintage. It was not too difficult to spot the fabulous '47; brilliant golden syrup colour, complex nose of honey and beeswax, mouthful of concentrated fruit – ripe pears, quince and apricot, all still lively and developing. It will last another 50 years *sans problème*.

ANDRÉ FOREAU, Le Clos Naudin, Vouvray.

Phillipe Foreau, son of André, was one of the young generation of Vouvray wine-makers who impressed me most strongly with his technical know-how and enthusiasm for traditionally made still Vouvray.

The family's 12 hectares are all on the high ground and mostly on clay/silex soil. As with all like-minded Vouvrillons, picking is done manually, and great importance is attached to getting the grapes, whole and undamaged, as quickly as possible to the press. Pruning is very severe, and yields are consequently low.

Fermentation takes place here, as in Philippe's uncle, Gaston Huet's cellars, in traditional wooden *fûts*. The period in cask varies between 2 and 2½ months, and the temperature of the must stays around 15°. During this time, the wine is racked (transferred away from the lees into clean casks) twice, and fined once – clarified with bentonite – in February; in mid-April the wine undergoes a light

sur-plaques filtration and is then bottled. Philippe considers that this springtime bottling is most important; if the wine waits any longer, he says, it loses freshness and finesse, and starts life too deep and yellow a colour.

When the must does not reach the required degree of 12.5° for making good still wine, then champagnisation is the order of the day. Vinification for *méthode champenoise* base wine is exactly the same as for still wine, except that a heavier filtration is employed.

Philippe Foreau studied oenology in Champagne, but said he found little need for change when he took over the wine-making from his father André in 1983. The only major innovation has been the acquisition of a hydraulic press, which Pierre says gives a much more gentle and evenly distributed pressure.

They commercialise all their own wine, of which about 35% is exported; the traditional shipping firm of Loeb in London is their main United Kingdom outlet. The balance of their production is sold to the restaurant trade and private customers on the home market.

In the depths of their deep, rock-hewn cellars there is a circular tasting-room, with a round wooden table set on the base of an old press. On the day of my

The tasting-room in the cellars of André and Philippe Foreau

visit, however, which was very hot, we retired to Philippe's office, and tasted with the french windows open on to the beautiful gardens.

We tasted three dry wines, three *demi-secs* and two *moelleux*, and it was interesting to see the evolution of these different types of still Vouvray over varying periods:-

Tasted: Sec 1985. Pale greeny gold. Fresh, flowery nose with distinct carnation. Lots of freshness, but very complex. Very young and closed – Philippe says it will take 10 years to evolve properly. Very long in the mouth.
Sec 1981. (A year of very low yield – 18 hectos/hectare.) Similar colour to '85; good rich fruit on nose. More astringent in mouth, but good, concentrated flavour; already showing well, but will give its best in two to three years.
Sec 1957. Lovely deep gold, but not too brown. Bouquet good and rich, with smokiness and a touch of quince, which is apparently unusual for a dry Vouvray. In the mouth the wine was still fresh, with nice fruit, but no great length. The nose developed more and more with aeration, giving off a lovely hint of rum and vanilla. Excellent for a *petite année* with 19 years bottle age.
Demi Sec 1985. Very light gold, nose beautiful with mixture of fruits – a definite whiff of tangerine! Excellent balance of fruit and acidity, a well-made wine, not over-rich, and with excellent length.
Demi-Sec 1981. Same light gold as the '85. Good nose of flowers summer fruits. Clean and well-balanced, still very fresh but more evolved than the *Sec* from the same year. Philippe says it will keep and improve more than the *Sec*.
Demi-Sec 1976. Nice medium-deep gold. Nose ripe and spicy, with a whiff of rum as the '57 Sec. Still has freshness, but lots of lovely well-ripened fruit and excellent balance. Length good.
Moelleux 1985. Pale, pale gold. Bouquet quite heavy, still closed, but honey there and promise of much to come. Fine, grapey richness, but tremendously concentrated and undeveloped still. Philippe says this could be a 50-year wine.

Moelleux 1976. Brilliant, deep gold – shades darker than the *Demi-Sec* of the same vintage. Wonderful bouquet, redolent of rum, vanilla and sun-ripened fruit. In the mouth, fatter richer and sweeter than the *Demi-Sec*, with lots of *pourriture noble*.

DANIEL ALLIAS, Le Petit Mont, Vouvray. Daniel and his sister are the fourth generation to make wine at Le Petit Mont, the vineyard at the highest point of the slopes forming the Vallée Coquette. The soil is clay/limestone, the exposure and micro-climate excellent; Daniel proudly showed me, if proof were needed, the orange trees growing, thriving and bearing fruit in front of his house. Daniel is yet one more of the young group of Vouvrillons who will keep the true character and reputation of the *appellation* alive, and he has a son who will carry the flag of quality into the fifth generation.

The Clos du Petit Mont vineyard rises up behind the Allias' homestead, and the cellars are carved into the rock beneath. All is picked by hand here, and Daniel is most careful about chemical treatments and fertilisers used in the vineyards. 'Did you know,' he asked me, 'the anti-pourriture grise treatment, effective though it is, delays the ripening process by a whole week?'

The section of the cellar devoted to the storage of wine in bottle has neatly labelled 'streets', using the traditional white-on-blue French street-signs; the culmination of this web of galleries, each of which is named after a particular section of vineyard, is a large rock chamber, christened the Salle des Carrés, which houses not only the Allias family collection of fabulous old Vouvrays, but also a marvellous display of fossilised shellfish, wood and other petrified objects found in the vineyard. There is also a huge, old stone fireplace, with a flue that goes up through the rock to the vineyard above, and I could picture some jolly gatherings of friends here in winter-time to taste, enjoy a *casse-croûte* and a gossip around a roaring fire of vine prunings.

About two-thirds of the wine from their 10 hectares of vineyard goes, in a good year, into the production of *vins tranquilles*, and a third into *méthode champenoise*. Almost all their sales are to private customers, many of whom have bought their Vouvray from the Allias family for years; they sell a little to the better local restaurants, as this is a good shop window for them, and they are also starting to export a little – their wine may be found in Harrods, and in one or two small private wine-merchants' lists.

We tasted the Petit Mont 1985 Moelleux; this had a lovely light greeny-gold colour, and a beautiful, aromatic nose of cooked fruits and honey. In the mouth there was a marvellous complexity and concentration of fruit flavours, with just the right level of acidity. All in all, one of the most accessible 1985 *moelleux* I tasted.

This was followed by the 1976 Petit Mont, of which the colour was still surprisingly pale and young. The bouquet was lovely with lots of rich *pourriture*, fruit and hints of beeswax. Excellent, rich and ripe in the mouth, with medium length. Good to drink now.

Daniel's final offering was given to me 'blind', and I was asked to guess the year. Lovely, deep golden-syrup colour, backed up by a fabulous waft of Christmas pudding and quince on the nose. Lots of richness and complex flavour in the mouth, and a lot of undeveloped potential, led me luckily to plump correctly for the 1959 as opposed to the 1947 vintage.

PIERRE LOTHION, Rue Gambetta, Vouvray.

I spent a thoroughly enjoyable morning with Pierre Lothion, and learnt a great deal from him. A man of around 65, Lothion comes from a long line of wine-makers; his grandfather Jamain became very ill at the age of 50, thought his time had come and sold up. To his and everybody else's surprise he recovered, and within five years had bought back everything, started again and became extremely successful, winning many prizes for his wines at the fairs.

This same indomitable spirit undoubtedly motivates Pierre. He came out of the army having qualified as a physical training instructor, which was to stand him in good stead. The family wine business was doing quite well and needed to enlarge its cellar space; Pierre Lothion did what the Vouvrillons have done for a thousand years and more – he took his pick and shovel, and dug himself a cellar. Twenty feet wide, eight feet high and 200 feet deep makes 60,000 cubic feet of rock – an almost superhuman achievement. The moment when he chipped the date, 1950, beneath the bottle above the door of his new cellar at the end of one and a half years of backbreaking toil, must have given him a sense of satisfaction felt by few people.

He works now in semi-retirement, aided by his son and grandson, and has very few hectares under vines

of his own. Lothion is a *négociant*, and buys in from local growers with whom he has dealt all his life. He loves and believes in his wines, but does not take either them or life too seriously. In his private cellar, reached by a curving stairway from the new cellar, again hacked out by his own hand, he keeps a *bibliothèque* of 90 bottles of every vintage since 1950. Judging by his kindness to me and the many spaces in the bins, it is a library that is oft referred to, and sadly the books cannot be returned!

My son Christian was with me, taking photographs, and Lothion took me aside to ask the year of his birth. When I told him it was 1960, he shrugged and said, 'Not a good year for Vouvray, but we might have a good surprise.' He opened a bottle of 1960 Demi-Sec, and it was certainly alive and well, with lots of freshness and concentrated ripe fruit, showing no signs of tiredness whatever. Pierre told us that this was one of the great delights and mysteries of Vouvray; if the wine is basically sound and well-made, even the poorer vintages can become very respectable with a long period in bottle.

Before we left he opened a bottle of his 1955 Demi-Sec, a much better vintage, but still not one of the classics. We drank it and discussed the problems of the world in Lothion's tasting-room – 'mon temple' – where he meets often with friends and colleagues for tastings and *casse-croûtes*. The wine had a deepish golden colour, but still looked very lively. The bouquet was honeyed and delicious, and the flavour rich, ripe and long. Lothion compared 1955 with '85, and if the latter endures in a similar way I shall not hesitate to put away a few bottles of Pierre's wine in my own cellar. I hope I shall have the patience, and the good health, to wait the necessary 30 years!

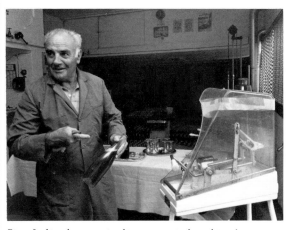

Pierre Lothion demonstrating dégorgement *in the making of sparkling Vouvray*

VERNON-SUR-BRENNE

GILLES CHAMPION, Vallée de Cousse, Vernou-sur-Brenne. The pretty village of La Vallée de Cousse, its houses built on the slope of the valley facing the sun, lies about 3 kilometres north of Vernou-sur-Brenne. At the time I visited M. Champion there was much agitation over the 'rape of Vouvray' by the coming of the new TGV railway line; it is true that there was much evidence of earth-moving plant on both sides of Vernou, but I feel that the eventual loss of a few hectares of vines will be more than commercially compensated by the shortening of the journey from Tours to Paris to one hour.

The commune of Vernou, in which the Vallée de Cousse lies, is the second-largest in the Vouvray *appellation*. The soil, as in Gilles Champion's 10 hectares, tends to be a clay/limestone mix, giving wines with some weight, body and keeping qualities.

Gilles is the third generation of the Champion family to make wine here in the Vallée de Cousse, and his son, who works with him, will continue the tradition. They run the 10 hectare vineyard with the help of one worker, and their wine is their sole livelihood. Gilles took me to look at his vines, which are all around the village; no weedkiller is used, and I was struck by the immaculate condition of his vineyard compared with some of his neighbours.

As with his vines, so with his wines; everything is done cleanly and correctly, and excellent wines are the result. The Champions make the whole gamut of Vouvray wine – *pétillants*, full *méthode champenoise*

and *tranquilles* – and within these three types the wines are *sec* or *demi-sec*, and in the great years *moelleux* for the still wines. To make a classic *moelleux vin de garde*, Champion told me, the wine should start with an acidity factor of between five and six, and this is extremely difficult to achieve when there is a lot of *pourriture noble*, the other *sine qua non* of a great Vouvray vintage; to arrive at such a result requires ideal growing conditions right up to the start of the vintage, usually in mid-October, and then three or four weeks of perfect *arrière-saison*, with morning mists clearing around 11, followed by warm sunny days to encourage the spores of the noble rot. It is not difficult to understand why, on average, only one year in 10 produces these great wines. 1985 was such a year; I tasted the Champion *moelleux* of this year, and learnt from him that it was fairly typical of 1985 Vouvrays, in that it was very advanced and was already like a wine with two years bottle age.

Champion has won many prizes with his wine; his '85 Demi-Sec won a gold medal at Tours. He also allowed me to taste an older prize-winner, his 1973 Demi-Sec, which gained him the Silver in Paris. Like the '85, it had a lovely fresh nose of ripe fruit, and, although somewhat lighter, had the same depth of flavour and great length.

Gilles sells between a half and one-third of his production in bulk to the *négociants*, about one-third on the export market – mainly America, with a little to the UK – and the rest is sold to a regular private clientèle.

In spite of the difficulties involved, which include a very high frost risk in this corner of the *appellation*, Champion clearly loves the way of life and believes

Protest sign at Vernou-sur-Brenne, Vouvray – the new high-speed railway has arrived nevertheless

fervently in the quality and future of his wines. He is President of the Vernou Syndicat and an officer of the Confrérie des Chevaliers de Chantepleure. I know that all such brotherhoods and societies are founded and exist for the noblest and best-intentioned reasons, but surely they could have thought of a better title for this one? Should I ever be enthroned as a Chevalier of this noble brotherhood, I would rather be a Knight of the Chenin Blanc, say, than a Knight of the Cask-tap.

APPELLATION: TOURAINE AZAY-LE-RIDEAU

The little town of Azay-le-Rideau owes its existence to the lovely sixteenth-century château on the Indre. One of the loveliest of the Loire castles, Azay draws hundreds of thousands of visitors each year from all over the world. It is curious, therefore, that Azay-le-Rideau is the smallest and one of the least known of all the *appellations* of Touraine. It is true that the wines are not great, but they are of a pleasant and fresh nature, and it is not difficult to imagine a marketing strategy, tied in with the tourist industry, that would improve their image and widen their market.

CHEILLÉ

ROBERT DENIS, La Chapelle St Blaise. I visited but one grower in the *appellation*, Robert Denis in the village of La Chapelle-St-Blaise, part of Cheillé, one of the eight communes entitled to make Touraine Azay-le-Rideau. M. Denis has been president of the *appellation*'s Syndicat Viticole for 18 years, and he is alone in commercialising all of his wines himself. Apart from these two distinctions, he is fairly typical of the average Azay wine-maker; he has 4 hectares of vines, but is also engaged in other forms of agriculture, including beef, cereals and fruit growing. Most of the scant 100 hectares of AC vines is divided into plots of this size; an exception is the Château de l'Aulée, a 15-hectare vineyard belonging to the Champagne house of Deutz and Geldermann, where they make Touraine Azay-le-Rideau Blanc and Touraine sparkling, using grapes and must purchased from surrounding growers, as well as their own produce.

Only white wine made from the Chenin Blanc, and, more recently, a rosé from a mixture of Grolleau, Gamay, Cot and Cabernet, are entitled to the *appellation*. The Grolleau, or Groslot, as it is sometimes spelt, must comprise at least 60% of the blend for the rosé wine. The balance can be made up of a mixture of the other varieties, though no more than 10% of Cabernet may be included. Robert Denis is an ardent supporter of the Grolleau, but believes in curbing its highly productive tendencies by severe pruning – a very low yield of 35 hectolitres per hectare results. His rosé is made from 95% Grolleau with the remaining 5% Cabernet Franc. Both rosé and white wine are vinified in wood, and the Denis wines are clean, well-made and, at best, possessed of considerable charm and elegance.

Quite a large amount of Robert Denis' wines are sold in cubitainer to a faithful clientèle of private customers; he also sells to the Paris restaurant trade, and, enterprising for a small grower, he is exporting 50-case lots to Denmark, Belgium and the United Kingdom, where David Baillie Vintners and McKechnie Wines are his importers. Robert told me that many growers sell part or all of their produce, either as grapes or must, to the Château de l'Aulée, or the firm of Monmousseau in Montrichard, also owned by a champagne house; most wine sold thus is destined for vinification into sparkling Touraine or Crémant de Loire. Robert Denis produces a little sparkling wine himself, but I get the feeling that he regarded this as the soft option; of a total annual output of around 20,000 bottles, only 2,500 will be sparkling.

I tasted three vintages of his rosé, all of which had nice fruit, some finesse and a pleasing dry finish; the '85 was especially good, but needed a little more time. I then looked at three examples of his Blanc Sec, starting with the 1983, which had a nice quincy Chenin bouquet, a light, greeny colour and a nice balance of fruit and acidity. The 1985 was shown next; not surprisingly this was altogether a bigger and richer wine, with a great deal of promise, and should be a cracker in two or three years. The last dry white was the 1981; this was a tiny vintage in terms of quantity – Robert recorded only 8 hectolitres per hectare – but the wine is beautiful and in harmony now. Feminine, elegant with fruit and acidity well-balanced, it would drink marvellously with fish 'au Beurre Blanc'.

APPELLATION: CHINON

Otherwise known as La Rabelaisie (see below), the countryside around the mediaeval town of Chinon on the Vienne is some of the prettiest in the Loire Valley. Chinon itself is a charming old place, with a maze of cobbled narrow streets and what the estate-agents call 'a wealth of exposed timbers'. Dominated by the Château de Chinon, which is in fact the ruins of three separate castles, finally razed to the ground on the orders of Cardinal Richelieu, Chinon makes an excellent centre for exploring the central Loire valley. Angers, Tours and Saumur are within easy reach, as are all the most lovely Loire châteaux – Azay-le-Rideau, Ussé, Loches, Amboise, Chenonceau . . . the list is endless. There are hotels and restaurants to suit every taste and pocket, and my personal discoveries, for what they are worth, may be found at the end of the section on Touraine, and in the chapter on the Relais & Châteaux.

The riverfront in Chinon is bustling and lively with bars, restaurants, cafés and shops; there are few more enjoyable ways of killing time on a warm day than to sit outside one of the many bars, drinking a glass of Chinon or a *pastis*, and just watching the world go by. In spite of all this twentieth-century bustle, the feeling in Chinon is of antiquity. The statue of Rabelais, born nearby at the Closerie de la Devinière in the parish of Seuilly, stands on the waterfront looking in at the town, happy no doubt that his name is synonymous, after 500 years, with mirth, good living and good wine. Only 50 years before Rabelais' birth, Joan of Arc was granted an audience with Charles VII at the Château de Chinon, when she was trying to persuade him to take back the throne of France and be crowned at Reims. In earlier times the castle was visited frequently by the Plantagenet Kings of England, Henri II and his sons Richard the Lionheart and John.

The vinous history of the area dates back to Gallo-Roman times, and in the 11th century there is a mention in the text of the *Life and Miracles of St Maximes* of a Chinon proprietor shipping his wine down the Loire to Nantes. This practice of shipping wines the whole length of the Loire Valley to Nantes, whence it found its way to the important markets of Brittany and Northern France, continued as long as the river remained a navigable waterway.

Production of Chinon is almost entirely red, but a little rosé is made, also from the Cabernet Franc; unlike Bourgueil, white Chinon may be made, but very little is actually produced, and, although I saw the Chinon Blanc vines growing in Cravant les Coteaux, I was never offered any white wine to taste.

The *appellation* is spread along the north and south banks of the Vienne from Crouzilles in the east to Savigny-en-Véron in the west, only a couple of kilometres from the confluence of the Vienne and the Loire. There are 19 communes entitled to the Chinon *appellation*, but three of these, St Benoît la Forêt, Thenieul and Tavant, have made no *déclarations de récolte* in recent years; the main communes are Savigny-en-Véron, Beaumont-en-Véron, Chinon itself, Cravant-les-Coteaux (responsible for 45% of the entire production of the *appellation*),

Panzoult, Rivière and Ligré. Sazilly, one of the smaller communes in terms of area under vines, produces wine of exceptional quality, which comes almost entirely from one grower, Charles Joguet.

There are currently around 1,500 hectares planted, a figure which has doubled over the past twenty years and is still growing; there is a possibility of doubling it again within the limits of the area as defined by the INAO. It is largely an area of small growers; some 75% of all the wine made in Chinon is commercialised by the *négociants*, and a large number of growers are general farmers, who grow grapes as just one of several crops. The *négociant* system does not work to the detriment of the *appellation* to the same degree as elsewhere in the Loire, since a major influence to the good is exercised by the Chinon *négociant* firm of Couly-Dutheil. This firm is headed by Pierre Couly and his brother Jacques, who have the good of Chinon very much at heart. They own 50 hectares of the best vineyards and exercise control, through regular buying contracts with growers, over a further 100 hectares. Roughly a tenth of the total production of Chinon, therefore, passes through a very quality-conscious company, and less wine is sold through the larger, less caring *négociant* houses outside the area than from other Loire *appellations*.

The soil on which the Chinon vines flourish best falls into three categories:

1 Gravel and sand on the lower land along the banks of the Vienne, which gives light, fruity wine, ideal for drinking young, 'dès qu'ils ont fait leurs Pâques'.
2 Clay-limestone, on slopes and plateaux, giving wine of body and backbone with more ageing potential.
3 Clay-silex, also on slopes and plateaux, giving wines of delicacy and finesse.

As elsewhere in the Loire, where *vignerons* tend to have vines in different parts of the *appellation* and on different soils, various policies are adopted. Some growers, for instance, who have a substantial amount of vines on the coteaux, with clay/limestone soil, might prefer to keep this wine separate from their 'sandy gravel' wine, and sell it as a laying-down wine under its own vineyard name. The other, more widely followed system is for the grower to make an *assemblage* or blend of the different sorts of wine to produce a harmonious style with a combination of the characteristics of the individual vine plots. The latter practice obviously applies to the majority of *négociant* wines, except in cases such as Couly-Dutheil, who own one or two very special named vineyards, and which they always vinify and sell as such; these wines are treated very much as the flagships of the fleet.

Maximum permitted yield is low – 45 hectolitres per hectare – but this may be increased by up to 20% in certain years on application to the INAO. Pruning is Guyot-Simple, and limited to seven buds, and two buds on the next year's spur. Vinification is fairly traditional, with de-stalking almost universal before a long fermentation, usually about three weeks, at an average temperature of around 25° to 28°C. Various materials are used for the fermentation vats, but I noted a marked tendency towards stainless steel in newer installations, with the Puisais-designed *système de pigeage* wherever it could be afforded. The use of wooden *fûts* and casks for ageing after the malo-lactic fermentation is fairly standard, but the length of time that the wine spends in wood varies according to the requirements of the vintage and the individual preference of the wine-maker. The time of bottling is also a matter for the decision of each grower or *négociant*; there is always a voguish demand for the 'new wine' in the spring, and early sales help cash-flow. Sadly it is not only the wines from the sandy, gravelly low ground that are bottled and sold early; often economic pressures force a *vigneron* to sell his better wine in this fashion – wine from the coteaux which would benefit greatly from more time in wood before being bottled and sold. The wiser and more successful operators, however, will age their best wines in wood for up to a year before bottling, and some, like Couly-Dutheil with their top *crus*, will not put their best wine on the market till it has spent a further period maturing in bottle.

The spirit of Chinon is perhaps best illustrated by the wine fraternity, Les Entonneurs Rabelaisiens de Chinon. This merry band of souls in their mediaeval robes, steeped in history since their formation in 1962, meet four times a year in the famous caves Painctés in Chinon; they are dedicated to the propagation of the knowledge and appreciation of the wines of Chinon, and believe in setting a good example. The clue to their activities lies in the name of the brotherhood; Mr Harrap gives two separate meanings to the verb *entonner*, the first being to sing, chant or intone, the second to swig wine. Rabelais would have enjoyed their evenings. There are over 4,000 members of the Bons Entonneurs scattered over the face of the globe, and their number includes many giants of the arts, politics, business and the professions – among them Elizabeth Taylor and Madame Giscard d'Estaing, to name but two. They hold four main Chapters, or meetings, a year: in January for St Vincent, the feast of Quint-essence in March, the Fête de la Fleur in June and the Vendanges in September. In addition the Entonneurs meet whenever and wherever the interests of Chinon may best be served. Under the leadership of their Grand Master, Pierre Couly, the Good Swiggers raise their glasses, emblazoned with the Chinon motto 'Buvez Toujours, Ne Mourrez Jamais', and quote from their patron, Rabelais:

> Chinon, Chinon, Chinon,
> Petite Ville, grand renom.
> Assise sur pierre ancienne,
> Au haut le bois, au pied, la Vienne.

(*Pantagruel*, Book 5.)

CHINON

MAISON COULY-DUTHEIL, 12 Rue Diderot, Chinon. The Dutheil family originate from the Corrèze, one of the poorest parts of France. To the Corrèzien the work ethic is strong, and they are no strangers to success, especially in the wine business. Driven from their homeland around Tulle by poverty, many Corrèziens drifted south-west towards Bordeaux; some, like the Moueix family of Pomerol and Château Petrus, cousins of the Coulys, stopped at Libourne and there established their dynasty. Others journeyed on to Bordeaux, where many took jobs as salesmen with the *négociants*, travelling all over northern France, hitherto untapped territory, and meeting with great success. Many of them formed their own *négociant* companies;

some, like the Theils at Château Poujeaux, became proprietors and some, like the Bories and the Moueix family, combined both activities and became pillars of the Bordeaux establishment.

From such sterling stock came the Dutheils, who became established here in Chinon as proprietors and *négociants*; it was Pierre and Jacques Couly's father who married Madeleine Dutheil, apparently a *grande dame* of the wine business. Under her sons' direction the business goes from strength to strength, and continuity is assured in the person of Bertrand Couly, son of Pierre, who is already actively and keenly involved in the company.

The activities of Couly-Dutheil are twofold, in that they are vineyard owners and *négociants*. Their own property, which adds up to a sizeable 50 hectares, includes some very fine vineyards which they vinify and sell under their own names; the 17-hectare walled Clos de l'Echo enjoys a fine position across the road from the Château de Chinon as you enter the town. The lavender bordered drive leads up the steep, south-facing slope beside the vines to the neat, white house where Jacques Couly lives. Clos de l'Echo, named after the echo that bounces back from the castle walls when you shout from the top, is reputed to have belonged to Rabelais' family. It was abandoned in favour of cereal-growing until the Coulys took on the monumental task of restoring and re-planting it in 1952.

The Domaine René Couly is another family property, some 22 hectares of vines on the plateau of St Louans, a hamlet to the west of the town, where the soil is clay-silex as opposed to the clay and limestone of the Clos de l'Echo. The wine is somewhat lighter in style than Clos de l'Echo, with a lot of finesse, and more attractive when young. There is a rather touching story attached to the Domaine vineyard; during the war, when petrol and vehicles were impossible to come by, the Coulys used a horse called, curiously, Mouton, to do their local deliveries. When peace came there was no work for poor Mouton, and the knacker's yard loomed. Luckily René Couly was very conscious of his debt to the old nag, and so he developed a special hilly bit to his vineyard, inaccessible to tractors, just to keep Mouton in work.

Other Couly-Dutheil labels include the Clos de l'Olive, also their own small vineyard in the commune of Chinon, on the road to Cravant, and Les Gravières d'Amador, Abbé de Turpenay, a group of vineyards mostly situated on the sandy soil along the banks of the river or the gravelly plateau. The *crème de la crème* is the wine that bears the name La Baronnie Madeleine. Every year the two brothers and their sons hold a blind tasting of all the various three-year-old wines; notes are compared, and the wine winning most votes is labelled La Baronnie Madeleine, named after Pierre and Jacques' mother, Madeleine Dutheil. When you drink a bottle of this wine, therefore, it may be Clos de l'Echo, Clos de l'Olive, Domaine René Couly, etc.; it will be at least three years old, having spent all that time in wood or bottle in the Couly-Dutheil cellars; above all, it will be the best Chinon that this fine house can produce.

In addition to their own properties, Couly Dutheil have regular buying contracts with a number of growers, some of which they bottle under the vineyard name, such as the Domaine des

Bouquerries, Domaine du Puy, Domaine de Versailles and the Domaine de la Haute Olive, all of which, with the exception of La Haute Olive in Chinon, are in the commune of Cravant les Coteaux. With their own properties, vineyards that they rent and the wine that they buy on regular contract, the firm commercialises and, more important, controls the making of more than 10% of Chinon's entire production. Most of the wine bought in under contract comes in as finished wine for its *élevage*, a nice word for the period between fermentation and distribution, which could be freely translated as its 'schooldays'. A fine 'school' this is for the raw young pupils, be they the sons of the house or the children of others. All the equipment is of the best, and the 'teachers' have generations of experience, yet are not so embedded in tradition that they will not utilise the best of modern technology.

Fermentation is carried out in stainless-steel vats, all equipped with the Puisais *système de pigeage* (see p. 168 for explanation). There are also ranks of cement tanks lined with glass which are used mainly for storage and bottling. The alcoholic fermentation is usually of 3 to 5 weeks' duration at a maximum temperature of 28°, and the malo-lactic fermentation is then allowed to take place naturally in vat before the wine is transferred to wood or to other vats to await bottling.

Fermentation vats with système de pigeage in the cellars of Couly-Dutheil

The Domaine wines all spend varying times in wood before being bottled, depending on the nature of each vintage and the type of each wine. The Clos de l'Echo, for example, will spend from three to nine months in oak casks, as well as a period before this in oak *tonneaux* or tuns of much greater capacity.

Whilst in wood, the wine will be 'racked' off its lees and transferred to clean casks every three months, and will undergo a fining with whites of egg. The wine is never bottled until nine months after the first racking, and then has to rest a further nine months in bottle before it is released on to the market.

The company are in the throes of some very interesting experimental research to determine which type of oak is most beneficial for the large *tonneaux*. Each vat is labelled with the name of the forest from which the oak came – Châteauroux, Blois, Tronçais and Jupille. I tasted wine from the three latter; the Tronçais gave the harshest tannins, and the Jupille had the best nose of the three, but a slightly disagreeable taste. They hope eventually to use oak from the Chinon forest, as this would be the 'natural' way.

I also tasted the 1985 Les Gravières, which spends no time in wood. It had a good, ruby colour, and a round, blackcurrant nose from the Cabernet Franc. In the mouth the wine was rounded, fruity and

perfect to drink now. We then looked at the La Baronnie Madeleine 1981, which still had a very dense, dark red colour, a perfumed *cassis* nose and lots of fruit and good tannins to keep it going and improving for many years. 1981 was a small vintage quantity-wise, but there was nothing wrong with the quality.

Approximately half the production of Couly-Dutheil goes to the restaurant business and wine shops, 40% to private customers and only 10% is exported. You do not have to take my word for the quality of Chinon's wine, just look at the wine lists of great Paris restaurants such as Fouquet's and the Tour d'Argent. If only we in England were more adventurous, what pleasure there is to be had from the red wines of the Loire for comparatively little money!

CRAVANT-LES-COTEAUX

GÉRARD SPELTY, Le Bourg, Cravant-Les-Coteaux. Very dark and Celtic-looking is Gérard Spelty; indeed his ancestors were coal-miners from Wales, who emigrated to Northern France in pursuit of work in their chosen trade. Gérard's grandfather had enough of the mines, and changed to the equally hard but healthier life of a farmworker. Gérard's father came to work in Cravant-les-Coteaux

Gérard Spelty takes a sample from the cask

as a farmer's boy, and ended up marrying the farmer's daughter at Le Bourg in 1946. He died in 1978, and now Gérard runs the mixed farm with 10 hectares under Cabernet Franc vines, with the help of one other worker, his wife, and his mother who handles the telephone and the office work.

Spelty has four hectares on the clay/limestone of the *coteaux* and six on the gravelly plain nearer to the river. He grows 100% Cabernet Franc, and it is almost entirely vinified as red, though he makes a little rosé occasionally; the lesser years like 1984, he confided, are better suited to rosé. Contrary to what one might suppose, the wine from the flat land is the better one, and is sold as Clos de Neuilly at a price about F5.00 a bottle more than the *ordinaire* which is a blend of young vines from the *graviers* and wine from the *coteaux*. The secret of the quality of this 'lowland' wine lies in the high average age of the vines, many of which are between 30 and 40 years old. We drove around the vineyards of the plain to look at his ancient vines, and I was most impressed by the vigour of his vines and the neat, weed-free vineyard.

In the vat-house there is just about every material in current use; stainless-steel, which is his preference, is soon to take over completely, but, until he can afford to replace the older vats, Spelty still uses wooden *cuves*, as well as epoxy-lined cement.

After fermentation, all Spelty's wines are transferred to wooden *fûts*, where they stay until they are either bottled or sold to private customers in cubitainers straight from the wood. The room where these *fûts* stand is kept immaculately clean, and the rows of gleaming oak vats look extremely attractive. The Clos de Neuilly is all sold in bottle, but the 'normal' blend may be purchased either in bottle or cubitainer. The advantage of buying in 'cubi' for the purchaser is considerable – F14.00 per litre against F20.00 per bottle – but the customer always runs the risk of spoiling his wine through lack of expertise in bottling. Most growers would prefer to bottle 100% of their wine, thus protecting their reputation and making better profits, but they have to tread softly with their faithful customers who come back year after year to buy their wine *en vrac*.

Practically all the Spelty wine is sold to private customers, of whom Gérard has a long and very faithful list. He has the Celtic gift of the gab, and I have observed him at work on customers who call. Even if he did not make excellent wine, it would be hard to resist his particular brand of charm.

We tasted both the *normale* and the Clos de Neuilly of 1985. The *normale* had lovely deep ruby colour, a rich blackcurrant bouquet; it was an excellent, mouthfilling wine, with lots of ripe summery fuits and supple tannins and a lovely long finish. The Clos de Neuilly was deep, bluey red, and the nose was still very closed. Huge mouthful with lots of complexity and developing tastes and aromas; lovely, soft tannins. Should be kept, and will make a superb bottle.

The next two wines were given to me blind. The first was deep purplish red with a very open, ripe and generous bouquet of *cassis*. In the mouth it was rounded, fat and easy, full of lovely ripe fruit. Drawing on Bordeaux experience, I made a lucky stab at 1982. This was followed by the 1983 *normale*, which was a lighter wine in colour, smell and taste. It had a touch more femininity and elegance than the 1982, and drawing again on Bordeaux, I got it right!

On a later occasion I begged a bottle of Spelty's 1981 Clos de Neuilly for a comparative tasting of some 10 to 12 Chinons of that year; by general consensus it was placed among the top four in that not very good vintage.

JEAN BAUDRY, La Perrière, Cravant-les-Coteaux. The Baudry family have a long tradition of wine-making in the area; there is a document dated 1398 in which this very piece of land, known for the last 300 years as La Perrière, passed from the ownership of a M. de Remeneuil to a M. Baudry, surely an ancestor of Jean, the present incumbent.

Jean's son is working with him, and the beautiful old house next to the cellars in the rock of the Coteau de Sonnay is being totally and lovingly restored for his occupation. Near the cellar also lives a legend, Jean's uncle, Gaston Angelliaume; although well into his eighties, this *savant* still takes a very active part in the vinous life of Cravant-les-Coteaux, and anything he doesn't know about Chinon, says Jean, simply is not worth bothering about. It is one of my regrets that I did not get the chance to meet M. Angelliaume, but I hope to remedy this before very long.

Baudry has 35 hectares of vines, a large holding by Chinon standards; his vines are mostly grouped around his house on the gravelly land near the river, though he has some *coteau* and *plateau* vines as well. The wines from the latter lack the easy, youthful charm of the *graviers* wines, but have the ageing potential so necessary to the blend. He grows almost 100% Cabernet Franc, with a very small amount of Cabernet Sauvignon; although he admits it to be a useful *cépage* in years when there are spring frosts, he is not a lover of the Cabernet Sauvignon and will eventually phase it out. Jean has the chance to plant a further 4 hectares of AOC Chinon vines, but that is the limit.

When Jean and his wife took over the running of La Perrière from his parents in 1963, the *encépagement* picture was somewhat different. Only half the present area was planted with Cabernet Franc, and there was a mixture of other varieties from which *vin de table* was made.

Although Jean Baudry's cellar in the tuff is about as old-fashioned and traditional as it could possibly be, the vat-house at La Perrière goes just as far the other way toward modernity and hi-tech. The range of automatic temperature-controlled stainless-steel fermentation vats would not disgrace the most up-to-date Californian winery. Cooling is by automatic sprinklers on the exterior walls of the vats, and there is a dual system for heating, either by circulation of hot water through pipes built into the vats, or by hot-air heating of the vat-house; both are run off the wood-burning domestic hot-water and heating apparatus.

There is a range of *demi-muids* – wooden casks of 600-litre capacity – for serving the cubitainer customers at La Perrière, though this operation is duplicated up at the old *cave*. In winter the fire is lit, and customers are given a *casse-croûte* of hot bread and cheese while they wait for the cubitainers to be filled.

Nearly 50% of Baudry's wine goes to the cubitainer customers, and about 25% is sold in bulk to the *négociants*. He also does a little restaurant business, exports a small amount and sells about 10,000 bottles to a merchant in Paris.

Toward the end of the morning we retired to the cellar in the hillside of the Coteau de Sonnay, near the Château of that name. Baudry was having a lower cellar excavated, and I was fascinated to see twentieth-century quarrymen at work; they were cutting out huge blocks of stone with a machine like a vast mobile chainsaw and removing them with a forklift truck. It is work that demands a knowledge of and a feel for stone, perfect judgment and split-second timing if fingers, hands, arms or indeed whole bodies are to avoid being crushed.

In the upper cellar, the scene of a famous publicity photograph for Cravant-les-Coteaux, in which some fifty growers are featured in various postures and states of inebriation, we tasted three cask-samples of Baudry's 1985 wine; all were good, but the last was from 100% old vines and was markedly better and finer. His 1982 had the full colour and generous, rounded bouquet and flavour of the vintage, and had better tannins and more ageing possibilities than others I have tasted. Finally we drank a glass of the 1978, which still had a good deep colour; the nose and taste were of summer fruits, and there were some good tannins to keep this beauty going for years.

GÉRARD ET DANIEL CHAUVEAU, Domaine des Pallus - Beauséjour, Cravant-les-Coteaux and Panzoult.

The Chauveau family came originally from Ancenis, but have been Parisians for three or four generations, where they have followed one or other of the professions, mostly legal or medical. Gérard and Daniel own and run the Domaine des Pallus-Beauséjour, which is partly in the commune of Cravant-les-Coteaux and partly in Panzoult. Their father, a doctor, still very much alive and alert at 90, bought the Domaine des Pallus some 50 years ago, mainly as a weekend retreat and holiday home. The Domaine de Beauséjour, which has 22 hectares of vines on the high ground, and about 40 hectares of private forest, was acquired later; this part of the estate passed into Gérard Chaveau's hands in 1968, while brother Daniel lives at the Domaine des Pallus farmhouse.

Since my visit the two brothers have decided to split the operation, and the wines of each are vinified and commercialised separately.

Daniel is and always has been the full-time wine-maker, whilst his brother Gérard is a successful architect with a busy Parisian office; this is not to say that Gérard takes no interest in the wine business. He is very commercial-minded and a great upholder of the quality and the traditions of the Chinon *appellation*, and the estate has benefited greatly from his professional skill, both in the jewel of a house he has built on the tree-line, and in the masterly and functional *cuverie* he has designed and had carved out of the hillside.

My visit to Daniel and Gérard Chauveau and their inclusion in this book were totally unplanned. My son and I were driving from Chinon towards the *autoroute* one beautiful Saturday morning in August, en route for a relaxing weekend at his house in

Fontainebleau with a good week's work behind us. The sunshine roof was rolled right back, and Christian was standing with his head and shoulders out of the car, keeping an eye out for good photographic shots. We were driving along the minor road on the north side of the Vienne, intent on crossing the river at L'Ile Bouchard; half-way between Cravant-les-Coteaux and Panzoult my photographer signalled for me to stop. I looked up to my left, where he was pointing, to see the Domaine de Beauséjour, a lovely stone house set at the top of the marching rows of vines, with the deeper green of the forest for a backcloth. We took our pictures, and I determined to return and find out who was the owner of this idyllic place.

Two weeks later I was lunching with Gérard and his attractive wife in front of a huge open fire, on which delicious lamb chops were grilled. Making their acquaintance was one of the big pluses of my trip, but it had not come about easily. I had called at the manager's house on my return from Fontainebleau to find out the name of the owner, and was directed up to Gérard Chauveau's house. 'Do not,' emphasised my informant, 'do not, on any account, get out of your car. Sound your hooter and wait.' Knowing the French propensity for keeping savage dogs did not in any way prepare me for the experience that followed. There is a book by Stephen King, now a film, called *Cujo*. It relates the story of a rabid St Bernard that keeps a mother and child imprisoned in their car for two days. I think Mr King may have visited Gérard Chauveau for the purposes of research. The creature that launched itself on to the bonnet of my car was a hound of hell; with slavering jaws agape, it tried to gnaw its way through the very glass of my windscreen, and, had not M. Chauveau made a timely appearance, would surely have gained entry and torn me limb from trembling limb. Gérard was in bed when I arrived, convalescing after a heart attack, and I fear my visit, complete with honking horn and baying hound, can have done his condition no good at all. Suffice it to say that he was kindness itself, and invited me to come back for lunch and a proper visit.

In the office down the road at Domaine des Pallus I met M. Chauveau *père*, who at 90 years of age was as bright as a button and did not miss a trick. Sadly Gérard's brother Daniel was in hospital at the time, having had his leg crushed in an accident whilst excavating the new cellar. There are 10 hectares down here at Les Pallus, and wine is kept in wooden

fûts for the passing cubitainer customers. The Chauveau wine business is fairly heavily orientated toward the private customer – some 400 hectolitres, equivalent to about 53,000 bottles, is sold to the cubitainer customers. The private business does not stop there, however, for the Chauveaus have a mailing list of some 3,000 customers who have their wine delivered in bottle, which accounts for a goodly proportion of the 100,000 bottles sold in an average year. The rest of the bottle sales are to the restaurant business, with a little going for export to Germany, Belgium, Holland and the United Kingdom.

Before lunch Gérard took me to see the *cuverie* which he had designed. There are, or very shortly will be, 20 stainless-steel vats of 160-hectolitre capacity, housed in the 500 square-metre vat-house. They have been designed and installed in such a fashion that they can be moved easily to make room for further vats; the split level of the vat-house and *pressoir* means that the grape must only moves by gravity, thus avoiding unnecessary fatigue and oxidation. Alcoholic fermentation is automatically temperature-controlled, and the wine is later brought down to 20°, so that the malo-lactic fermentation can be completed in vat.

Over lunch we tasted three wines, the '85, which needs a little time, but will be very good, the '83, which is drinking well, and finally an exceptional '75, a Gold Medal winner with a splendid ruby colour and plenty of fruit and life.

PATRICE DE FOUCAUD, Château de Sonnay, Cravant-les-Coteaux. The last of the Cravant wines that I looked at is, in my opinion, one to watch. Patrice de Foucaud took over from his father in 1979, since when he has replanted over half of the gravelly vineyard on the lower ground.

I did not have the time to visit the property, but tasted the wine on two occasions. The 1981 was part of a comparative tasting of a dozen different growers' wines from that vintage. It came out somewhere in the middle of the range, but it was hardly fair to judge that vintage, since Patrice de Foucaud had only just taken over.

The results of his efforts were really apparent in the 1985, of which I tasted an April bottling; the colour was almost black, and the bouquet promising, but still very closed; in the mouth the wine was huge, with lots of excellent Cabernet Franc flavour and lovely ripe tannin. It will make a really superb bottle in four or five years.

SAZILLY

CHARLES JOGUET, Sazilly. Though one of the smallest of the Chinon communes, Sazilly nonetheless enjoys a unique reputation for the quality and individuality of its wines. Charles Joguet, artist, sculptor, poet and wine-maker *extraordinaire*, is, to all intents, Sazilly. His love for and dedication to his wines is transparently obvious; it is thanks to this passion that Joguet's wines are known and appreciated all over the world, for he is his own best and most energetic ambassador.

Some two-thirds of Joguet's vines are on chalky clay soil around his home in Sazilly, a quiet little village on the south bank of the Vienne, opposite the vineyards of Cravant-les-Coteaux. These vines are ungrafted, and it is probably this, allied to the lateness of the vintage in Sazilly, more than all the care lavished upon them, that makes Joguet's wines so very individual.

Charles Joguet sells his wines under four different labels. The produce of the young vines, which he vinifies both as red and as rosé, is sold as Cuvée du Clos de la Curé; the Clos du Chêne Vert is a vineyard next to the Clos de l'Haute Olive in the commune of Chinon, and is always vinified apart from the Sazilly wines. Les Varennes du Grand Clos is a blend from the Sazilly vineyards, whilst the Clos de la Dioterie is the best wine from the oldest vines on the estate, and is possessed of the most amazing ageing potential.

Picking is still done by hand, and plastic baskets are used to minimise bruising of the fruit; the bunches are carefully de-stalked, and then undergo a slow alcoholic fermentation and maceration period in the special rectangular stainless-steel vats, complete with automatic temperature-control and *système de pigeage*, which were designed by Joguet in collaboration with Jacques Puisais and the manufacturers, Ets. Guérin. All Joguet's wines spend varying times in wooden *fûts*, according to their individual needs.

I tasted the Cuvée du Clos de la Curé 1985, which was bottled in March and was already drinking nicely. The '85 Cuvée des Varennes du Grand Clos had a lovely depth of colour. The nose was still very closed, and the wine still had far to go, although good fruit and soft tannins were there a-plenty.

We then went to a little cellar in the rock, down country lanes so convoluted that they were their own security. Within slumbered ranks of older vintages, mostly of the Clos de la Dioterie. We tasted by the light of a guttering candle the '82, '81 and finally a mind-blowing 1976; all were wines of considerable breeding and elegance, and the '76 could hold its head up high in a tasting of fine Bordeaux.

LIGRÉ

PAUL AND JEAN-MARIE DOZON, Ligré. Tradition rules on the romantically named 'Wolf's Leap' estate. Paul Dozon and his son Jean-Marie make their wine, albeit with meticulous care and attention to hygiene, much as it must have been made here for the past hundred years. Fermentation is in oak vats, and the wine all spends up to eighteen months in casks of 220 litres before bottling. The cellars, carved into the tuff, give perfect conditions for the storage and evolution of wine, with a constant year-round temperature between 12° and 14°.

The Clos du Saut au Loup vineyard itself extends to 13 hectares, all in one piece, and the Dozons have a further 7 hectares elsewhere in the Ligré commune. The soil here is of two distinct types – clay-silex at the top of the slopes, and clay-chalk lower down. The soil and Dozon attitude to vinification combine to produce achetypal Ligré Chinon – a wine of some finesse that is slow to develop but ages well.

My appointment was with M. Dozon *père*, who was suffering from an acute case of *gueule de bois* (hangover). There were some small children playing very noisily in the courtyard outside his office, and it was evident that their merry cries were causing *le maître* some considerable distress. The effort of getting up and remonstrating with them seemed too much, however, so he resigned himself to his sufferings and answered my questions with good grace.

Paul explained to me that he and his son Jean-Marie divided the responsibilities of running the business very clearly between them. He, Paul, is the wine-maker, whilst Jean-Marie, bearded like an apostle, attends to all aspects of viticulture. They sell about half their wine in bottle and half in bulk, of which only 5% goes to the *négociants*; as one would expect from such a traditional house, the major part of their bulk sales is to long-established private customers, who buy year after year in cubitainers and do their own bottling.

In the *cuverie* we tasted the 1985 vintage from five different vats. The Dozons do not make an *assemblage* of their wines, but bottle the different vats in rotation according to the state of their maturity; thus the more ready and appealing wine from the younger vines will be sold first, and the best of the old vines of the Clos du Saut au Loup vineyard may not be bottled until eighteen months after the vintage. I would have liked to have tasted a maturer vintage, as the 1985s were still very tough.

SAVIGNY-EN-VÉRON

JEAN-MAURICE RAFFAULT, Savigny-en-Véron. Jean-Maurice Raffault's wine and spirit business is based at La Croix in Savigny-en-Véron, but his 30 hectares of vines are spread over six of the Chinon communes – Chinon, Avoine, Savigny-en-Véron, Beaumont-en-Véron, Rivière and Ligré. His wines are always sold under their Domaine or vineyard name, of which there are eight – Les Morillères, Clos des Lutinières, Les Galluches, Domaine du Puy Rigault, Beaulieu, Les Picasses, Domaine d'Isoré and Clos du Galon. The last three are the longest-lived. Les Picasses, from a chalky tuff soil, was my particular favourite – the '82 was beautiful, and already giving of its charms, whilst the '81 was by way of an experiment. Jean-Maurice had aged the wine for 12 months in 100% new oak casks, and the wine was still almost black, with huge depth of flavour, and tannins like a young St Estèphe – a

fascinating exercise, but strictly non-commercial. We finished up with the 1969, amazingly lively and young in all respects for an 18-year-old.

The cellars where we tasted these wines are in the tuff beneath the Château de Danzay in Beaumont-en-Véron, where the Domaine wines age in oak casks. There is also a large stock of bottled wines, and in one room there are some very old vintages laid out on the floor in seemingly haphazard fashion; the bottles are covered in mould, and give the curious impression of mummies lying in some ancient tomb. A feature of Raffault's cellar is an extraordinary pink marble spitoon of gargantuan proportions, surmounted by a marvellous Heath-Robinson arrangement of rotating copper pipes which spray water in the basin, keeping everything clean.

Jean-Maurice is also a distiller, and produces a delicious Poire William eau-de-vie, as well as a respectable grape brandy sold as Marc des Coteaux de la Loire. The purity of the latter was demonstrated by setting light to it and by rubbing it vigorously between the palms of the hands; in neither case could any caramel – often used to give false colour – or any other impurity be detected on the nose.

A keen and active promoter of Chinon's wines, Raffault exports an unusually high proportion of his production. Some 30% is sold to Belgium, Germany, Holland, Canada and a little in the United States.

Old bottles in Jean-Maurice Raffault's cellars under the Château de Danzay

APPELLATIONS: BOURGUEIL & ST NICOLAS DE BOURGUEIL

It must be a very personal taste, for few people either here in England or in the Loire Valley agree with me, but for me the best red wines of Touraine come from the communes of Bourgueil and St Nicolas de Bourgueil.

The area of the *appellations* is a long, right-angled triangle on the north bank of the Loire, halfway between Langeais and Saumur. The communes entitled to the Bourgueil *appellation* are, starting in the east and working along the riverside, southern edge of the triangle: St Patrice, La Chapelle-sur-Loire and Chouzé-sur-Loire, then, turning north, we come to St Nicolas de Bourgueil, which for no discernible reason has its own *appellation*; here is the right-angle of our triangle, and we turn back east and go through the best vineyards of Bourgueil, in the communes of Bourgueil itself, Benais, Restigné and Ingrandes de Touraine, a couple of kilometres up the D35 from our starting point.

The soil of the *appellation* is divided into three types on three levels, which give three distinct sorts of wine. The flat, sandy land nearest to the river gives light, elegant wines, best drunk young; the slightly higher ground, between the sand and the *coteaux*, is older alluvial soil with more stones and gravel on the surface, from which comes wine of more finesse and breeding; the top level in terms of altitude and quality, is the *coteaux* soil, known as tuff, composed of clay and limestone, from which come wines of greater breeding, body and longevity.

There is but one grape grown in the 1,600 hectares of the *appellation*, and that is the Cabernet Franc; a little Cabernet Sauvignon is permitted by the INAO regulations, but very few growers will give it house room. One *vigneron* in St Nicolas de Bourgueil summed up the general attitude to the Cabernet Sauvignon when I asked him if he grew any. 'Yes,' he said, 'I believe there is one vine which the nursery delivered by mistake.' On the other side of the coin, the firm of Lamé-Delille-Boucard in Ingrandes de Touraine have 10% of their vineyard planted with Cabernet Sauvignon, since they find it gives backbone to the wine in the less successful vintages.

Within the seven communes that make up the Bourgueil *appellation*, a grower will often have his vines spread over more than one commune; in any case, a large percentage of Bourgueil is sold through the excellent *négociant* house of Audebert et Fils or vinified at the local Cave Co-opérative. The nett result is that the vast majority of Bourgueil is a homogenised blend of *sables*, *graviers* and *coteaux* wines.

Generally speaking this works to the benefit of the *appellation* and its reputation, since the majority of the wines are on the lower ground, which produces wines of less character, which in turn benefit from blending with their nobler, tougher cousins from the higher slopes. We shall, however, meet one or two growers from the higher ground who insist that their wines are vinified, bottled, and sold under their particular vineyard label, and, in my view, rightly so; these conscientious and dedicated wine-makers have something very special to offer, which will benefit both the public and the Bourgueil *appellation* alike.

Both Bourgueil and Chinon suffer less from the 'tarnished image' sometimes given to other *appellations* by the big *négociant* houses. There are two reasons for this: first, both *appellations* have their own 'in-house' *négociant* firms of great integrity and honesty, and secondly neither area has much problem in selling its wines. A bottle of Bourgueil or St

Nicolas de Bourgueil may often prove too young, but it will rarely disappoint. Being by education and inclination a Bordeaux lover, I cannot but think that Bourgueil, made from the classic Bordeaux Cabernet, has an unexploited market and will find a warm welcome in the cellars, and stomachs, of those British wine-drinkers who can no longer afford the inflated price of young clarets.

Château de Villandry with its famous vegetable garden

BOURGUEIL

AUDEBERT ET FILS, Bourgueil. The old-established *négociant* and wine-making house of Audebert et Fils in Bourgueil seemed a logical place to start my visits since they own one of the most famous vineyards in the *appellation* and, by dint of their activities as *négociants*, they probably sell more Bourgueil than any other business in or out of the area.

I spent a morning with Georges Audebert, father of Jean-Claude, who in turn has a son of 18 to follow him. Georges, who is now in semi-retirement, comes from a family of wine-makers in Restigné; the Bourgueil vineyards were the property of his wife's family, but they have been well loved and cared for by the Audeberts.

I learnt from Georges that the Cabernet Franc is also known locally as Le Breton, dating probably from the days when the Loire was navigable, and a good market was to be found in Brittany. The family business has 30 hectares of vines, which includes the nine-hectare Domaine du Grand Clos, up on the slopes beneath the blue windmill, as well as six hectares in the sister *appellation* of St Nicolas de Bourgueil. They also buy in, either as grape must or finished wine, large quantities of Bourgueil and St Nicolas de Bourgueil, Chinon and Saumur-Champigny, to satisfy their large French clientèle, who have come to look to this house for the best of the red wines of the Loire. Their home market is mainly in northern and western France and Paris, and they have as yet found little need to do much on the export market. A gesture towards the world outside France was made in 1985, however, when Audebert et Fils sent a special commemorative *cuvée* of their Bourgueil to mark the refurbishment and 100th Anniversary celebrations of the Statue of Liberty on Long Island.

I was curious to know why so little effort was made to export Bourgueil. Jean-Claude said it was difficult for foreigners to pronounce and they did not understand what it was. These seemed to me to be fairly easily surmountable obstacles; firstly, the name is easily said, if mispronounced, so does it really matter? Secondly, it is not beyond the bounds of possibility for the combined powers of the CIVT, SOPEXA and the local Syndicat to mount a tasting in London and other wine-consuming capitals, showing people just what the potential of Bourgueil's wine is. I, as an importer, will certainly do my bit.

There are 15 permanent staff on the Audebert payroll, who, augmented by regiments of relations, cope with the vintage which is still done entirely by hand. It is this ready availability of labour which has kept them from purchasing a picking machine, though both father and son acknowledge that many have already made the change without detriment to their wine.

Georges then took me in his car to look at Le Grand Clos, 1.5 kilometres north of the town, across the D35 road. The nine hectares are all on the upper slopes or *coteaux*, and give a toughish wine with lots of tannin, breeding and backbone that needs five to 10 years in bottle to give of its best. There is little risk of frost here, as the slopes are protected from the cold north winds by the hills and forests behind them. From the top of Grand Clos there is a stunning view of the surrounding countryside; the mediaeval Castle of Saumur can be seen away to the west, and the vineyards of Bourgueil and St Nicolas are spread like a carpet at your feet. Every prospect pleases, and only the Centre Nucléaire at Chinon is vile. In fact Georges assured me that it was totally safe, and that the vast mushroom-shaped cloud ascending from it was only steam from the seven reactors. This was the oldest nuclear power-station in France, he said, it had been there for 30 years, so surely it must be safe? The French government is deeply committed to nuclear power, and the public are not told much of the risks involved. The Chernobyl fiasco hardly merited a mention in the French newspapers until the world media made it impossible to ignore any longer. I suppose it is inevitable that these monstrosities are built in the great wine regions, for great rivers go with great wines, and great volumes of water are needed for cooling purposes. Cheap electricity is, of course, important, but I cannot help

A typical rock cellar in the Bourgueil region

feeling that a large number of people would rather pay a little more for their power, and rest assured about the future of their wine – and their children!

On the way back into Bourgueil we stopped off to look at the vinification cellar, hacked out of the rock beneath the Grand Clos. Audebert installed a range of stainless-steel vats in 1976 in preference to the old conical wooden ones that used to be the norm in this region. Fermentation lasts 5–6 days, and temperature is maintained at between 25° and 28°C by running cold water on the exterior of the vats to cool or by serpentine with hot water to warm up the must.

As we drove back to his offices, Georges Audebert talked to me of the gastronomy of Bourgueil. Our progress through the town was impeded by a Garlic Fair. Garlic, opined Audebert *père*, was fine, for it gave something extra to meat, and it was meat that the Bourgueillois liked. Salads and vegetables were, he said, 'herbes pour les vaches'; the proper stuff for the wines of Bourgueil was rillons, rillettes, andouillettes, roast meats, a good coq au vin, and game of all descriptions.

Before leaving, we tasted the 1985 Domaine du Grand Clos. It had a nice, deep, bluey-red colour, and a pleasing, fruity nose of Cabernet with some *cassis*. Rounded, well-made, with some good tannin and plenty of fruit, it will make a splendid bottle in five years.

MESSRS THOUET AND LORRIEUX, Clos de l'Abbaye.

Suitably enough, the ancient Abbey of Bourgueil has been for the last 100 years a convent for the Sisters of St Martin. It is St Martin who is reputed to have bought the vine to Touraine, and whose donkey, so the legend goes, discovered that pruning the vine improves the grapes. Before the good sisters took over, the abbey was in Benedictine hands, who made no liquor but licorice, and also kept silkworms. The sisters were faithful to the precepts of their founder, and made wine here until 10 years ago, when Messrs Thouet and Lorrieux rented the 6½ hectare walled vineyard from the Abbey. The good nuns ran a school here, and were never short of pickers.

Sadly the infant *vendangeurs* are not available to M. Thouet and his partner, but picking is still done by hand, and, being in the centre of the town, there is not too much difficulty in finding the necessary labour. The Thouet accent is very much on tradition in the cellars as well as in the vineyard. Of the five fermentation vats, four are the traditional conical wooden type, though the fifth is a brand new stainless-steel model, complete with the automatic *pigeage* system on top. This is an apparatus, invented by the great oenologist Jacques Puisais, by means of which the 'cap' of skins and pips can be broken up at will by the action of hydraulically-operated plungers preventing the must from overheating and encouraging lazy yeasts to do their work.

The wine always spends a minimum of nine months in wood; a little is bottled in June to meet the demand for the new wine, but Thouet prefers to bottle in September or just after the next harvest is finished. Careful and patient vinification, allied to the soil, sheltered vineyard and a large preponderance of vines that are 60, 70 and even 80-years-old, produce a wine of exceptionally high quality. This is true Bourgueil, and, though it has its attractions in youth, should really be kept for five years or more to give its best.

I tasted both the 1985 and the 1984 vintage; the former had a deep, purple colour like young Bordeaux, and a powerful nose of blackberries and blackcurrants. It was tannic, mouthfilling and well structured, and will make a lovely bottle in 1990. The '84 was amazingly good for the year, with the same depth of colour, with lots of good fruit and ripe tannins, probably right for drinking in 1989.

Young M. Thouet also runs his own family vineyard, the Domaine Thouet-Bosseau, on the outskirts of the town. He is helped here and at the Clos de l'Abbaye by his attractive and capable young wife. They took over the running of the family vines from his father recently, and are now commercialising the *vieilles vignes* wine themselves, selling in bottle to restaurants and private customers; the produce of the younger vines is still sold to *négociants*.

Judging from the 1985 Vieilles Vignes that I tasted, they have a great future with their five hectares. The wine was a deep bluey-red, with a nice fruity bouquet just beginning to open. In the mouth there was plenty of good fruit and tannins to keep it well, with an interesting *goût de terroir* (tang of the soil).

JEAN GAMBIER, Bourgueil.

Jean Gambier's fine old creeper-clad farmhouse, the Domaine des Galluches, is about a kilometre from the centre of Bourgueil on the Restigné road. Quiet, unassuming and helpful, Gambier's knowledge of the *appellation* and its growers was encyclopaedic; this is hardly surprising, since he is the fourth generation of his family to have made wine here, and he is also Secretary of the local Syndicat Viticole.

There are 10 hectares of vines on M. Gambier's estate; the name Les Galluches means flat limestone pebbles, which is curious as the soil here is mostly silex. Vinification is along traditional lines; following a three-week period in vat, the wine spends an average of one year in oak before bottling, giving a wine with the typical Bourgueil scent of raspberries and cassis, and excellent ageing potential. The grape variety is 100% Cabernet Franc, and I remember tasting the 1985 from the cask and finding it similar to a fine young St Emilion. No tasting notes survive, since the electricity failed in the middle of the *dégustation*, which was completed in Stygian darkness, but none the worse for that.

BENAIS

PIERRE-JACQUES DRUET, Benais. Every once in a while in the course of my vinous travels I meet special people like Pierre-Jacques Druet. He is, first and foremost, a perfectionist; he is also highly professional, hard working, dedicated to, and in love with, the whole business of making good wine. He is much more than the sum of these parts, though; he is outgoing, friendly and his enthusiasm and pursuit of excellence are totally infectious. I have enjoyed tastings and meals with Pierre-Jacques, his pretty wife, Martine, and their children, that I will always remember; stronger still will be the memory of nights spent helping him, and learning much, during the fermentation of the 1986 vintage, when temperatures were low, fermentation difficult and much use was made of the *pompe à chaleur* to encourage the reluctant yeasts to their task. More than any other of the many wine-makers I have met, Pierre-Jacques showed me the extraordinary degree of attention to detail and sheer physical graft that goes into the making of good wine, and I thank him most profoundly.

A relative newcomer to Touraine, Pierre-Jacques is the only *viticulteur* in the whole Bourgueil *appellation* to have all his vines on the *coteaux*, or high slopes. He has 13 hectares in the Benais commune, a large part of which is situated in the two best vineyards of Beauvais and Le Grand Mont, where he has an unusually high proportion of very old vines. Pierre also has 1.5 hectares of vines in Chinon at the

Château de Danzay in the commune of Beaumont-en-Véron, where the vines are all between 50 and 80 years old. Vinification of his Chinon wine takes place in Benais, and he produces an average of 8,000 bottles each year of Chinon of quite outstanding quality; it may only be labelled as plain Chinon, with no reference to Château de Danzay or Beaumont-en-Véron, because it is vinified here, outside the Chinon *appellation*

His Bourgueil wines are vinified in the same way as the Chinon, and the Beauvais and Grand Mont wines are always vinified, aged, labelled and commercialised separately; the produce of the younger vines and the less good vats are sold as Cuvée Réservée.

Pruning in all Druet's vineyards is severe, and *rendement* or yield per hectare is consqently low, particularly among the very old vines; it is this deliberate sacrifice of quantity that counts here, as in all great vineyards, in terms of the quality of the eventual wine. All picking is done by hand. Fermentation is carried out mainly in the most modern of stainless-steel vats; these are conical in shape, and equipped with the *système de pigeage* already described, and were made especially to Pierre's specification. There are also one or two of the old wooden, open-top conical vats in use. The ideal temperature for fermentation, in the gospel according to Druet, is between 22° and 25°C, and should never exceed 30°. After the alcoholic fermentation is over and just before the wine is 'de-vatted', he raises the temperature of the wine to 35° for a period of half an hour.

All Druet's wines are then aged in oak casks in his cellar in the tuff beneath the Grand Mont vines. He is most insistent on oak, and violently anti the chestnut so often used in Touraine; it is the disagreeable tannins from chestnut wood that give a wine the unpleasant bitterness at the back of the mouth which are occasionally found in red Loire wines. The wine is racked at three-monthly intervals, fined with whites of egg and undergoes a light Kieselguhr filtration – never *sur plaques* – before bottling. This takes place at varying times for the different wines – the Chinon wine and the Bourgueil Cuvée Réservée are usually bottled in September, the Beauvais in November or December, having spent over a year in cask, and the Grand Mont is bottled last of all in January or February.

The viticulture, vinification, care and attention given to Pierre-Jacques Druet's wine are equal to any that I have observed, even in the great Bordeaux châteaux. He bounced in here barely half-a-dozen years ago, all boyish good looks, enthusiasm and oenological qualifications; at first he was regarded with cynical amusement by his peers, but it is by now clear to anyone who tastes his wines that Druet is a force to be reckoned with.

I tasted all the '85 from the cask in the Grand Mont *cave*, and was uniformly impressed by their fruit, structure and non-aggressive tannins; the Chinon and the Grand Mont were particularly fine.

Pierre put on for me a range of all the vintages that he has made here, and the quality was so outstanding that I have reproduced my notes in full.

Tasted: Cuvée Réservée 1984. Good medium bluey red. Attractive open nose. A well-made 1984 with good fruits and tannins.

Cuvée Beauvais 1984. Same good colour. Bouquet more spicy, and still quite closed. Well-structured wine with excellent length and tannins to the fore.

Cuvée Grand Mont 1984. Slightly more ruby in colour. Bouquet more rounded and open than the Beauvais. Tannins more pronounced, but not harsh. Excellent mouthful of aromatic fruit and tremendous length.

Cuvée Réservée 1983. Good deep colour, with hint of orange. Bouquet redolent of *cassis* and blackberries. Lovely full fruit in the mouth, but tannins a bit harsh. Pierre says this was caused by hail just before the grapes turned colour.

Cuvée Grand Mont 1983. Very dark, dense red. Nose good, but still closed. A big, black, strapping mouthful of wine. Very tannic, but huge fruit and very aromatic. An astonishing wine for the Loire. 10 out of 10. To drink in 1993 and beyond. Hurrah!

Cuvée Réservée 1979. (Not vinified by Pierre-Jacques – and it showed.) Colour light compared with others. Slight over-ripeness on the nose (Pierre-Jacques puts the character of this wine down to lack of control at fermentation time). Flavour okay but very short, leaving a bitter after-taste in the back of the mouth. ('Typical chestnut wine!' says P.-J.)

Cuvée Grand Mont 1980. Lightish red, turning to orange. Light and pleasing bouquet, easy to drink now, with good balance of fruit and tannin.

Cuvée Réservée 1982. Deep, purplish colour, with a rounded and open *cassis* bouquet. Fat, rounded and fruity with good ripe tannins.

Cuvée Grand Mont 1982. Blackish red. Very closed on nose at first, but, with aeration, began to give off good and exciting perfumes. Very shut-in and concentrated still in the mouth, but huge potential there, with lots of fruit and good tannin. Will make a marvellous bottle in 2 or 3 years time.

The 1982 and 1983 wines compare with each other in the same way that these two vintages compare in Bordeaux. The '82 is fat and round and agreeable; the '83 more reserved and will perhaps, eventually, give the most pleasure.

Congratulations and many, many thanks to Pierre-Jacques Druet for showing me what can be achieved with the Cabernet Franc in the Loire Valley.

M. AND MME CASLOT- GALBRUN, La Hurolaie, Benais.

Mme Caslot-Galbrun is the Mayor of Benais, and she is also a very capable wine-maker and businesswoman. She and her husband have 15 hectares of vines, of which part is a walled *clos* in Restigné called the Clos de la Gaucherie. They also have a large part of their vines on the tuff, some on the lower slopes and the best on the *coteaux*, which is commercialised under the name of the vineyard, Les Rossés, and is their best wine.

Only the wines from the tuff vineyards are bottled, the remainder being kept for sale in cubitainers to private customers who like to save a few francs by doing their own bottling. This method of sale is more common in Bourgueil and Chinon than anywhere else I have visited, but more and more quality-conscious growers are tending to abandon the practice. Firstly, they have a better control over the eventual quality of their wine, thus ensuring a faithful clientèle; secondly, and just as important, the bottled wine fetches a higher price and is more profitable. The *coteaux* and mid-slope wines are bottled and commercialised by the Caslot-Galbruns and are sold to private customers and restaurants; a little is exported, and Christopher Tatham buys for the English market.

All the Caslot-Galbrun wines, whether destined for bottle or cubitainer, spend a whole year in wooden casks in their cellar in the rock of the *coteaux*. The *cave* is spacious, damp and keeps a perfect, constant temperature throughout the year, and here Madame, handling pipette and cask-hammer as well as any man, gave me a tasting of her entire range of '85s from the cask.

Firstly, the *sables* wine, from vines grown on the lowest level of the Bourgueil *terrasse*, where the soil is very sandy; the wine had a good, if light, colour and a nice open nose with hints of raspberry. A well-balanced mouthful with plenty of good fruit. I complimented madame on such a good wine coming from sand, and she told me that there was a good deal of clay not far from the surface.

The *vin de tuffe* had a much deeper colour, with a rounded and more open nose. A much fuller wine with more flavour and good length.

I then tasted the *coteaux* wine, Les Rossés; the colour was similar to the *vin de tuffe*, the nose more closed; in the mouth there was more finesse and elegance, but the wine had a long life ahead.

Finally, we looked at Le Clos de la Gaucherie. My dictionary defines *gaucherie* as, among other things, clumsiness. What a misnomer! This Gaucherie had lots of breeding and delicacy, but it was still closed in and shy. It will make an excellent bottle in a few years.

Mme Caslot-Galbrun in her cellars in Benais

I was surprised to discover that the only wood used in this cellar was chestnut. Maybe they renew the barrels regularly, or the wine stays a shorter time in wood than chez Druet, but at any rate I did not get a hint of the *arrière-bouche* bitterness I had been warned of.

INGRANDES-DE-TOURAINE

LAMÉ-DELILLE-BOUCARD, Ingrandes-de-Touraine. Monsieur Lamé-Delille has about 28 hectares of vines around the commune of Ingrandes, approximately 24 of which are in production at any one time.

Vinification is entirely in wood, fermentation taking place in a splendid range of wooden, conical vats with open tops; a mobile gantry with a hydraulic plunger is moved between the rows of vats for the purpose of breaking the 'cap'. Following the maceration period in vat, the wine is transferred into large oak *fûts*, and some into smaller casks, where it spends varying lengths of time dependent on the needs of each vintage.

The rock cellar, where the casks lie and where M. Lamé-Delille has his tasting room, is a real hobgoblin's cave. There is not a level surface anywhere, and everything is festooned with a copious growth of black mould or fungus, of which the proprietor is inordinately proud. He could not have been more hospitable, but he refused point-blank to allow me to photograph the mouldy tasting corner. 'The flash, monsieur, you understand. It makes the mould to vanish.' I was not too sure of the scientific soundness of this theory, but it was his cellar, so I naturally complied.

We sat on the mouldy goblins' chairs, and tasted four vintages of his excellent red wine – he also makes a little rosé. The first wine was his 1984, which had a good, deep ruby colour and a nice open bouquet. A really well-made, balanced wine, very agreeable to drink now. The reason for his success with this mediocre vintage, affirmed M. Lamé-Delille, is that he is one of the very few *viticulteurs* who still grow a significant proportion of Cabernet-Sauvignon; the 10% that he grows always gives that bit of extra backbone to the *petites années*. We then tasted the '83, which was much darker; the nose was quite closed, but there was some good, slightly peppery fruit there. A well-structured *vin de garde*, with loads of fruit and good tannins. Will keep for

A vintage scene showing grapes with the 'Noble Rot'

Château de Saumur and the Loire

The steep vineyard of the Coulée de Serrant and Château des Roches aux Moines, Savennières

Château among the vines

The old-fashioned way

years. The 1982 was a more open and friendly wine, lighter in colour, and with pleasing fruit; excellent for current drinking. Finally we tasted the 1981, for me the best of the four. Brilliant light red, and an intoxicating raspberry-strawberry-blackcurrant bouquet; well-balanced and harmonious, lovely long aftertaste. A cracker!

I found the Lamé-Delille wines really well-made, and a fine example of what can be produced in the old-fashioned way from the mixed *coteaux* and *graviers* soils of this commune. Sadly only a small proportion of the production is exported, and that mainly to Belgium and Switzerland, but this will change!

RESTIGNÉ

MARC MUREAU, Lossay, Restigné. The affable and highly voluble M. Mureau has 15 hectares of vines around Restigné, which he runs from his house and office in the hamlet of Lossay, aided by his son Régis. There is a *boîte* in their courtyard, from which they sell a large part of their production to private customers; the wines are well-packaged and free tasting is offered. Like most Bourgueillois, something in excess of 90% of their wine is red; a little rosé is produced, mostly in less good years. About 20%, a high proportion for the *appellation*, is exported to Belgium, Holland, Germany and the United States of America.

Mureau's cellars are, like most in Bourgueil, well hidden, off one of the secondary roads leading up to the *coteaux*. Ivy and virginia-creeper hang around the entrance to yet another one-time quarry, and within, barrels and binned bottles abound. Mureau also boasts a troglodyte tasting-room, complete with fireplace, table and seven chairs hewn from tree-trunks. I expected at any moment to hear the Seven Dwarfs approaching from some far corner of the cave, singing 'Hi ho! Hi ho! It's off to work we go!'

Seven Dwarfs or not, some very serious and effective work has evidently been carried out in these rocky cellars. Marc Mureau opened three bottles of his wine for me to taste – 1982, 1976 and an amazing 1959. The '82 was comparatively light and open, with nice fruit and good length; the '76 had an extraordinary depth of colour with no hint of brown, a powerful bouquet of ripe fruits, and was still very young and lively in the mouth, with tremendous body, fruit and backbone. The year 1976 was a

M Lamé-Delille in his cuverie at Ingrandes-de-Touraine

Marc Mureau opens a bottle of his 1959

splendid vintage in the Loire, and I found throughout the region countless examples of red wines and *demi-sec* and *moelleux* whites that had aged marvellously; none of them had that distinct trace of end-of-life fatigue that afflicts so many Bordeaux of that year.

Mureau's *pièce de résistance* was his 1959 red; if anybody had told me that I would one day drink a 27-year-old red wine from the Loire and mistake it for a five-year-old, I would have laughed at them. The colour was even denser than the '76, and the bouquet was almost overpowering, with a mass of ripeness and blackcurrant and blackberries. Huge, mouthfilling wine, with plenty of life and spine still, and an aftertaste that went on and on forever. Extraordinary!

ALAIN RENOU. Before leaving the hospitable purlieus of Bourgueil, I must thank Alain Renou of Restigné. I was, in fact, looking for his uncle, Georges Renou, a man of such importance and such a busy schedule that I never managed to meet him at all; he is President of the Syndicat des Producteurs de Bourgueil et de St Nicolas de Bourgueil, as well as being in charge of the Cave Co-opérative, where growers take their grapes for vinification, to be subsequently returned to them in bottle for labelling and commercialisation. I am sorry not to have met him, for if he is half as charming, articulate and welcoming as his brother Jean's son, Alain, he is a man not to be missed.

I called in on Alain, uninvited and unknown, at midday to ask where his Uncle Georges might be found, hoping to find the elusive wolf in his lair at feeding time. His home, I gathered, was just down the road, but he was, not surprisingly, away at some important function. On learning the purpose of my visit, Alain insisted that I stay for lunch, and he and his wife made me most welcome. We had a simple and delicious meal of steak and salad, washed down with his excellent rosé, followed by a bottle of his '82 red with the cheese.

Alain is now totally responsible for his father Jean's vineyards, which amount to about 12 hectares in the communes of Restigné and Benais, with a little in Bourgueil itself. He is another of the 'young wolves', and Bourgueil need have no fears about its future as an *appellation* if it is entrusted to the likes of Alain Renou and his peers.

St Nicolas de Bourgueil

JEAN-PAUL MABILEAU, St Nicolas de Bourgueil. St Nicolas de Bourgueil abounds with Mabileaus – Madame Blanchet's directory lists 13 growers of that name. Jean-Paul is to be found near the church, and the search is well worth the trouble. He was extremely kind, makes very good wine, and gave me much useful information about St Nicolas.

Given its own separate *appellation* in 1937, at the same time as Bourgueil, St Nicolas de Bourgueil has currently around 600 hectares of vines in production. Apart from a higher proportion of *graviers* soil and less *coteaux* than the rest of the Bourgueil *appellation*, there does not seem to be any very good reason for setting St Nicolas apart. It has been suggested that the granting of an eponymous *appellation* was, more than anything else, the result of the civic pride of a well-connected mayor of the town at the time; if so, *tant mieux* for St Nicolas.

From 13 hectares, which is a large area by St Nicolas standards, Jean-Paul produces an excellent red wine from 100% Cabernet Franc grapes. His wines are mainly on the *graviers* soil of the *terrasse*, but he also has some vines on the *coteaux*, where the clay-limestone mix gives body and backbone to the wine.

Although his sales are about 90% to the home market, Mabileau exports a little to England, Belgium, Germany, Luxembourg and America. He has rather a special tie with England, in that there is a restaurant called Mabileau at 61 The Cut, London S.E.1. The owners came on a visit with their friend and wine-merchant, J.P. Corliss of Brissac Wines Ltd., and were so well received and so impressed by the quality of Jean-Paul's wine that they asked his permission to name their restaurant after him, to which he readily agreed. If you would like to taste some older St Nicolas de Bourgueil, I am assured that the Mabileau's cellar contains every vintage of Jean-Paul's wine back to 1974.

As well as being a skilled and enthusiastic wine-maker, Jean-Paul is a keen promoter of St Nicolas de Bourgueil in general and his own Domaine du Bourg wines in particular. He is a staunch and active member of the Bourgueil brotherhood, La Commanderie de la Dive Bouteille de Bourgueil et St Nicolas; the Commanderie holds public meetings twice yearly, on the last Sundays in April and November, at which wine lovers may taste and learn.

I tasted three 1985 wines *en cuve*: the Première Cuvée, the wine from the *graviers* soil, and that from the clay-limestone slopes. The samples were all good, and I could see how the parts would form the whole, the tougher more robust wine from the high ground giving body and ageing potential to the lighter more delicate wines from the sand and gravel of the lower ground.

As 'one for the road', Jean-Paul opened a bottle of his 1977; though not a great vintage, the wine had a pleasant and fresh smell, but the colour was becoming pale red to orange. There was still lots of ripe fruit, but the finish was short. Best drunk, with great enjoyment, in the next twelve months.

PIERRE ET JEAN-JACQUES JAMET, Le Fondis, St Nicolas.

My next visit, after an unbelievable value-for-money lunch in the Routier in the square – 5 courses, wine and coffee for F36.00 – was to one of the last growers within the area of the *appellation* before you cross into Anjou.

The Domaine du Fondis is to be found on your left as you drive out of St Nicolas in the direction of Allonnes and Saumur. Jamet is yet another numerous wine-making family in St Nicolas, whose roots go back as far as the records and beyond. The main branch of the family are the Anselme Jamets at Clos le Vigneau, the head of the family by tradition always being christened Anselme, rather like the Alphonse Mellots of Sancerre.

Pierre and his two sons, Jean-Jacques and Francis, are cousins of the Anselmes; indeed, it was Pierre's grandfather Anselme who is recorded as exporting wine regularly to China as long ago as 1891, an example that might well be noted and followed by more of today's growers in Bourgueil and St Nicolas.

Le Fondis is a vineyard entirely on sandy gravel, with a uniform depth of about three metres. The wines produced are light, elegant and fruity but they age very well. They have 20 hectares of productive vines, with a possibility of enlarging to 25. Ninety-five per cent of the vines are Cabernet Franc, but the Jamets too are believers in a little Cabernet Sauvignon to help the poorer years.

Slow fermentation and long maceration in closed vats of cement lined with glass is the Jamet policy. This ensures the maximum conservation of aromas with the minimum of oxidation. The wine remains *en cuve* for a year, and then spends a period in oak before bottling on the premises.

In the true Jamet tradition, a lively export market is enjoyed. England and Holland are large customers through the Dutch importers, La Française Exportation; Germany, Belgium and Switzerland are also importers, as well as Japan, though sadly China has dropped out of the list. Domestic sales are largely to private customers, of whom nearly half buy their wine in cubitainers to bottle themselves.

JOËL TALUAU, Domaine de la Chevrette, St Nicolas.

Chevrette is a hamlet in the commune of St Nicolas high up on the *coteaux*, near to the tree-line. On the way up to Joël Taluau's house you pass that of his father, Albert. Almost all of Joel's vines are up here on the clay-limestone of the high slopes, and his wines are among the best I tasted in either Bourgueil or St Nicolas. He is in a fortunate position for a St Nicolas grower, for there is only a very small proportion of *coteaux* – some 15% – in the *appellation*, but it is not simply a question of soil that makes the Joël Taluau wines so special.

Joël is, as Suzanne Blanchet puts it, a *jeune loup* – a young buck and a bit of a rebel. He believes passionately in the *appellation* and in his own wines, and takes infinite pains from vineyard to bottle to ensure that nothing goes out under his label but the very best. Like every good wine-maker, he believes in rigorous pruning and strict selection at every stage of vinification; a long period of maceration in vat is allowed, so that the malo-lactic fermentation can take place in its own good time. It is at this stage of proceedings that Joël flies in the face of tradition, for none of his wines spends any time in wood. He started this policy after long and careful experimentation in 1985, and the results are certainly proving him right.

There are 12 hectares in production, 10 of which are on the *coteaux*. I asked Joël if he grew any Cabernet Sauvignon, and he told me that there was one vine, which he thought must have been a mistake on the part of his *pépinièriste*. Fifteen per cent of his production is exported all around Europe, and his wine is sold by the Wine Society in England; the domestic market is split roughly equally between private customers and the restaurant business. The restaurant at the Château de Rochecotte, where I was lucky enough to stay during my three months in the area, happily had a selection of his half-bottles on their wine list, which cheered many a solitary dinner.

Having inspected the modern vinification plant beside his house, and said hello to his wife, Clarisse, who was busy bottling some wine, we drove to his cellar which was a couple of kilometres away, deep in the rock with its entrance almost hidden by vines and creepers. On the way there, Joël told me proudly that he was the only grower in the *appellation* who put his wife's name beside his own on his wine labels. She does her share of the work, he reasoned, so she should have her share of the credit.

The tasting that followed was one of the most interesting of those I was given in the Loire Valley. It was also a very long session, but I really did see a large white rat running along a crack in the rock, and it was not the wine that made me take an hour to find my way back to Rochecotte, three miles away!

Most of the wines tasted had been open for more than two days, which made them even more remarkable. I should also explain that Joël bottles his wines under three labels – Jeunes Vignes, the wine from the young vines, Domaine de la Chevrette, a blend of wine from the gravelly soil and the *coteaux*, and Vieilles Vignes, the wine from the old vines.

Tasted: Jeunes Vignes 1985. Good, brilliant scarlet. Nose good, but a bit closed. A bit muted, but good fruit there. Only bottled in August, so wine was a little bottle-sick.

Domaine 1985. Nice deep red, with a fine, fruity bouquet. Good fruit, tannins and length. Well balanced. Will be very good.

Vieilles Vignes 1985. (This had been open for 5 days.) Good deep red, nose open and not oxidised. Still really good, with lots of backbone. This was the first year that Joël had heating and cooling equipment for controlling the fermentation.

Vieilles Vignes 1982. Same very deep colour. Nose very ripe. Rounded, open and more accessible than '83. Lovely to drink now.

Jeunes Vignes 1978. Still very good bouquet of raspberries and nice colour. Good fruit and tannins. Holding up well.

1976. (Bottled after 1 month in wood.) Deep red still. Open, fruity nose. Still really good and well structured with lots of life and length.

1976. (Bottled after 20 months in wood.) Colour orangey. Nose and taste completely oxidised – over the hill.

Everything in this tasting went to prove Joël's theory about wood, though whether this holds good with wine from less uncompromising soil is open to question.

LA CURIEUSE CAVE TOURISTIQUE ILLUMINÉE DE BOURGUEIL. Signs for this strange attraction are to be seen everywhere. In a snobby sort of way, I kept thinking to myself that if it was for the tourists, then it could not possibly have any interest for a serious wine writer. In fact it is a very well-run centre from which to start a tour of the Bourgueil vineyards for any stranger to the area.

Situated about 2.5 kilometres from the centre of Bourgueil, the Cave is yet another disused quarry in the tuff rock, just by the vineyard of Le Grand Clos, near the Moulin Bleu that dominates the Bourgueil skyline. There is lots of parking space, a shop where you can buy wine and other souvenirs – hopefully this book, one day – and the Cave itself. Entrance costs F9.00 for individuals, but only F8.00 if you are in a party. This entitles you to a tour of the *cave*, which is certainly *illuminée*, but not, I thought, particularly *curieuse*; you also get a glass of wine from one of the local growers, plus a commentary on the photographs and various exhibits which include a collection of old cooperage tools, vats and wine-presses. A useful leaflet gives you names and addresses of all the growers in the *appellation* by commune, general information about Bourgueil and its wines and gastronomy, a map and advertisements from local restaurateurs and *vente directe* growers. Thus informed, fortified and equipped, the tourist may sally forth into the Bourgueillois countryside.

VDQS: CHEVERNY

Cheverny produces VDQS wines of middling quality from a large area on the south bank of the Loire, which stretches from Condé in the west to a point some 15 kilometres upstream from Blois, with Cheverny itself at the southern edge. Whites are made from the

Romorantin, a grape introduced from the Burgundy region by François I in the sixteenth-century; Chenin Blanc, Chardonnay and the Pineau Menu are also used, but the dominant variety is the Sauvignon. Reds and rosés come mainly from the Gamay, but Cabernet Franc and Cabernet Sauvignon, Malbec and Pinot Noir are also grown in some measure. A little sparkling wine is also made.

VDQS: VALENÇAY

In the south-eastern corner of Touraine, the small vineyards of Valençay are spread over 15 communes. Nice refreshing reds and rosés are made from mainly Gamay, though the Cabernets and Malbec may also be used; they are at their best when drunk young. The white wine must be made from at least 60% of Pineau Menu, Chardonnay or Sauvignon, and up to 40% of Romorantin or Chenin Blanc may also be incorporated. I have tasted an excellent example from Hubert Sinson; the wine was fresh and crisp, with a nose of white peaches and a slightly quincy flavour; I drank it rather dubiously on the recommendation of a *sommelier* in a restaurant in Tours, who told me that it would go well with a hot *foie gras* dish; to my surprise he was absolutely right.

APPELLATION: JASNIÈRES & COTEAUX DU LOIR

A relatively small area of vineyard within the Coteaux du Loir district is entitled to the Jasnières *appellation*. Jasnières is always white, and made exclusively from the Chenin Blanc. It is mostly very dry, of excellent quality, and is best left in bottle for four or five years; a little *demi-sec* is also made. The best-known grower is Joël Gigou, who has vines on the favoured chalky slopes around the little hamlet of Jasnières, not far from Lhomme. The high quality of this little known wine is partly due to the very low permitted yield – only 25 hectolitres per hectare, the same as for Sauternes.

The Coteaux du Loir white is to all intents and purposes the same as Jasnières, having the same permitted yield and the same grape variety, but it may come from a slightly wider area on both banks of the River Loir, not to be confused with the much bigger Loire some 25 kilometres to the south.

André Fresneau makes all types of Coteaux du Loir, and the general quality of his wines is of a high standard. In his rock cellar he gave me a tasting, and I was particularly impressed with the reds; the preferred variety for red wine is the Pineau d'Aunis, though Cabernet, Gamay and Malbec are also permitted. I had the distinct impression that this was an area in which the reds are more attractive in the hot years; the 1982 was certainly better than the '83 or the '85. There is also some quite pleasant rosé made in the Coteaux du Loir, which is made from the same varieties as the red, though a maximum of 25% of Groslot may be added to the blend; Fresneau's rosé had a pleasing lightness, and a nice level of acidity, and was deliciously dry.

TOURAINE:
GUIDE TO HOTELS & RESTAURANTS

From poets to package holiday operators, people have been extolling the virtues and beauties of Touraine for hundreds of years. It is not the function of this book to add to their panegyrics, but it would be selfish not to pass on some of the places from which I derived such pleasure.

Touraine has everything to offer the tourist at every level – the châteaux, the wines, the endless beauty of its rivers and countryside as well as more energetic forms of leisure; you may sail, windsurf, canoe or fish the rivers, play golf, shoot, ride in the forests, join bicycle tours, go up in a balloon or even walk. To rest you and sustain you there are châteaux, hotels, *gîtes, chambres d'hôte* (bed and breakfast), camping and caravan sites galore, as well as restaurants, cafés, pizzerias, crêperies and hamburger joints – yes, there are hamburgers in Tours – to suit every palate and pocket. You do not have to be a foodie to come to Touraine; not even the most philistine fish-finger reared, beer-swilling *rosbif* could fail to be seduced by the lovely country cooking and the endless variety and simple charm of the wines.

Entering Touraine, as I did on my vinous odyssey, from the Paris direction, you can turn off the A10 autoroute at the Amboise exit and visit the château there; from here it is a pleasant cross-country drive to Chenonceaux, loveliest perhaps of all the châteaux, with its long gallery spanning the River Cher like a bracelet on a lovely woman's arm. Time your visit so that lunch or dinner at Le Bon Laboureur et Château reward you at the end of your tour. Louis-Claude Jeudi's cuisine leans toward the traditional rather than the nouvelle, so a healthy appetite helps. (tel: 47.23.90.02).

The south-eastern sector of Touraine has many châteaux like Montpoupon, Montrésor and Loches, but, as my business was with the wine-makers of the Loire, my observations must be confined to those areas, and I will leave you to discover the delights of non-vinous Touraine for yourself.

Les Hautes Roches is a unique restaurant/hotel on the banks of the Loire in Rochecorbon, opened in early 1989. The restaurant specialises in fish and the white wines of the area, particularly Vouvray, and is owned by Philippe Mollard, also owner of the superb Château de Marçay near Chinon. The setting is quite stunning, with marvellous views over the Loire, and the guest rooms are mostly 'troglodyte' caves, high up in the rock. The telephone number is 47.52.88.88.

I spent some time in Vouvray, where I ate in the Grand Vatel in Vouvray (tel: 47.52.70.32), a very traditional French hotel, where the food was good, the wine-list well stocked with Vouvrays from the best growers, but the service indifferent. Undoubtedly the best value for eating-out that I found in Vouvray was La Cave Martin (tel: 47.52.62.18), a restaurant in a chalk cave in the hamlet of La Vallée Coquette, entirely surrounded by vineyards. Fresh local produce and regional cooking are the keynotes, and the prices are extremely fair. I spent a couple of nights at the Hôtel les Fontaines (tel. 47.52.50.02) in Rochecorbon, where the rooms are comfortable if a bit old-fashioned; there is no restaurant, but the chief attraction of Les Fontaines is the kindness, charm and welcome of the owner and his wife.

Across the river from Vouvray lies the wine town of Montlouis, where I ate a better than adequate lunch at the Auberge Tourangelle (tel: 47.50.81.15), on the river road. I heard much about a Vietnamese restaurant, very small and very, very good in Montlouis, but alas it was so small that I never managed to find it – next time, perhaps.

Without a doubt the best restaurant and hotel in Tours itself is the Hotel Le Parc de Belmont, which houses the Restaurant Jean Bardet, owned and run by the great chef Jean Bardet and his capable wife Sophie. Formerly a private residence, the hotel has been beautifully extended and adapted to provide 15 luxurious bedrooms and suites. It is situated in the smart, northern residential part of Tours known as St Symphorien, and stands in three hectares of lovely garden and park, with its own swimming pool. The rooms are comfortable, spacious and tastefully decorated, all with splendid bathrooms. The room-service is discreet, friendly and professional, and the breakfasts, served in your room, are the work of art that you would expect from Bardet.

Jean Bardet transferred his two Michelin rosettes here from his famous restaurant in Chateauroux at the end of 1987, and the citizens of Chateauroux' loss is definitely the Tourangeaux' gain. He is not only a great chef, but a man of charm and considerable presence. His passionate belief in the skill and individuality of the wine-makers of the Loire, and the importance of maintaining such ability and character, can only work to the good of the growers.

On the occasion of my visit, M. Bardet prepared the following menu, and I have shown the accompanying wines alongside:

Amuse-Bouches	Vouvray Pétillant
Millefeuille de Foie Gras	Vouvray Demi-Sec 1976 Audebert
Le Saumon Sauvage Légèrement Fumé	Chinon Blanc 1985 Olga Raffault
Le Pintadeau Fermier aux Shitakés	St Nicolas de Bourgueil 1986 Joël Taluau
Fromage Fermiers	Chinon 1981 Olga Raffault
Le Millefeuille au Chocolat	Late-bottled Vintage Port 1978

– Café –

A really memorable meal, the only slight criticism being the choice of a glass of port to go with the miraculous chocolate millefeuille – but complementing chocolate is a virtual impossibility.

Reservations, Chez Bardet, are essential (tel: 47.41.41.11).

Bardet apart, Tours itself did not draw me into its urban bosom very often, as firstly I do not like big towns and secondly there is not much wine made within the city limits. There are numerous restaurants of all types and qualities, and tremendous efforts have been made in recent years to create an atmospheric pedestrian *quartier* in the old town. The effect is seen to best advantage in the Place Plumereau and its surrounding streets; the square is surrounded by quaintly leaning sixteenth-century timbered houses, and the ground floor of almost every one is a restaurant, pizzeria, bar, café or ice-cream parlour – there is even an English pub with unrecognisable sparkling bitter. There is something faintly Venetian about the place, and it is easy and stressless to sit outside one of the many bars on a summer night, just watching the tourists and the Tourangeaux at play. In the centre of the square is an open space, where impromptu cabarets take place. The amateur rock musicians often make up in decibels for what they lack in talent, which proves a source of annoyance to the elderly residents who have apartments on the upper floors; this can add spice to the evening, as the gendarmerie are frequently called out to remove the noisemakers, and merry chases ensue.

A superb new golf course has recently opened, Le Golf d'Ardrée, at St Antoine du Rocher, 12 kilometres north of Tours. It has been laid out in the beautiful parkland of the Château d'Ardrée, which is shortly to be opened as a château-hotel by Philippe Mollard of the Château de Marçay and Les Hautes Roches. The clubhouse is modern, and extremely well designed, with every convenience for the golfer and his guests. Good bar and restaurant facilities are offered, and green-fees, though quite expensive to English eyes, are competitive by French standards(tel: 47.56.77.38).

Some thirteen miles south of Tours on the RN10 lies Montbazon which offers three jewels to the sybarite. The legendary Château d'Artigny (tel: 47.26.24.24), a Walt Disney seventeenth-century castle which is dealt with in my chapter on the Relais et Châteaux. In Montbazon itself is La Chancelière (tel. 47.26.06.57), a temple of gastronomy in which I was lucky enough to worship in the company of a charming American couple, husband and wife, both attorneys from San Francisco. They were generous enough to buy me the dinner of a lifetime, and I only hope they will give me a chance to play a return match when they come to England.

A short distance back along the road to Tours and off to your left lies the Domaine de la Tortinière (tel: 47.26.00.19), one of the most comfortable and attractive places in which I have stayed. The rooms, both public and private, have been decorated with flair and taste by the owner, Madame Denise Olivereau-Capron, and the new chef has assured the continued excellence of the cuisine.

Within easy striking distance of Montbazon is the lovely village of Saché, on the back roads between Montbazon and Azay-le-Rideau. Home of the writer Honoré de Balzac, Saché has played host to the arts in more recent years; the American sculptors Alexander Calder and Jo Davidson made Saché their home, and one of Calder's works, a gigantic mobile, stands in the car park as a permanent reminder that its creator lived here and loved the place. I trust my blimpish comment may be forgiven, but I find the car park a peculiarly apt site for what, to my philistine eye, resembles a giant roadworks 'stop-go' sign.

Art in one of its more tangible and accessible forms may be appreciated at the Auberge du XIIème Siècle (tel: 47.26.86.58) where Jean-Louis and Marilynne Niqueux, who used to work at the Château d'Artigny, offer food and service equal to anything I have eaten in France in the seductive atmosphere of this ancient hostelry. There is a lovely walled garden at the back, where the house apéritif, champagne and peach brandy may be enjoyed in total tranquillity. Perhaps fortunately, there are no bedrooms at the Auberge, for this is truly one of my favourite restaurants in France, and a long weekend there could easily prove to be my last.

Tragically, at the time of going to press, Jean-Louis Niqueux had just been killed in a car accident, and the fate of this wonderful restaurant hangs in the balance. There is a Niqueux brother, Jacques, who also cooks like a dream. His restaurant, the Poêle d'Or, is largely and unjustly ignored by the guides; it is to be found in St Cyr-sur-Loire, a couple of miles outside Tours on the N152 Saumur road, but keep your eyes peeled or you will miss it. Inside, you will be warmly welcomed by the very attractive Madame Niqueux, your palate will be seduced by her husband's superb cooking and your eyes will be rested by the sight of the Loire running beneath the windows of the restaurant.

If your visit to Touraine includes a little vinous appreciation, your natural route after the Poêle d'Or will take you straight on along the river road towards the red wine *appellations* of Bourgueil and St Nicolas de Bourgueil. Having turned off the N152 just after Langeais, following the signs to Bourgueil, you will come to St Patrice, the smallest of the wine-producing communes of Bourgueil. Here you will find the relatively newly opened Château de Rochecotte (tel: 47.96.90.62 or 47.96.91.28), a hotel of surpassing loveliness, comfort and charm, with cuisine and cellar to match. The rooms, all of which have well-appointed bathrooms *en suite*, are light and spacious, the beds large and comfortable; to wake up in Suite 2 on a spring or summer morning, and to see from your bed the lovely countryside of the Loire Valley spread before you, bathed in the very special light that seems to illuminate the Garden of France, is a source of never-ending surprise and pleasure. Perfectly situated as a centre for a touring holiday of Touraine, Saumur and Anjou, Rochecotte is a delight. The restaurant is not cheap, neither is it expensive, considering the standard of cooking and service; the rooms are extremely reasonably priced for a *château-hôtel* of this quality. It is, perhaps, the warmth of the welcome you receive at Rochecotte that puts it into a class of its own. Monsieur and Madame Pasquier, who own and run the hotel, have

that very special knack of making you feel at home without ever intruding on your privacy; in this they are charmingly assisted by their pretty daughters Cristalle, Isabelle and Emmanuelle, though which was which I was never able to establish, even after two months' stay! I have already thanked this family for giving me a 'second home' in Touraine during my researches, and I do so again. If you don't believe in such a fairy-tale place, go there and find out for yourself.

If you are looking for bed and breakfast with a difference, you could try the Château de Cinq-Mars-la-Pile (tel: 47.96.40.49), Madame Untersteller, the owner, is a diminutive old lady of great charm and infinite kindness, and an artist in ceramics of some renown. The château itself, now in ruins, is one of the historic monuments of France. The Marquis de Cinq Mars, a young man of singular good looks, was born here in 1620; after a meteoric rise to favouritism in the Court of Louis XIII, he appears to have upset the powerful Cardinal Richelieu, who had him executed at the tender age of 22, and had the castle reduced to its present ruinous state. Madame Untersteller lives in the long, low *maison bourgeoise* alongside the castle, and has three comfortable rooms available. You will take your breakfast with her, and she is a fund of interesting local information and gossip.

In Bourgueil I found but one restaurant, Germain (tel: 47.97.72.22), where the food is good and the service friendly rather than professional. The wine list has a good but limited selection of the best wines of Bourgueil, with a nod of acknowledgment to the existence of Chinon.

Before crossing the Loire to Chinon, I would mention the Château des Réaux (tel: 47.95.14.40). This moated fifteenth-century castle, near Le Port Boulet on the N152, offers *chambre d'hôte* accommodation of the very highest standard. Florence Goupil de Bouillé and her husband, Jean-Luc, are very professional hosts; if you give notice, you can dine with them in the château, and they keep a good table.

Across the river and just past the oldest and largest nuclear power station in France, you enter the wine-producing area of Chinon. I have stayed on past visits at the Château de Danzay in Beaumont-en-Véron. The rooms have been beautifully converted and the comfort of your stay is assured by the friendly Monsieur and Madame Safarti; they have worked extremely hard to make this a success, and my only criticism is that they have pitched their prices too high for this type of accommodation.

In Chinon itself there is a wealth of accommodation and eating places of all sorts at all price levels. Le Plaisir Gourmand (tel: 47.93.20.48) at the foot of the castle has an excellent reputation, though I have not eaten there myself. A few miles south of Chinon, but still in the *appellation*, is the delectable Château de Marçay (tel: 47.93.03.47), which is dealt with in the chapter on the Relais & Châteaux.

Returning to Tours via Azay-le-Rideau, with its enchanting castle circled by the River Indre, you can eat very well at the little restaurant called L'Automate in La Chapelle St Blaise; the name is a little off-putting, conjuring up images of money-in-the-slot restaurants in New York, but it actually refers to the fascinating collection of toys which decorate the dining-room.

Off to the left of the D751, as you leave Azay in the direction of Tours, lies the splendid nineteenth-century Château du Gerfaut (tel: 47.45.40.16). The Marquis and Marquise de Chenerilles have six very comfortable rooms in which you can stay on bed and breakfast terms. They occupy only half the château, the other part being lived in by their daughter and containing self-catering accommodation for seven people. The de Chenerilles are old-school French aristocrats, and farm about 400 hectares as well as owning some 800 hectares of forest. The estate originally formed part of the lands of the Marquis de Billancourt of Azay-le-Rideau. One of the family's forebears married an Englishman named Blunt, who founded the Société Générale and also started the first railway company in France, the Compagnie du Chemin de Fer du Nord; being an Englishman, he had his trains running on the left, as they do throughout France to this day.

I thoroughly enjoyed my stay with the de Chenerilles, but it went somewhat against my class-conscious English grain to have my very heavy suitcase carried up three flights of stairs by a marquis, and a septuagenarian to boot; the bill, however, overcame my principles.

Hotel Château de Rochecotte

ANJOU & SAUMUR

CONTENTS

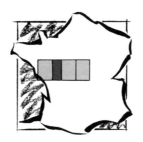

Anjou & Saumur

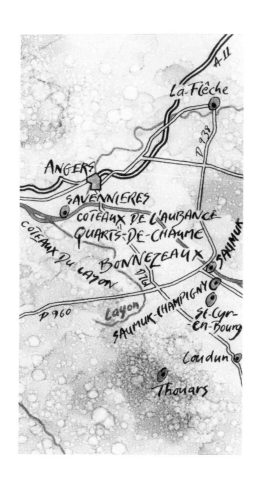

Appellation: Anjou

The vast vineyard of Anjou encompasses Saumur and other *appellations* such as the Coteaux du Layon, Quarts de Chaume, Bonnezeaux and Savennières. There are some 20,000 hectares of vines, of which about 75% are *appellation contrôlée*; of the balance, much of the wine is now being sold as Vin de Pays du Jardin de la France, a label created in 1981 to improve the quality of the non-AC wines of the Loire Valley.

Representing about 4.5% of all the AC vineyards in France, Anjou and Saumur produce around 9,000,000 cases of wine in an average year. Of this huge volume, nearly half is represented by the various forms of Anjou Rosé, and a further 20% consists of plain Anjou red and Anjou white; sparkling wines in the form of Saumur Mousseux and Crémant de Loire account for 15% and the 'quality' *appellations* make up the balance.

Anjou and Saumur are very much the mirror of wine-drinking trends. Up to the 1950s, production was largely of still white wines, which were either sweet or medium sweet; in the '60s and '70s the taste was for pink wine, and within that short time the vineyards were almost entirely replanted and the words rosé and Anjou became synonymous. As the wine-buying public becomes more sophisticated, taste goes from sweet to dry, and production now swings towards red wines and quality dry *méthode-champenoise* sparklers.

Conversion from white or rosé wine-making to red is not an easy transition, but very serious efforts are being made; the reds of Saumur, particularly those of Saumur-Champigny, merit serious attention and great strides are being made with the vinification and eventual quality of the reds of Anjou – Anjou Rouge, made from the Cabernet, Anjou Gamay and the new *appellation*, Anjou Villages.

As we shall look at the wines of Saumur and other *appellations* in their own right, let us take a general view of the Anjou wines. The *vignoble* of Anjou stretches from Ingrandes-sur-Loire in the west to Montsoreau, halfway between Saumur and Chinon, in the east, where the Vienne flows into the Loire; the longest north-south axis runs some 75 kilometres from where the river Sarthe flows into the Maine-et-Loire *département* down to a point south of Montreuil-Bellay. All the up-market *appellations*, with the exception of Savennières, are to the south of the Loire; although much AC Anjou wine is made within these *appellations*, the bulk of the Anjou rosés comes from the north bank.

Since Anjou AC, whether pink, red or white, accounts for two-thirds of the region's total production, let us consider the different types of wine within these broad categories. By far the greatest volume of Anjou's entire output of wine is, despite changing fashion, pink, representing about half of all the wine made including all the *appellations* within Anjou and Saumur, both still and sparkling. Around four and a half million dozen bottles are made annually, divided into three types:

1 Rosé d'Anjou, the commonest form, is usually medium-dry and made principally from the Groslot; Cot and Pineau d'Aunis may be used without restriction.

2 Cabernet d'Anjou is medium dry to, in good years, *moelleux*. As the name implies, it is made from only Cabernet, usually the Franc rather than the Sauvignon, and it can age remarkably well.

3 The most recent runner in the Anjou pink colours is sold as Rosé de Loire, which is always dry, and must be at least 30% Cabernet, with Gamay, Cot, Groslot and Pineau d'Aunis. *The appellation* for Rosé de Loire was created in 1974, when it was realised that the demand was tending towards drier wines. It does not appear to have worked, though it is my favourite of the three types; perhaps drinkers whose taste is beginning to go for drier wines gravitate more readily to dry white than dry pink.

White AC Anjou is now being more and more vinified as a dry wine, whereas a mere twenty years ago only *demi-sec* or *moelleux* was produced. I had the pleasure of tasting one or two nice young wines, though they are not particularly easy to make. The Chenin Blanc, or Pineau de la Loire, which must comprise at least 80% of the make-up of Anjou Blanc, is not quick to give of its charms; it tends towards unpleasant astringency in extreme youth, which is when most people seem to want to drink white wine, and when most growers are obliged to sell it. The permitted additional varieties are the Sauvignon or the Burgundian Chardonnay, which a still wine maker can use to good effect, dulling the adolescent awkwardness of the Chenin.

Anjou Rouge, which is currently being produced from about 2,500 hectares, is made principally from Cabernet Franc; the Cabernet Sauvignon and the Pineau d'Aunis are also permitted, but not widely used. The other red AC wine produced under the Anjou label is Anjou Gamay, which is made from that grape, and may be produced anywhere in the Anjou *appellation* except in Saumur.

Before passing on to Saumur and the smaller *appellations* of Anjou, it is interesting to look at market trends and selling patterns pertaining to this huge area. In ten short years the production of red wines has trebled, and now represents nearly the same proportion of the total as sparkling wine; in 1976 it was less than 7% of the whole.

There are some 1,000 *viticulteurs* in the region, whose livelihood comes entirely from the vine, and a further 3,000 *polyculteurs*, farmers who may have just a few rows of vines as part of their general agronomic structure. As more and more young 'oenocrats' are attracted to wine making, there is a tendency for the size of the vineyard to increase, and there are now many viable units of 12 hectares and more. With such a pattern of production, it is hardly surprising that Anjou is a centre of the *négociant* or merchant business. Many of the small growers lack the knowledge or commercial initiative to handle their own sales, and are happy to rely on one of the 50 or so *négociant* houses to give them a fair deal; of these 50 firms, there are perhaps only 10 of any size, and between them they handle 80% of all the business.

Sales of Anjou and Saumur wines are divided about 70% to the home market and 30% export. The export market is growing in a very healthy way, and has risen from 10% of production in 1968 to 34% in 1984. The United Kingdom is the biggest importer of Anjou/Saumur with 34% of the market, of which the greater part is rosé, with the reds fast gaining ground. It is my opinion that red wines like Saumur Champigny, Saumur Rouge and well-made Anjou Rouge and Anjou Villages will find an increasing demand on the Bordeaux-orientated Anglo-Saxon export market, as prices for Cabernet-based wines from the Gironde continue to spiral.

APPELLATION: SAUMUR-CHAMPIGNY

The best red wines in Anjou are made in the nine communes covered by the *appellation* Saumur-Champigny. These communes run along the river from Montsoreau, through Turquant, Parnay, Souzay-Champigny and Dampière as far as Saumur on the eastern side of the River Thouet, Varrains, Chacé and St Cyr-en-Bourg.

Some 600 hectares are currently planted within the *appellation*, almost exclusively with Cabernet Franc, although Cabernet Sauvignon and Pineau d'Aunis are also permitted. The soil is varied, and usually has a subsoil of chalky tuff which gives, as elsewhere in Touraine and Anjou, not only character to the wine but also perfect conditions for vinification and evolution in the many miles of quarried cellars that honeycomb the area. As the soil varies, so do the owners and their approach to and philosophy concerning the making of wine; it will come as no surprise, then, that we find within the *appellation* more than one type of wine. Saumur-Champigny can be vinified to give the drinker great pleasure when it is still young, or it can be treated like a great Bordeaux, developing slowly in cask for a couple of years, and then in bottle for many more until it achieves a dignified and aristocratic old age. This same variability is one of the attractive features of red Loire wines, and gastronomically they are very adaptable; young, served cold, they can be delicious with fish dishes, whilst mature wines will marry beautifully with the finest roast meats and game, and a Saumur-Champigny, Saumur Rouge, Anjou Rouge, Bourgueil or Chinon can be found to complement any of France's 360-odd cheeses.

As with the wine of Bourgueil and Chinon, I believe strongly that well-made Saumur-Champigny has great marketing potential as an alternative to the more fashionable and expensive Cabernet Franc-based wines of St Emilion and Pomerol.

The confrérie of the Commanderie de Taste Vin de Saumur

PARNAY

PISANI-FERRY, Château de Targé, Parnay. Taking the communes of the *appellation* as I came to them from Chinon, my first visit was to the impressive four-turreted Château de Targé, set high on the cliff-face in the village of Parnay. Edouard Pisani-Ferry's family have lived at the château in an unbroken line since 1655. Through this distinguished family, who number among their members such noted politicians as Allain Targé, Guyet de Targé, Charles Ferry and Edgard Pisani, runs a common thread of love for the property and its vineyard.

Each generation of the family seeks to improve some facet of the property, and Edouard has certainly made his mark. After a hazardous, hooting drive up the multi-hairpin lane to the château, and having successfully negotiated my way past a softly growling German shepherd-dog, I was met by a member of the staff and was led to see the young master. We made our way through an upward-leading zig-zag of tunnels in the tuff, finally emerging in the vineyards above. Here Edouard has constructed a brand new, hi-tech, insulated vat-house. There are 12 stainless-steel *cuves* with automatic built-in temperature control, as well as two oak vats of 61.10 hectolitres purchased from Cognac. The whole installation has been operational since 1979.

Edouard is fiercely and rightly proud of his wines. He is a qualified agricultural engineer and a graduate of the Ecole de Montpellier. He oversees vinification in person, and every *cuve* bears a chart plotting each stage of fermentation, maceration, treatment and heat changes. During the critical weeks after the vintage, Edouard and his enthusiastic work-force frequently spend several sleepless nights in constant attendance at the fermenting vats.

Château de Targé wines spend a variable amount of time in wooden *foudres* which line the seemingly endless passages of the chalk cellars. This period varies according to the needs of each vintage.

We tasted 1985, 1984, 1982, 1981 and 1975. The '85, as one would expect, had a deep ruby colour, and a powerful *cassis* bouquet. Quite high in alcohol, it had excellent fruit and the right tannin to turn it into a great bottle in a year to eighteen months.

The 1984 was a *tour de force*. A difficult year for red wines in Saumur, and in many other places, '84 is a vintage by which a wine-maker's skill can be assessed. It is a sign of confidence if you are offered this vintage to taste at all, and this one was really well made. The

The church at Parnay

colour was a palish scarlet, and the nose, though muted, was clean and pleasant. A light wine with nice fruit – no great length, but really good to drink now.

The 1982 was in perfect condition for current drinking; it had a nice bright colour and an open raspberry bouquet. In the mouth the wine was rounded with nice fruit and a good long aftertaste.

After the 1982 it was difficult to judge the '81 fairly, for it is an altogether smaller, lighter wine and is beginning to thin out; it was, nonetheless, a good example of a well-made wine in a small year.

The last wine Edouard offered me was 'blind'. The nose suggested some age, though the colour was still good and deep with no trace of brown. There was good fruit and some nice tannin still in the mouth, but not a great deal of length. I guessed it, wrongly, to be 1976. It was '75, and very good too.

The Pisani-Ferry wines were among the best Saumur-Champignys I tasted. He exports quite a bit – some to the USA, Japan, Belgium and England.

CHAMPIGNY

RATRON FRÈRES, Clos des Cordelliers, Champigny. Bernard and Michel Ratron represent the third generation of their family to make wine at the Clos des Cordelliers. Their grandfather bought the property in 1932, and they now have 15 hectares of vines, which are exclusively Cabernet Franc. Most of the vineyard is on small knolls and enjoys good exposure to the south and south-west; the soil is chalky clay, and the Ratrons pride themselves on the distinctive *goût de terroir* that this gives to their wines.

The Clos des Cordelliers is one of only a handful of wine properties situated in the commune of Champigny itself, as opposed to the much larger one of Souzay-Champigny; the other vineyard in Champigny of any size is the neighbouring walled Clos Cristal, named after Père Cristal, a previous owner, who donated the property to the Hospices de Saumur and contributed much to the *appellation* of Saumur-Champigny.

Parts of the *vignoble* here are very exposed and subject to the dangerous spring frosts, and the Ratron brothers have found that the best protection is to prune the vines much higher off the ground than is generally practised in the area. Vineyard and wine-making buildings are all in an immaculate state, and, as may be expected from such outward signs, the wines are well-made. Only Saumur-Champigny is made here, whereas most local growers devote at least a portion of their crop to the easier option of making plain AC Saumur Rouge or Blanc and a little *vin de base* for sparkling wine. All Clos des Cordelliers wines are aged in *foudres* of chestnut or oak in the chalk cellars beneath the property; the time that a particular vintage will spend in wood will vary according to the needs of that year. The Ratrons attach great importance to the date of bottling; they reckon that June is generally the best month for this work, but some bottling is also done in September and a little after the vintage.

A good proportion of the Ratrons' sales are to a large and faithful private clientèle, and there is a cheerful tasting-room with a mural of the property on the wall behind the bar. On the day of my visit there was a constant stream of visitors, all of whom were given a tasting of the excellent 1985, most stayed for a chat about past vintages they had bought and about the prospects for the '86, and the atmosphere was more that of a friendly local *estaminet* than a wine-

shop. It was easy to see how the brothers have built up and kept such a good relationship with their customers. About 40% of their production is sold to the private customers, 25% to restaurants and the rest to *caves spécialistes* and *clubs de dégustation*.

The 1985 had a beautiful deep colour, and an open nose with some blackcurrant. It was aromatic and had the slight earthy taste that is typical of the property. A very well-made wine that will benefit from keeping a little longer.

Before leaving I was given a rare treat: a bottle of a very special *cuvée* of their 1976. This had spent a full two years in wood; the colour, like so many really good red Loire wines from this vintage, was still astonishingly deep with no trace of browning. The nose, though closed at first, came out strong and well with aeration. In the mouth this was an amazing wine, with backbone, fruit and tannin equal to a fine Bordeaux, and all the necessary constituents to keep it going for another 10 years – a real star!

VARRAINS

CLAUDE DAHEUILLER, Domaine des Varinelles, Varrains. Aside from having one of the most unpronounceable names for the Anglo-Saxon tongue I have ever encountered, Claude Daheuiller also makes some very good wines. He and his pretty blonde wife, Marie-Françoise, live in an attractive *maison bourgeoise* on the main street of Varrains, the largest of the nine communes in the *appellation* of Saumur-Champigny.

They have a substantial 23 hectares of vines, 18 of which are devoted to the production of AC Saumur-Champigny; the balance of Daheuiller's production is made up of Saumur Blanc, Rosé de Loire and Saumur Crémant, though the champagnisation is not carried out here.

Claude makes two separate blends of Saumur-Champigny, one the standard wine and the other exclusively from the produce of older vines, sold as Vieilles Vignes in numbered bottles.

Vinification is a complete mixture of ancient and modern; above ground there is an enormous, newly-constructed *cuverie*, with eight stainless-steel vats, two of which are equipped with the hydraulic *système de pigeage*. The *cuvaison* usually lasts from two to three weeks, and the temperature is kept below 30° during the alcoholic fermentation; when the alcoholic fermentation is finished, the wine is racked into clean vats and left there until the malo-lactic fermentation is completed early in the new year.

Below ground there are deep cellars in the tuff, which house bottled stock, wine in wooden *foudres*, and a range of old-fashioned fermentation vats in glass-lined cement. About half the Daheuiller wines spend some months in wood, the quantity and the length of time varying according to the needs of each vintage. The Daheuillers are perfectly prepared to make use of the new technology, but only when they are quite convinced that it will be for the long-term benefit of their wines. As an example of this philosophy, 1986 will be the first year that Claude has allowed a picking machine in his vineyards; although he certainly has the acreage to justify the use of one, he insisted that this was only an experiment.

I tasted the '85 Saumur Blanc, which was a nice clean, dry and straightforward young Chenin Blanc; good to drink now with fish or as an aperitif.

We then looked at the '85 Saumur Champigny, both the standard blend and the Vieilles Vignes. The former had a nice scarlet colour and a pleasant summer-fruit nose. Good fruit and length, not a heavyweight, but will benefit from a year or so in bottle. The Vieilles Vignes was a totally different cup of tea, with a far deeper, bluey-red colour, and a fatter and more assertive bouquet. More wood was evident in the mouth; this was an altogether more 'structured' wine that needs at least two years in bottle, and will probably be even better after five.

As I was preparing to leave, Claude's son came in from the vineyard. Apparently, the night before, he and his wife had presented Claude with his first grandson, so it was decided to wet the baby's head, probably not for the first time since the birth! This momentous occasion was marked with a bottle of the 1976 Vieilles Vignes, which was excellent, though I found that it had more 'hot weather' characteristics than other wines of this vintage I have tasted.

DAMPIERRE

BERNARD DE TIGNY, Château de Chaintres, Dampierre. Chaintres is a lovely, sleepy old village full of stone houses and walled gardens, where time appears to stand still. The Château de Chaintres is the most attractive of these houses, and I had determined to visit it, if it had even the remotest vinous connection, from the moment I

first spied the sun-warmed stone façade through the frame of the gateway.

Bernard de Tigny has traced the history of this jewel of a property back to the end of the sixteenth century, when it belonged to one Robert Guyelet, squire, Lord of Chantonays, and his sister the Demoiselle Marie Guyelet. They sold their estate in 1601 to a King's counsellor called Jean Sapinault, and it changed hands several times over the next three-quarters of a century. In 1675 Sieur Alexandre Milon, Seigneur of Chaintres, sold it to the religious order of Les Pères de l'Oratoire de Saumur, to whom it belonged until the French Revolution in 1792. When the property of the Oratoriens was put up for sale by the new administration, the Château de Chaintres and the Grand Clos – the walled vineyard as it still is today – became the property of Jacques Huard-Duvigneau, whose son inherited and kept it until the mid-nineteenth century. On his death, the estate passed into the hands of the de Fontenailles family and changed owners several more times before Bernard de Tigny's father bought it in the late 1930s.

Following his father's death in a concentration camp in 1945, the property was run by Madame de Tigny, Bernard's mother, during the post-war years. Until Bernard took over in 1960, the wine made at Château de Chaintres was all rosé. This was not an unusual situation, for the *appellation* Saumur-Champigny had only been in existence for a couple of years, and Anjou Rosé was the order of the day for this area. Bernard set about re-planting the vineyard, which extends to some 15 hectares, all enclosed within the original wall. Today production is mainly of Saumur-Champigny from 100% Cabernet Franc vines, with a little Saumur Blanc made from Chenin Blanc.

Picking is still done by hand, and fermentation takes place in cement vats, in which the red wine stays until the malo-lactic fermentation is completed. The wine is then transferred into wooden *foudres* or casks, where it spends varying lengths of time according to the individual needs of each vintage.

All Château de Chaintres is sold in bottle; about 30% goes to private customers and 70% to the restaurant trade. We tasted the 1985 both in magnum, which is a speciality of de Tigny, and in bottle; the bottle size had been bottled longer than the magnum, yet the wine from the larger-size bottle was tasting much better. It had a very deep colour, an open nose with good fruit, and was quite hard and tannic but with plenty of fruit to give it a long life.

DOMAINE FILLIATREAU, Chaintres, Dampierre. Filliatreau is the name most likely to be known to English wine-drinkers in connection with Saumur-Champigny. Paul Filliatreau has 27 hectares of vines, 25 of which are dedicated to the growing of Cabernet Franc for Saumur-Champigny and 2 hectares of Chenin Blanc go into the production of Saumur Blanc. According to *Les Vins du Val de Loire* by Suzanne Blanchet, Filliatreau is by quite a long way the biggest volume-producer of red wine in the *appellation* with an annual average of 1,000 hectolitres.

His vat-house is certainly one of the most modern, and considerable investment has gone into the ranks of thermostatically-controlled stainless-steel fermentation vats. The heating and/or cooling medium is an in-built system of serpentine tubes that run round the surface of the vats, and through which water of the desired temperature is run to warm or cool the must within. The temperature sought for the alcoholic fermentation is relatively low at 24°, and 20° for the malo-lactic. The interiors of the vats have been fitted out with a *système de pigeage* to give automatic breaking of the cap of skins during fermentation.

Filliatreau makes three red wines under the Saumur-Champigny *appellation*: the first is Saumur Champigny, Domaine Filliatreau, Jeunes Vignes which, he boldly says in his publicity leaflet, comes essentially from young vines between the age of 10 and 50 years. Next is Vieilles Vignes, from older vines between 50 and 100 years old; and the third, Saumur Champigny, Lena Filliatreau, comes from 10 to 60-year-old vines grown on clay-silex as opposed to the clay-limestone of the other two.

As far as I could determine, the Jeunes Vignes wine sees no wood at all, and is best drunk young and fruity; the Vieilles Vignes spends some time in *fûts*, and can be kept in a good cellar for up to 20 years. The Lena Filliatreau, due to its more gravelly soil, is more fleshy and tannic in style; it spends eight months in wood, and has a good life of ten years or more in bottle.

Domaine Filliatreau combines all that is best in modern wine-making and marketing with the love and respect that are the *sine qua non* of this, one of man's oldest and most valuable arts. Paul Filliatreau sells the majority of his wines to the restaurant business, and around 35% to regular customers. The Belgians, who know a good thing when they taste it, and the English, are his premier export customers. In the United Kingdom his wines are sold by Robin Yapp of Mere in Wiltshire, a good recommendation in itself.

CHACÉ

FRÈRES FOUCAULT, 15 Rue de l'Eglise, Chacé. In the life of every man there are certain 'red letter' days that remain always fresh and special; I know that my visit to the Foucault brothers will always be such a day for me. There was a dream-like quality about the men themselves, their cellars and their wines that makes the entire episode totally vivid to me six months later; I can see colours, smell smells and taste flavours as if it all happened this morning. The whole visit had about it such a curious magic that I would not be a bit surprised to go back to Chacé and find that the old premises in the Rue de l'Eglise had been empty and abandonded for half a century.

The Foucaults have been making wine here for many generations, and making it very well. Jean-Louis and Bernard's great-grandfather showed tremendous initiative as long ago as 1900; when phylloxera virtually wiped out the Fench vineyards, he took himself off to Bordeaux to study how the *vignerons* there were setting about the replanting and grafting. He was also one of the first in the area to

The brothers Foucault tasting in their cellar at Chacé

bottle his own wines, which he sold in wicker baskets fastened with chestnut leaves.

The respect held by their ancestor for the doings of the Bordelais is present in the two brothers today. They are engaged in a fascinating experiment with the 1985 vintage which I, for one, will follow with the greatest interest and admiration. All their red wine is being aged for eighteen months to two years in casks of one vintage from Château Margaux. I have come across one or two growers in the Loire prepared to go to the expense and trouble of using second-hand casks from Bordeaux châteaux, but Jean-Louis and Bernard insist that it must only be casks of one vintage, and from a *premier cru*; as if these specifications were not exacting enough, they will only buy from Margaux, because they are one of only two châteaux who still employ their own cooper, who selects his own oak for the casks. We tasted the '85 from several of the distinctive Château Margaux casks, and found an amazing variation of flavours from different casks; all had one thing in common, an outstanding richness and complexity of fruit, allied with the vanilla taste and perfume of young oak. How I look forward to tasting the *assemblage*, and then the final result in five, ten and even twenty years time.

My confidence in the future of the Foucault '85 Saumur Champigny was reinforced by the tasting that followed. Admittedly the first wine that we tried could hardly have been made by the brothers, since they would, at the most, have been schoolboys at the time, and they would not even have been born when the second one was made. The third, a white Coteaux de Saumur from 1928 was a stunning Chenin Blanc dessert wine for which I have no yardstick; it was a clear, orangey gold with a rich, complex nose of quince, which filled the mouth with richness and sun-warmed opulence; the finish was dry, long and memorable.

To return to the reds, the first wine was their 1964, one of the great 'once-every-ten-year' vintages of the Loire Valley. The colour was a deep, almost black ruby. The bouquet was rich and full of fruit with a touch of the farmyard. A lovely, rich mouthful of ripe fruit was followed by a long aftertaste – a wine that will be around for many, many years.

The *pièce de résistance* from the Foucault's liquid treasure-house was a wine from the 1937 vintage. The most amazing feature of this wine, like most of the old red Loire wines I have been lucky enough to taste, was the fantastic depth of colour, with no trace of the browning that one would expect to find in a Bordeaux or Burgundy of comparable age. The bouquet was still quite alive and assertive, with that same farmyard hint I found in the '64. There was still a mass of fruit and good tannin in the mouth, and I saw no immediate signs of deterioration in the wine. What a privilege!

The two brothers, both with walrus moustaches and the same blue jackets and trousers that the previous three or four generations of Foucaults must have sported, accompanied Michel Sébéo of Marc Brédif and myself to the Auberge du Thouet in Chacé, where we had a memorable lunch. If there is anything wrong in the world of wine and men that we did not put to rights that day, it was not worth bothering about. I thank them both, and hope to see them again soon – in England I hope.

ST CYR-EN-BOURG

ROBERT & REGIS NEAU, St Cyr-en-Bourg. Robert and his son Régis Neau (pronounced No) run a sizeable and varied wine business from their fine seventeenth-century house in the centre of St Cyr. The Domaine de Nerleux extends to some 35 hectares, 22 of which are planted with Cabernet Franc, 10 with Chenin Blanc, 2½ with Chardonnay and 1 with Sauvignon.

A wide variety of wines and styles is produced at the Domaine; the major part is Saumur-Champigny from 100% Cabernet Franc, and in 1985 a special *cuvée* was made called Cuvée de Chatain from a special corner of the vineyard which boasts very old vines and superb exposure. From the Chenin Blanc, Chardonnay and Sauvignon the Neaus produce between 10,000 and 15,000 bottles of very high-quality sparkling wine. They also make some fine still white wines, which vary from dry to *moelleux*, though the latter can only be made in exceptionally good years like 1985, 1976, etc. In common with Vouvray and Coteaux du Layon, the volume of sparkling wine made here in any given vintage is in direct inverse ratio to the quality of that year. This is a reflection of the characteristics of the Chenin Blanc, a variety that in a good year can be made into still wine of great quality and keeping potential, whether vinified dry, *demi-sec* or *moelleux*; in less sunny years, like 1984 for example, when the sugar-content is down, the rather astringent wine is best suited as *vin de base* for champagnisation.

The maximum permitted quantity of Chardonnay is included in the *vin de base* for the *méthode champenoise*, since this gives added finesse to the wine. The dry sparkling Saumur d'Origine that Régis gave me to taste was certainly among the best of its genre that I came across. We also looked at the two Saumur-Champignys of 1985 – the standard blend and Cuvée de Chatain mentioned above. I found both to be of fine quality, but the wine from the old vines had much more skeleton and structure for keeping and improving. The last wine tasted was an '85 Coteaux de Saumur Moelleux. It was a pale golden colour and had a rich bouquet of ripe pears; I found it interesting, but as yet totally undeveloped. There was a great deal of concentrated and complex flavour there, which will take several years to reach its undoubted potential.

CAVE CO-OPÉRATIVE DES VIGNERONS DE SAUMUR, St Cyr-en-Bourg.

Most of the Domaine de Nerleux production of white wine, as well as a good proportion of its red, is sold through the Cave Co-opérative des Vignerons de Saumur, also in St Cyr-en-Bourg. The co-operative, run by Marcel Neau, a cousin of Régis, has been a runaway success since its foundation in 1957. This is a supreme example of how a co-operative should be run, what its aims should be and how they are best achieved. From fifty members at its inception, there are now around two hundred and thirty. The equipment, cellars and buildings are the envy of wine-makers throughout the Loire, and the oenological know-how and technical expertise on which the co-operative can draw is second to none. It is no exaggeration to say that to a large extent the success of the *appellation* of Saumur-Champigny can be laid at the door of this co-operative, though they make equally good white wine, Saumur Rouge, Anjou Rosé and the entire range of *méthode champenoise* sparkling wines.

Madame Blancher comments in her book that the stone extracted from the quarries that now forms the co-operative's extensive cellars is reputed to have been used to repair Westminster Abbey after it was damaged in the Fire of London in 1666. Already, she says, the English had begun to appreciate our products!

This may or may not be so, but what is certain is that we English have been given a good introduction to Saumur-Champigny and other wines of Anjou through the good offices of the co-operative, which now exports 50% of its considerable output all over the world.

Château de Saumur has a commanding view above the Loire

APPELLATION: SAUMUR

The mediaeval town of Saumur is perhaps best known for its dominating Grimm's fairy-tale castle, the famous Cadre Noir riding and dressage establishment, and the sparkling wines that have been such an essential part of its economy for the past 177 years. The area from which the grapes for sparkling Saumur may come is spread over 93 communes, all on the south bank of the Loire; and the variety which dominates is the Chenin Blanc, though up to 20% of Chardonnay and/or Sauvignon may be used; there is also a selection of white-juiced black varieties permitted – Cabernets Francs and Sauvignons, though these may not make up more than 20% of the blend.

A new *appellation* was created for sparkling wines as recently as 1975; Crémant de Loire, which is widely produced in Saumur, may also come from Anjou, Touraine or Saumur; the permitted yield per hectare is lower than for sparkling Saumur, the time that the wine spends in bottle before disgorgement longer, and the wine therefore tends to be of higher quality and more expensive. Sadly, the new name was not given sufficient exposure, and the wine-buying public do not really appreciate the difference, so it has met with limited success.

ST HILAIRE – ST FLORENT

ACKERMAN-LAURANCE, St Hilaire-St Florent. My first visit in Saumur was, appropriately enough, to the ancient house of Ackerman-Laurance in the suburb of St Hilaire-St Florent on the River Thouet. I say appropriately for it was the founder, Jean Ackerman, who was the first to adapt the *méthode champenoise* to the wines of Saumur. Ackerman, a member of a banking family from Anvers, arrived in Saumur after some time working and studying in Champagne. He was immediately struck by the suitability of the local wine for champagnisation and by the availability of miles and miles of cheap and perfectly adapted cellars in the old quarry workings that honeycomb the tuff all around Saumur. He was at the same time struck by the suitability and the beauty of Emilie Laurance, daughter of a local banker. The cellars were bought, the marriage solemnised, and the firm of Ackerman-Laurance was formed in 1811.

For 37 years Ackerman was the only one to use the Champagne principle in Saumur, but from the mid-nineteenth century onwards he has had an ever-increasing number of competitors and imitators. In those far-off and less bureaucratic days there were no regulations as to the use of the word Champagne, and until 1919, as witness old advertisements used for England, Ackerman-Laurance quite openly marketed

'Dry Royal Champagne, Finest Imported from Saumur!' Later advertisements, which were always very tastefully done, and with the accent on sporting activities, were toned down somewhat; there is one which bears the words 'Not a cheap sparkling wine, Not an imitation Champagne, but the best value in sparkling wine'. Even this would not be allowed under today's strict labelling and advertising regulations; the very mention of 'Champagne' would result in all the legal guns in Epernay opening fire without hesitation. Within the next five years, even the words *méthode champenoise* will be outlawed for any wine that is not the genuine article, and producers of quality sparkling wine are hard put to it to find exactly the right and permissible wording for their labels. 'Saumur d'Origine' is the best that the Saumurois have come up with, since it is felt that the word *mousseux* implies an inferior sparkling wine made by pumping CO_2 into the wine in vat.

In those early days of sparkling wine production in Saumur there was a two-way traffic between here and Champagne in the base wine for champagnisation, and the Saumurois are proud to tell you that more of their wine went to Champagne than vice-versa. Today Ackerman-Laurance, headed by Philippe Treutenaire, is still one of the major producers and exporters of sparkling wine from Saumur. The company is closely associated with Remy-Pannier, whose premises are next door, the largest *négociant* business in the Loire Valley, and one of the biggest in France. Ackerman-Laurance handle very little still wine, since most of this business can be channelled through Remy-Pannier. Their business is sparkling wine, of which 70% is *brut* and 30% *demi-sec*; about a third of their production is exported, and their principal importers are the United Kingdom, Belgium, Holland and the United States.

Although M. Remy has some family vineyards, the vast majority of the base wine for Ackerman-Laurance is bought in from certain regular suppliers, either as grapes, unfermented must or finished wine. The grapes and must are vinified, and afterwards the wine is given the champagne treatment of secondary fermentation in bottle, *remuage*, *dégorgement* and *dosage*; all this takes place in the seven kilometres of cellars in St Hilaire-St Florent, where the company is geared to receive visitors from all over the world.

LANGLOIS-CHATEAU, St Hilaire-St Florent.

Like Ackerman-Laurance and most of the important sparkling Saumur firms, Langlois-Chateau have their offices and cellars in St Hilaire-St Florent. The company attained its 100th birthday in 1985, having started its existence as the Association Viticole de Muret-Saumur under the ownership of the Delandes family. Edouard Langlois, who worked for the Delandes, married Jeanne Chateau, and took over the running of the company in 1912, and the firm bears their joint names to this day. The company was acquired by the Champagne house of Bollinger in 1973, and is today run by Michel Villedey who is married to a Bollinger, and Jean Leroux, a direct descendant of Jeanne Chateau.

Langlois-Chateau have always interested themselves in quality above all else, and this applies to the range of still wines from all over the Loire Valley that they make and sell under their own label, in addition to their excellent sparkling Saumurs and Crémant de Loire. It was most probably this pursuit of excellence that attracted Bollinger, for their policy also has always been to concentrate on the top end of the market.

My visit happily coincided with that of Simon Leschallas, a director of Mentzendorff & Co. Ltd, English agents for Bollinger as well as Langlois-Chateau. I say happily, for Simon and his party were still lunching when I arrived, and I was able to join them for coffee and a lovely glass of 1959 Coteaux du Layon. Michel Villedey was also kind enough to

invite me to join them all for dinner that evening, which we took at Le Prieuré at Chênehutte-les-Tuffeaux. The view over the Loire from the hotel's wooded grounds is magnificent, and the food, starred in Michelin, definitely *mérite un détour*.

To earn this pleasure I had worked industriously but enjoyably with Michel Villedey and Jean Leroux all afternoon. First Michel explained the workings of the company. About half their output is in sparkling wine, the three labels of Saumur and the Crémant de Loire, and half in still wine. They have their own vineyards behind the cellars for the production of red and white still Saumur of excellent quality, sold until recently as Château St Florent; the white is made of 80% Chenin Blanc and 20% Chardonnay and the red from 80% Cabernet Franc and 20% Cabernet Sauvignon. Since my visit in 1986, demand for the still wines of the Château, especially the white, has increased so much that it became necessary to buy another vineyard; this is about 7 kilometres away, 20 hectares in size, and in the same *appellation*. In view of this change, and the fact that the soil is different, Langlois-Chateau have abandonded the name Château de St Florent and bottle all their still Saumur wine at their new cellar in Varrains under the label Domaine Langlois-Chateau. This is typical of Langlois-Chateau's honest way of doing business, when they could quite well have legally continued to use the Château St Florent name.

They also have a four-hectare vineyard, Domaine de Grand' Maison, near St Fiacre, where an excellent Muscadet de Sèvre et Maine sur Lie, is produced. The company's most recent acquisition is the Château de Fontaine Audon in the commune of Ste Gemme in Sancerre. Wine is also bought and commercialised from other Loire *appellations* – Pouilly Fumé, Chinon, St Nicolas de Bourgueil, Saumur Champigny and Coteaux du Layon.

Of the million or so bottles of top-quality wine issuing from Langlois-Chateau's cellars, 45% is exported, and the list of importers is impressive, from a comprehensive selection of European countries to such far-flung outposts of civilisation as Hong-Kong, Singapore and Guinea. The French market is mainly composed of sales to restaurants and *caves spécialistes* in the Paris area, as well as in the locality.

Michel took me on a tour of the Château de St Florent vineyard and press-house, which impressed me with their cleanliness and well-run appearance. In the vineyard, each row of vines has a plaque at the end showing the variety and date planted; this would prove an indispensable aid to navigation for me, since, even after having inspected hundreds of thousands of vines, I find the greatest difficulty in telling one variety from another.

Jean Leroux kindly organised a tasting of a whole range of Langlois-Chateau's wines:

Tasted: Langlois. Sparkling Saumur, Blanc de Blancs, Brut. (90% Chenin Blanc, 10% Chardonnay – no vintage on label, but the wine was 100% 1984.) Excellent light golden colour, good small mousse. Light, with very pleasing balance of fruit and acidity.
Langlois. Sparkling Saumur, Blanc de Blancs, Brut, Reserve 1982. (A special *cuvée*, made to celebrate the centenary of the company in 1985.) A much more Champagney style of wine, with some nice bottling-age and length. Good to drink with food.
Langlois. Sparkling Saumur Rosé, Dry. (70% Cabernet-Franc, 30% Grolleau.) Nice deepish pink. Light and fresh bouquet, slight raspberry hint. Quite full and rich in the mouth, with an agreeable touch of sweetness.
Domaine Grand' Maison, Muscadet de Sèvre et Maine Sur Lie 1985. Nice greeny-gold colour. Good fruit, slight CO_2 prickle; fresh traditional Muscadet, with nice length.
Château de St Florent 1985 Saumur Blanc. (Now Domaine Langlois-Chateau.) (80% Chenin Blanc, 20% Chardonnay.) Pale, greeny gold; nice nose with some rich fruit. Full, but dry, with good Chenin fruit and good length; could age well. Médaille d'Or, Concours de CIVAS.
Château de Fontaine-Audon 1985. (Sancerre – 100% Sauvignon.) Very pale colour. Green. elder-wood nose. Quite pleasing, but slightly oxidised. Jean Leroux explained that they did not take charge of vinification until the 1986 vintage.
Château de St Florent 1985 Saumur Rouge. (Now Domaine Langlois-Chateau.) Very nice deep colour. Good open nose with some *cassis*. A well-made wine with some length and power; needs a year in bottle. Cabernet Sauvignon will be reduced in favour of Cabernet Franc in future vintages to make the wine more approachable in youth.

BOUVET-LADUBAY, St Hilaire-St Florent. Bouvet-Ladubay, the second oldest of the Saumur sparkling wine firms, was founded in 1851. Etienne Bouvet very sensibly married his accountant, Mlle Ladubay, and the company acquired its present name. Etienne and his son Jules steered Bouvet-Ladubay into pole position as the largest exporters of sparkling wines, including the Champagne houses, by the end of the century. They did, in fact, own a small Champagne company in Epernay, but the bulk of the business was in the sparkling wines of Saumur; at their turn-of-the-century peak, the company was selling 5,000,000 bottles of Saumur sparkling and 2,000,000 bottles of Champagne. The business at this time appears to have been very largely in BOB (Buyer's Own Brand) wines, as witness the beautifully made ranks of revolving oak cabinets containing over 5,000 labels. Jules Bouvet died in the early 1900s, and his father soon after him; management of the company passed into the hands of Etienne's son-in-law, who died at the young age of thirty-three. Rudderless, the company drifted along until a sale was forced in the early 1930s. At this point the old-established Montrichard firm of Monmousseau bought Bouvet-Ladubay. Their objective in purchasing the Saumur business at that time is not entirely clear, since no great effort towards expansion seems to have been made until Patrice Monmousseau's father, Jean, was sent to run the company after the war. Bouvet-Ladubay continued as a low-key operation for another 25 years, until Jean's son, Patrice, took over in 1972.

When Patrice arrived in Saumur, sales were coasting along at around the 350,000 bottle mark. In 1974, the Monmousseau family decided to merge with Taittinger Champagne, which opened up expansion possibilities. Taittinger left management in the capable hands of Patrice in St Hilaire-St Florent; results have certainly proved the wisdom of this decision, for sales have reached the 2,000,000 bottle mark.

It is quality, image and PR that sell sparkling wine, and all three ingredients are present here. Quality is evident in the tasting-room, but for a more subjective yardstick one only has to look at the 30-odd gold, silver and bronze medals that Bouvet-Ladubay wines have won since 1972. Sponsorships have included the prototype Peugeot P4 jeep in the 1986 Paris-Dakar rally; the entry, christened 'Ville de Saumur' in the sailing Tour de France, and a racing hovercraft, built and piloted by Dominique Leglé, which took part in the European Championship in 1985, 1986, 1987 and 1988. On home ground, a liveried blue and silver horse-drawn *calèche* carries the Bouvet-Ladubay name and fame through the streets of Saumur, and there are others in Chambord, Fontainebleau and London. The English Vintage Car Rally from Bristol to Bordeaux has for two years made the house of Bouvet Ladubay one of its pit-stops; this represents an opportunity for Patrice Monmousseau to indulge two of his passions at one stroke – motor-cars and the promotion of his wine. This dual interest is further evidenced by the participation of the Bouvet-Brut Rondeau in the Le Mans 24-hour race; the car finished 13th in 1986 and 12th in 1987.

Patrice Monmousseau applies his interest in practical engineering to his own business. The automatic *remuage* machines are his own design.

Bouvet-Ladubay have currently five styles of sparkling wine – the standard Bouvet Brut, which is non-vintage, as is the Bouvet Rosé and the increasingly popular Bouvet Rubis; the jewel in the crown is the vintage Bouvet Saphir in its smart house colours of blue and silver. At the time of my visit, Patrice was very excited about his proposed new addition to the range, to be launched shortly under the name 'Trésor'; it will be made from 80% Chenin Blanc and 20% Chardonnay, and fermentation and a short part of the maturation will take place in new casks of Tronçais oak; a special heavy bottle will be used, with, one is confident, the usual quality presentation in terms of labels and capsule. The idea is an extension of Bouvet-Ladubay's policy of 'quality first', and sets out to prove that a de-luxe sparkling Saumur can be made as in Champagne. The wine will retail at a price around that of a vintage Champagne, and the first year's production will be limited to about 1,000 cases.

In addition to their sparkling wines, which represent the vast majority of their production, the company also markets Saumur Champigny, Saumur Blanc and, due to family connections, some Vouvray. The firm owns no vineyards in Saumur, but buys in grape must from about 150 different growers on a regular contract basis. They thus have total control of pressing and vinification in their 1.6 million litre capacity *cuverie*, where the very latest in stainless-steel hardware and thermostatic fermentation-controls are installed.

Bouvet-Ladubay is one of the few firms I visited in the entire Loire Valley that exports more that it sells on the home market. Sixty per cent of production goes overseas, mainly to the United States, where its share of the market is five times greater than that of its nearest rival. The prestigious House of Deinhard is the United Kingdom agent.

VEUVE-AMIOT, St Hilaire-St Florent.

Veuve-Amiot, another of the large sparkling wine firms in St Hilaire-St Florent, was started in 1884 by the widow Amiot. She was a pioneer of 'branded' wine marketing, registering her Crémant du Roi with the English Trademarks Office as early as 1886. After the First World War, the firm made a deliberate sales attack on France's many colonies, and it was not long before colonial sales comprised half the total turnover. After the Second World War, many of the colonial customers returned to the mother country, but retained their taste for the Amiot wines, and consequently this has always been a home-market orientated business.

Efforts are now being made on the export market, and this has been considerably helped by the acquisition of Veuve-Amiot in 1978 by the Italian vermouth giant, Martini-Rossi, with its ready access to world markets. Eighty per cent of production is still sold in France, but the export business is growing; Holland, currently importing around 220,000 bottles, and the United Kingdom, with retailers like Grant's of St James's and Stowells of Chelsea accounting for some 60,000 bottles, are two of the major growth markets.

Monsieur Pardessus, current Directeur Général, joined the firm in 1964 when it was owned by three grandsons of the original Veuve Amiot. These three worthies were all approaching retirement age, and had not one descendant between them to take over the reins, which is how, as he modestly puts its, Pardessus came to be in the driving seat. I got the impression that he is where he is through ability rather than default, and I am sure that a company the size of Martini would not keep a man in such a position unless he were more than equal to its challenge. As well as being evidently a man of great ability, he is also blessed with great charm, and I am grateful to him for the time and trouble he took over my visit.

Total production varies between two-and-a-half and three million bottles, and consists of 95% AC Saumur sparkling wines in *brut* (the driest), *sec* and *demi-sec*. The 5% balance is made up of other sparkling wine of the region. Two-thirds of the wine is vinified on the premises, being bought in from growers as grapes or grape-must, and one third is purchased as finished wine in bulk, ready for the champagnisation process.

There is evidently no lack of investment capital from the parent company, so I was surprised to note that in such a well-equipped winery only 20% of the 'remuage' is done on the mechanical *gyropalettes*. M. Pardessus told me that this was because much experimentation is currently being done in Champagne, which if successful will revolutionise, if not totally eliminate, the *remuage* stage of the *méthode champenoise*. This new method consists of introducing into the bottle, at the start of the second fermentation, tiny pellets that attract the dead yeast cells; when the second fermentation and ageing in bottle period is completed, the bottle is inverted in one move into the *dégorgement* machine; the deposit-encrusted pellets are then heavy enough to fall straight on the cork at once, leaving behind a perfectly clear wine. This will save weeks of work and expensive man-hours, and, dare we hope, may reduce the price of Champagne and sparkling wines.

SAUMUR

GRATIEN & MEYER, Saumur. If you approach Saumur from the Chinon direction, the distinctive 1920s architecture of Gratien & Meyer's offices and cellars, perched high above road and river, is one of the first impressions you receive. Visitors are encouraged, and are rewarded not only by the warmth of the welcome offered by one of the biggest and best of Saumur's sparkling wine producers, but also by the magnificent view from the terrace over the river and surrounding countryside.

The company was established here in Saumur by Alfred Gratien in 1864, who founded Alfred Gratien Champagne in Epernay at the same time. Jean Meyer, an Alsatian from Grunsbach, birth-place of Albert Schweitzer, joined Gratien in 1870, having left Alsace following the defeat of France by Germany in the war of 1870.

Alfred Gratien died in 1885, leaving a widow with four children. Having no business experience, she readily took M. Meyer into full partnership. Gratien's son Robert and Meyer's son Albert took full charge of the business in 1902; sadly Robert Gratien was killed at Verdun in 1916, leaving a widow who died only two years later. Albert Meyer, badly wounded in the

Remuage automatique producing the sparkling Saumur of Gratien & Meyer

trenches, nevertheless returned to assume full control of the company after the war; he remained, actively in charge, until his death in 1965. Meyer had a daughter who married Eric Seydoux, who, with his two sons Alain and Gérard, and their cousin Bernard de Bousquet, run the company today.

Legislation has changed frequently over the past hundred or so years, working ever more firmly on the side of the Champenois against other products of fine sparkling wine. The wheel has finally come full circle, and the great Champagne houses, recognising the hole in the lower end of the sparkling wine market, are increasingly making their presence felt in Saumur. Taittinger, through Monmousseau in Montrichard, are the owners of Bouvet-Ladubay and Bollinger S.A. owns the prestige firm of Langlois-Chateau. Throughout the vicissitudes of fashion and despite changing market trends, Gratien & Meyer is the sole company to have maintained a constant link with Champagne over the past century, via Alfred Gratien in Epernay.

The company is also unusual among the sparkling wine houses in that it owns substantial vineyards in the best communes of the Saumur *appellation*, though these are far from large enough to supply all the grapes needed for their huge production. Until 1972 only finished *vin de base* was bought from other growers for champagnisation, but now they have vastly increased their vinification capacity; only grapes or unfermented must are now purchased, giving this quality-conscious firm total control at every stage of the wine-making process.

Eric Seydoux and his large, friendly son, Alain, treated me to a horizontal tasting of all their sparkling wines, as well as the two sparkling 'cocktails' they have launched, Royal Framboise and Royal Orange.

Tasted: Gratien & Meyer Saumur Rosé. (100% Cabernet Franc.) Darkish pink colour, with a sweetish, flowery nose. Nice light mousse – a clean tasting wine with good fruit, on the medium side of dry.
Gratien & Meyer Brut. (70% Chenin Blanc, 30% Cabernet.) Nice medium gold colour with a fine mousse. Clean and fresh bouquet with good fruit. A wine of some body and a good level of acidity. Good to drink with food.
Gratien & Meyer Crémant de Loire. (Same grapes as for Saumur Brut.) Light gold, better mousse than Saumur Brut. Fine, clean nose, with slightly less fruit than the Saumur. A lighter style of wine, very pleasing and fresh – an aperitif. The quality stemming from the stricter regulations to this AC really shows through.
Gratien & Meyer Cuvée Flamme AC Saumur, Brut. (Same grapes but blend of older wine.) Deeper gold, with a good medium bubble. More body, pleasing taste of good fruit and the extra bottle age. Not, insisted Alain, a Prestige Cuvée, but a different style of wine to the straight Saumur Brut.
Gratien & Meyer Saumur Demi-Sec. (Same grapes again.) Mid-gold colour with a light mousse. Pleasing, ripe bouquet. Light and elegant, medium rather than sweet with no cloying on the palate. Lovely with fruit and desserts.
Gratien & Meyer Rouge Mousseux. (100% Cabernet Franc.) Dark red. Interesting nose with some sweetness, but definite Cabernet. Surprisingly clean and 'red wine' character, unlike many sparkling reds I have tasted, which tend towards the sparkling Ribena style. On the dry side of medium, would be an interesting aperitif, or perhaps an accompaniment to raspberries or strawberries.
Gratien & Meyer Royal Framboise. Pale pink with light mousse. Nose like Eau de Vie de Framboise. Sweet, clean, with distinct raspberry flavour. Not my cup of tea, but perhaps suiting the French taste for sweet aperitifs.
Gratien & Meyer Royal Orange. Golden colour with orange shades, and a nice light mousse. Orange flavour on nose and palate, but the grape dominates. Intended to drink with chocolate-based desserts or with coffee. At an excellent lunch with Alain Seydoux we drank it with both – and it works!

Over lunch, Alain spoke to me of the need to educate the wine-drinking public to a greater understanding of the quality and characteristics of the wine of the Loire Valley. His firm participates in the Loire Valley Wine Tour that takes in Muscadet, Savennières and Anjou, Layon, Saumur sparkling wines, Chinon, Bourgueil and Saumur Champigny. For the Saumur part of the Tour, travellers are received at the Gratien & Meyer hospitality Château de Beaulieu, for a tasting and buffet lunch following a

Château de Brézé, the home of the Comte de Colbert

tour of the cellars, and the last night of the trip consists of a formal dinner in the company's cellars, where diplomas are presented to all who have stayed the course.

Gratien & Meyer export about half their production, and the United Kingdom is their biggest customer; they also sell to the United States, Belgium, Denmark and Norway, and, rather surprisingly, to Australia and New Zealand.

BRÉZÉ

COMTE DE COLBERT, Château de Brézé, Brézé. The foundations of the Château de Brézé date back to the eleventh century, and in its day it has been home to Diane de Poitiers, wife of Louis de Brézé, the Grand Sénéchal of Normandy, and the Grand Condé, who exchanged it with the Dreux family, later Marquises de Brézé, whose descendants were hereditary Grand Masters of Ceremonies to Kings of France from Louis XIV to Charles X. The main part of the castle is, however, Renaissance, and the façade was much altered by the nineteenth-century architect Hodé. The yawning dry moat, 18 metres deep and 13 metres across, is the biggest in all France, and may well have been created in order to quarry out the stone of which the castle is built; it certainly also stood the inhabitants in good stead as a first line of defence.

The current occupant is the Comte de Colbert, whose family have only been here for a mere three hundred years. He makes some very good Saumur Rouge, Coteau de Saumur Demi-Sec, and Brézé Brut Blanc de Blancs Méthode Champenoise, but the jewel in his vinous crown is undoubtedly the Saumur Blanc, which is dry and has more character than all the rest of the still white wines of this *appellation* put together. There are about 24 hectares of vines, 14 of which are given over to the Chenin Blanc for his Vin Blanc Sec and Méthode Champenoise together with a little Chardonnay, and 10 hectares are planted with Cabernet Franc and Sauvignon for making the red wine. Vinification is very traditional, and much wood is in evidence in the cellars quarried deep into the rock at the bottom of the dry moat. Seventy-five per cent of the Comte's wines are sold to private customers, 15% to the French restaurant trade and 10% is exported. He is also proprietor of a Cru Bourgeois château in the Haut-Médoc, Château Saint Ahon near Blanquefort. I tasted the wine at the Château de Brézé, and look forward to a visit when next I am in Bordeaux. The Château de Brézé is not, strictly-speaking, open to the public, but if you are interested in wine, I strongly recommend that you pay de Colbert a visit.

APPELLATION: COTEAUX DE L'AUBANCE

Prior to writing this book, I must confess to never having heard of the wines of the Coteaux de l'Aubance. This is perhaps not entirely my fault, for it is not an easy wine to find even when you are in the *appellation*. The area covered is quite large – some 1,800 hectares are entitled to the name – but very little Coteaux de l'Aubance is actually made. The reason for this has been encountered elsewhere in this book; the *appellation* only applies to white wines made exclusively from the Chenin Blanc, with all its attendant problems, and the maximum yield has been set by the INAO at the low level of 30 hectolitres per hectare. As if all this were not sufficient deterrent, the name is not well known even in France, so it is not an easy wine to market even when you are able to make some. Small wonder therefore that the growers in the ten communes that make up the area of the Coteaux de l'Aubance lean towards the production of the 'softer-option' wines of generic Anjoux.

The vineyard area lies between the Coteaux du Layon to the south and the River Loire to the north, and takes its name from the tiny River Aubance which meanders lazily through the *appellation* on its north-westerly journey into the Loire, from Brissac-Quincé to the eastern limit at Denée. The northern boundary of the Coteaux is centred on the old river-port of Juigné-sur Loire, and the most southerly point is the village of Vauchrétien.

MELANIE-SUR-AUBANCE

CHRISTIAN PAPIN, Domaine de Haute Perche, St Melaine-sur-Aubance. My visit to Christian Papin at the Domaine de Haute Perche was a good introduction to the Coteaux de l'Aubance, for not only are his vineyards situated almost at the geographic centre of the *appellation*, but Papin is also a model wine-maker of the region. He has a total area under vines of 20 hectares, about average for the Coteaux de l'Aubance, and, although he makes an excellent white wine under the *appellation* label, the majority of his production is in red wines, two kinds of rosé and Anjou Blanc Sec.

For the AC Coteaux de l'Aubance, Papin has 6 hectares of Chenin Blanc, and the wine is usually vinified as *demi-sec* rather than *moelleux*, though in the great years, of which 1985 was one, great sweet wines can be made. Some of the Chenin Blanc is used for the production of Anjou Blanc Sec, plus a little Chardonnay and Sauvignon. For the red wines, Christian Papin grows chiefly Cabernets, though Grolleau and Gamay are also grown, the latter for the Anjou Gamay red, the former for the rosés.

Papin believes that the future for Anjou lies in red wine, and, in common with many other forward-looking wine-makers, is concentrating his efforts in that direction. He will be helped in this respect by the fact that the new up-market *appellation* for red wines, Anjou Villages, will take in the area in which his vines are grown.

The soil at the Domaine de Haute Perche is fairly typical of the Coteaux de l'Aubance, being composed of schist and a little clay. Papin prunes hard for quality, and picking is still done by hand, even for the red wines. Machines are totally impractical for picking the Chenin Blancs for the Coteaux de l'Aubance wines, and there is little point in going to the capital expense of buying a machine when nearby Angers provides a ready source of experienced pickers, who understand the system of picking the super-ripe grapes only.

His vinification is technically immaculate, and the equipment includes a good deal of stainless steel. For the white wines, especially the Blanc Sec, he believes that too much malo-lactic fermentation loses all-important acidity and fruit; like Yves Soulez at Château Chamboureau in Savennières, he solves this problem by allowing only part of the wine to go through this process. The vast majority of Papin's wine is sold on the home market to private customers and restaurants, half in bottle and half in cubitainers. For some years now, though, he has been pursuing a gradually expanding export business, and is currently selling to Belgium, Holland and a little to the United Kingdom.

I tasted his Anjou Blanc Sec, which had a nice fruit/acidity balance, and the finesse imparted by the Chardonnay was evident on bouquet and taste. Three vintages of Anjou Rouge, all Cabernet, followed; the '85 was rich and rounded, with some nice *cassis* on the bouquet and tannins quite pronounced. This will make a really nice bottle in a year. The '84 was well-made, lighter and less fruity than the '85, but this is what you would expect from the vintage – no faults, pleasant to drink now. 1981 was a small vintage in the Loire, and the red wine of Haute Perche was beginning to show signs of age; browning a little in colour, and showing age on the nose, it was still firm with some nice fruit in the mouth, finishing a little dry.

The *dégustation* now proceeded to a totally new and delightful dimension for me – three vintages of Coteaux de l'Aubance. Starting with the 1985, I was immediately impressed with the lovely bright golden colour, and the richness and fruitiness of the bouquet; I detected some good *pourriture noble* in the mouth, and a nice complex of rich aromas, lovely now, but promising great things for the years to come. The 1984 was a shade darker, with a more straightforward, approachable style, both on the nose and on tasting, Some nice richness, but less finesse and complexity than the 1985, as one might expect.

The kindly Monsieur Papin's parting shot was to open a bottle of his 1978 Coteaux de l'Aubance, a Gold medal-winner in Paris. The colour was a lovely mid-gold, and the nose had distinct dried-fruit and quince tones that typify ripe Chenin Blanc wines. A delicious, concentrated mouthful of rich ripeness, with a beautiful, long, echoing aftertaste. Papin said that the 1985 would be a better wine, having a little more Coteaux de l'Aubance *terroir* on bouquet and palate. My overall impression of these and other Coteaux de l'Aubance wines was that they are lighter and more inclined to *demi-sec* than *moelleux*, but that they have a definite place in my cellar in the future.

BRISSAC-QUINCÉ

HENRI BRAULT, Domaine de Ste Anne, Brissac-Quincé. The Domaine de Ste

Anne is run by M. Henri Brault and his son Marc, a family whose name has been synonymous with wine-making in the area for many generations. My appointment with M. Brault was for two-thirty in the afternoon, but I had some difficulty in arousing him from a post-prandial nap. When he finally awoke, he sent his wife scurrying off to fetch a bottle of his 1982 red Anjou Cabernet; this was opened and tasted with due reverence before we spoke a word, a kind of liquid introduction that spanned any possible gaps in language or communication of any sort. The wine had a beautiful deep ruby colour, and a generous nose of blackcurrant – in the mouth it was pleasing and rounded, but it had quite a bit of backbone, and excellent length.

Thus introduced, I was given more detailed information about the Brault operation. There are some 45 hectares under vines, nearly half of which is planted with both sorts of Cabernet for making into red and Cabernet Rosé d'Anjou, plus a little Gamay and Pineau d'Aunis; there are also about four hectares of Grolleau for Rosé de Loire. As far as white wine is concerned, there are around five hectares planted with Chenin Blanc, much of which is made into Anjou Blanc Sec, to which may be added a little Sauvignon or Chardonnay; a little *méthode champenoise* is also made, but only in the lesser years like 1984. Brault also makes some Coteaux de l'Aubance, of which he is very proud, but I got the impression that it was more a matter of honour than commerce that keeps him making this wine.

Like most aware growers in Anjou, Brault is concentrating his vinous and marketing activities on dry white and red wines rather than the traditional rosés of Anjou, as this is where demand now seems to lie. Ninety per cent of production is sold by the Braults directly, and the remaining 10% is sold in bulk. Eighty per cent of their sales are on the French market, of which the major portion is in cubitainers and bottles to private customers. Twenty per cent is exported, mostly to Belgium and the United States.

Before I left, Brault showed me his impressively capacious vinification installations, where a variety of materials are used for fermentation, including epoxy resin-lined cement and his own special design of stainless-steel vats. Fermentation is along fairly traditional lines, except that he uses *macération carbonique* for making his Gamay red; for this reason, the Gamay is the only red variety that is not picked by machine, since fermentation under CO_2 demands whole, undamaged grapes. The Chenin Blancs for

the Coteaux de l'Aubance are also picked by hand, as this wine has to be made with only super-ripe grapes.

In the large tasting-room, complete with bar, where Brault receives tourists by the coach-load, I tasted the Coteaux de l'Aubance 1985. It was very pale golden, with a bouquet that was still very shy and shut-in. There was a complex richness of flavour in the mouth, and some *pourriture noble* fruit. This will make an excellent bottle in a few years.

JEAN-PIERRE DAVIAU, Domaine de Bablut, Brissac-Quincé.

I am more than glad that I did not leave the Coteaux de l'Aubance out of my itinerary for various reasons, chief among which is having met Jean-Pierre Daviau of the Domaine de Bablut. It did not take us long to discover, over a simply amazing tasting of Coteaux de l'Aubance wines going back to 1919, that we shared a common passion for *la chasse*. Daviau insisted that I accompany him the very next morning on a day's shooting in the Duc de Brissac's forest. I lost not a second in accepting, swiftly changing all the appointments I had made for the following day.

It was a day that I shall always remember, a memory to treasure in darker days, when, too feeble of foot and rheumatic of shoulder to venture forth, I twirl a glass of Daviau's 1985 Coteaux de l'Aubance before a crackling log-fire, drawing from its amber depths the golden days of my life. We met at eight in the morning in an old stone cottage in the woods, where I was introduced to some twenty merry *chasseurs*, all armed to the teeth with weapons of varying age and type and each with a curly hunting horn slung across his shoulder. The function of these horns was explained to me. A complicated code of long and short toots indicated various items of news: one short 'I have seen a wild-boar'; one short, one long 'I have shot a wild boar'; two shorts, 'I have seen a roe-deer', and so on. This seemed an admirable practice, keeping all the participants properly informed of each other's whereabouts and of the movement of game, and, most important, adding to the general safety of all concerned.

Before setting off into the forest, it was necessary to take on board something in the way of nourishment to sustain body and soul until lunch-time. A *casse-croûte* of bread, cheese, saucisson, rillons and rillettes ensued, washed down with copious drafts of Daviau's Château de Brissac 1985 red Cabernet, or newly-fermented 1986 Sauvignon for the stronger stomach.

The *modus operandi* seemed simple enough. The huge tract of forest was divided into sections of about 50 acres with rides in between. The heavily armed and horn-toting hunters surrounded each sector, one at a time, whilst a formidable lady with a pack of beagles went into the undergrowth to flush out the resident population of deer and wild boar. The system, however, did not allow for the volatility of the Gallic temperament; every time a twig cracked, usually caused by one of the beagles, the nearest hunter let forth a mounting crescendo of notes on his bugle, completely unconnected with the aforementioned code of signals. Quicker than the walls of Jericho tumbling at the sound of Joshua's trumpets, every man jack of them was galvanised into action, which usually consisted of taking off at a gallop, cocked gun at the ready, in the direction in which each man thought the game was likely to appear. By lunch-time any kind of cohesive plan had completely disintegrated, and the beagles were in another forest altogether.

During the entire day I only saw one roe-deer. The Englishman, unarmed and useless, was standing directly in the line of fire between the creature and the nearest gun. I thought my hour had come, but mercifully my only punishment was verbal – and good-humoured – rather than ballistic.

Lunch consisted of a splendid *déjeuner sur l'herbe* beneath the autumnal golden umbrella of a giant chestnut, during which several more dozen of the Château de Brissac and '86 Sauvignon were interviewed. All that fresh air and running about had engendered gargantuan appetites, which was just as well since each man appeared to have brought enough food to feed all the others. There was, nonetheless, a slight *embarras de richesses* in the cheese department, and some extremely over-ripe Bresse Bleu became an utterly unwanted object in one of the messiest and smelliest games of 'Pass the parcel' in which I have taken part.

After another hour of rather more sluggish dashing about, it began to get dark. Jean-Pierre proposed an evening's duck-flighting on a nearby pond, for which activity the local butcher and I were the only volunteers.

Modesty forbids me to record the name of the man who shot one mallard, the entire bag for a whole day's shooting by 21 men and 15 couple of beagles, to say nothing of the cost of all that wine, bread, charcuterie, pâté and cheese. 'C'est le sport, n'est ce pas?' said Jean-Pierre.

To return to the wine-tasting and discussions of the previous day, Jean-Pierre told me proudly that there have been Daviaus making wine and milling flour at the Domaine de Bablut in Brissac-Quincé in a direct father-to-son line since 1546. It was Jean-Pierre's grandfather, M. Daviau-Rozé, who was among the first to plant Cabernets in this region after the ravages of phylloxera, and he believes that the family were definitely the first to vinify the Cabernet as a rosé wine for laying down and long keeping. They have always had a laudable policy of keeping back a decent proportion of their crop each year of this fine *moelleux* Cabernet d'Anjou, as well as their Coteaux de l'Aubance; this is binned away for sale in years to come to their 17,000-strong mailing list of private clients and restaurants. This means that they now issue a price-list with Cabernet Anjou Rosé and Coteaux de l'Aubance from 1943 right up to the present day. There are much older wines in the cellar, as I was later to discover, though I did not get a chance to taste the Coteaux de l'Aubance from 1911 which still slumbers there.

This is a big business, though still a very personal one. There are 90 hectares under vines, as well as 30 hectares of vineyards rented from the Duc de Brissac, where the superb red Cabernet, Château de Brissac, comes from. Their range of red wines consists of the Château de Brissac Anjou Cabernet, Domaine de Bablut, and an Anjou Gamay; the rosés are Cabernet d'Anjou and the dry Rosé de Loire; the whites are even more varied, from the luscious Coteaux de l'Aubance, through Anjou Blanc Sec, Blanc Sauvignon Sec, Blanc Chardonnay Sec to a *méthode champenoise* Crémant de Loire Brut. From this one estate, Jean-Pierre can find you a bottle that will complement to perfection any meal and any occasion.

Production is about one-quarter in white varieties and three-quarters red and rosé, with the accent now heavily on red. When his grandfather planted the Cabernet at the turn of the century, it was with the production of rosé in mind, and so it remained until trends and tastes shifted to drier wines and reds, a shift that has only occurred over the past 15 or 20 years. From the early Sixties, when they made the first red here, production of rosé has dwindled until it is now only one-fifth of the quantity of red.

The new red *appellation*, Anjou Villages, so Jean-Pierre told me, could really be quite accurately entitled Brissac Rouge, since the vast majority of the area covered by the *appellation* is here; the INAO, however, in their wisdom, hit upon the Anjou Villages name to avoid any possibility of jealousy on the part of surrounding villages.

All the Domaine de Bablut wines are presently commercialised direct by the family, only 8% going for export, the home market being divided between a huge private trade and some restaurant business. The whole operation is geared to the private customer, from the price-lists and tasting facilities in the converted mill to the special presentation wicker baskets and the 'Collection Prestige' selection case that Daviau has had designed; the latter contains one or two bottles of all the wines that they produce, with special labels by a talented water colourist called Lamotte featuring, surprise, surprise, game-birds, deer, hares and wild-boar for the reds and rosés, and fish for the whites.

The tasting which Jean-Pierre gave me in his comfortable living-room on the first afternoon was memorable. The only slight problem was the rather bumptious Daviau black Labrador that had developed over the years a technique for hurrying his master back to the shooting field; as soon as a glass of wine was poured, he would sneak up and nudge my right arm violently in an upward direction, spilling most if not all of the contents. I soon got wise to this, and the tasting proceeded.

Tasted: *Château de Brissac, Anjou Rouge 1985.*
(Cabernet Franc and Cabernet Sauvignon.) Fine deep colour. Good powerful *cassis* nose, with some raspberry. Lots of good fruit in the mouth, with ripe and non-aggressive tannins. Good for drinking now – and tomorrow, as it turned out – but has the structure to keep and improve for several years.

Coteaux de l'Aubance 1966. Golden syrup colour. Rich, quincey nose of mature Chenin Blanc, with a touch of honey. Complexity of rich, ripe fruit, and a pleasing dry finish, Would be superb with Salmon and Beurre Blanc Sauce.

Coteaux de l'Aubance 1919. Light golden syrup colour. Rich and quincy on the nose. Beautifully light and elegant on the palate, with lots of aromatic, ripe but understated flavours. J.-P. says it must have started with a very high acidity level.

Coteaux de l'Aubance 1955. Lightest colour of all so far, Chenin nose less marked than the previous two wines. Very fine and concentrated flavour still very undeveloped, has a long way to go still.

Coteaux de l'Aubance 1943. Darker golden colour. Very fine nose with rich dried fruits like raisins, sugar plums and figs. Rather like drinking liquid Christmas pudding – the Fortnum and Mason kind! The best tasted, and then still available at F130.00 per bottle.

Coteaux de l'Aubance 1928. Very dark golden-brown. Nose a bit maderised; still has great finesse and concentration of ripe richness in the mouth.

Cabernet Rosé d'Anjou 1959. Colour beginning to brown a little. Very special slight raspberry bouquet, quite unlike anything I have smelt before. Light, elegant, fruity and clean-tasting, with a good long aftertaste. Jean-Pierre gave me a bottle of this wine to take home for my wife. We made some guests drink it blindfold, and all thought it was white and from Bordeaux.

APPELLATION: COTEAUX DU LAYON

In this very pretty, half-forgotten backwater of the Loire Valley, the little River Layon runs about 70 kilometres from its source near Lake Beaurepaire in a meandering but generally north-westerly direction; it joins the Loire in the marshy lowlands near Chalonnes to the west of Rochefort-sur-Loire. I am no geologist, but it is not difficult to imagine that, in prehistoric times, this muddy little stream must have been a raging torrent; the valley which it has carved out often rises to 300 feet on either side of the river, and very steeply in places.

There is evidence of vine-growing all along the Layon, suggesting that wine has been a major part of the agronomy since the 4th century AD; this may well be ascribed to the steep nature of the terrain on which the vine is the only practicable form of agriculture. As in so many other parts of the Loire *vignoble*, it was the Dutch who first caused the expansion of the Coteaux du Layon wines. The Canal du Layon which ran from St Georges-sur-Layon to the Loire, was finished in 1779; built to carry coalbarges, it also served to open up a convenient shipping route for Dutchmen thirsty for sweet wine. The Layon wines of that day certainly bore no relation to the elegant creatures that we now know; the wines were quite coarse, often dry Anjou wines, made from any old grape variety and sweetened up with liberal doses of molasses.

The *appellation* Coteaux du Layon dates only from 1950; before then the wines were entitled only to the AC Anjou Blanc. This does not mean that superb dessert wines were not made prior to that date; one only has to visit the cellars of the grower *négociant* firm of Touchais in Doué-la-Fontaine, where over a million bottles slumber. Touchais has never subscribed to the rightness of the Coteaux du Layon *appellation*, and all his wines, many of which are entitled to the Coteaux du Layon label, are sold as Moulin du Touchais, Anjou. In addition to these 'renegade' wines, he also has stocks of white Anjou of truly amazing quality going back to the last century.

The area defined by the INAO in 1950 embraces no less than 25 communes on both sides of the Layon; from Cléré-sur-Layon and Les Verchers in the south to Rochefort-sur-Loire in the north there are currently some 650 hectares under vines. In 1955 the INAO granted a sub-division of the *appellation*; six communes were allowed the AC Coteaux du Layon Villages, and have the right to put their commune on the label. One stricter *appellation* was created at the same time, that of Coteaux du Layon Chaume; this is not to be confused with the even more limited Quarts de Chaume. Coteaux du Layon Chaume is geographically restricted to the clayey soil around the hamlet of Chaume, and permitted yield per hectare is only 25 hectolitres, the same as for Sauternes and 20% lower than plain Coteaux du Layon.

The six communes of the Coteaux du Layon Villages *appellation* are Faye d'Anjou, Rablay-sur-Layon, Beaulieu-sur-Layon, St Lambert-du-Lattay, St Aubin-de-Luigné, and Rochefort-sur-Loire. Although the villages of Rablay and St Lambert du Lattay are on the south side of the Layon, most of the best vineyards of the Coteaux du Layon, as well as the superior *appellations* of Bonnezeaux and Quarts de Chaume, are on the north bank, where they enjoy the more favourable south-westerly exposure.

The only grape variety permitted for the making of Coteaux du Layon is the Chenin Blanc or Pineau de la Loire. The options open to wine-makers in the Layon Valley are many and various. The Chenin Blanc, as we have noted elsewhere, is not an easy grape to live with. The best still wines from this variety are made by waiting until it is super-ripe; indeed, if you want to make the great *demi-secs* and *moelleux* for which the Coteaux du Layon are best known, you must wait until the grapes are, quite literally, rotten. This rot, though, has to be the right sort – the *pourriture noble* of Sauternes and Barsac, the Rhine and Mosel Valleys and the Tokay vineyards of Hungary. It is a mushroom spore that settles on the grape and shrivels the fruit without puncturing the skin, concentrating the flavours and natural sugars to the most extraordinary degree. The development of this 'noble rot', or *Botrytis cynerea* to give it its Latin name, requires very special weather conditions – a late summer and autumn with days that start misty and become warm and sunny around mid-morning. This is what is described locally as the *arrière-saison*, which translates almost exactly into the East Anglian 'back-end'. Unfortunately beautiful back-ends are rare, even

Melon de Bourgogne, the grape of Muscadet

The vineyards of the Pays Nantais from Château La Noë, Vallet

A fisherman by the banks of the Loire

The ruined Château de Clisson

An ancient wine-press outside the offices of the CIVOPN, La Haie-Fouassière

in the centre of France, and the longer you hang about waiting for one to happen, the greater the chance of total disappointment.

Fortunately, from the economic point of view, there is an alternative or additional course to follow with the Chenin Blanc. It may be harvested earlier, when the acidity level is high and the sugar content less advanced and vinified as *vin de base* for making into sparkling wine. Most of the Layon Valley growers do a little of both, since the production of genuine high-quality Coteaux du Layon is not only risky, it is also ruinously expensive, and the wines, though of the highest quality, are not always easy to sell at their proper price.

The third option for the grower is to devote a large part of his vineyard to the production of less sensitive varieties for making into the easier and more humble multiple *appellations* of Anjou – Rosé d'Anjou, Cabernet d'Anjou, Rosé de Loire, Anjou Rouge, Anjou Gamay, and Anjou Blanc Sec, Demi-Sec or Moelleux. Depending on the size and quality of the vineyard, many growers go for a combination of all three options.

FAYE D'ANJOU

SCA DU FRESNE, Château du Fresne, Mont, Faye d'Anjou. The SCA du Fresne is by any standards a large operation, and by Coteaux du Layon standards it is a giant. A total of 90 hectares of vines is exploited by the company, and the entire gamut of Anjou's wine is made and sold, from fine Coteaux du Layon through two types of Anjou Blanc Sec, three still rosés and two reds to *méthode champenoise*, *brut* and *demi-sec*, white and rosé. The 90 hectares is all rented land, but much of it is family property.

From the size of the vineyard and the huge range of wines produced, it might be assumed that this is some sort of wine factory, impersonal, computerised and soulless. This could not be further from the truth; SCA du Fresne belongs to the Robin-Bretault family; the château itself, an extremely old manor-house, is no longer inhabited though it is used for the

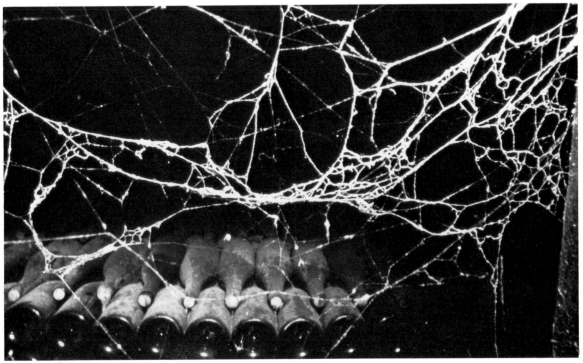

The cellars of negociants Touchais at Doué-la-Fontaine

reception of visitors and for meetings of the property's own Confrérie des Gourmandiers et Tasteviniers. The older generation is represented by the gentle Monsieur Robin; his daughter, Michelle, is married to one of two Bretault brothers, whose family vineyards in nearby Montbenault are run in tandem with the Robin vines. Michelle and her father run the office, private sales, tasting and commercialisation generally, while the two brothers are responsible for viticulture and vinification.

Not surprisingly, picking is done by machine, and has been since 1980, though not for the Coteaux du Layon for which careful handpicking of only the ripe and *pourriture*-affected grapes is essential. The vinification buildings and equipment are scattered and various in their composition, but all is under proper control. A large new vat-house equipped with stainless-steel fermentation vats and underground tanks is currently under construction, and was already in use for the reception of the 1986 crop during my visit.

Michelle Bretault did all the talking. The day was a real scorcher, and she seemed pleased to have an excuse to abandon the horrendous pile of paperwork that completely filled not only her desk but most of the office in the round tower of the château. Madame Bretault suggested a stroll in the vineyard. We walked for a very enjoyable hour in the warm afternoon sun, finally arriving at a farmhouse owned by a delightful octogenarian couple, M. and Mme Fribault, who used to farm the surrounding land, now part of the du Fresne vineyard.

A couple of their friends were visiting them, and we were ushered into the welcome cool of their kitchen. Having seated us at the huge kitchen table, bread and cheese were produced, and a dusty bottle, dripping with condensation from the cool, deep golden liquid within. It was a bottle of the Fribault's best Coteaux du Layon of the fabulous 1959 vintage from a special part of the vineyard called the Clos des Cocus. The colour was deep, deep gold, and the nose was rich and complex with a multiplicity of ripe fruit and flowers. In the mouth the wine was honeyed and concentrated. It had the most amazing structure, and will probably go on for another thirty years without any trouble at all. When I said that we had walked over to their house through the Clos des Cocus, there was much laughter, winking and nudging, which I pretended to understand. I thanked the Fribaults for their great kindness, and we took our leave.

Back at Château de Rochecotte that evening, I consulted my dictionary to find that I had sauntered with Madame Bretault through the 'vineyard of the cuckolds'.

On my return after the vintage, the Bretaults had laid on a magnificent tasting of their Coteaux du Layon Faye:

Tasted: *Standard Blend 1985.* Good intense colour, nose rich with some rot. Excellent concentrated richness in the mouth, with tremendous length and great potential.
'Pourriture Noble' 1985. More closed on nose than the first wine. Same brilliant gold. Rich, concentrated and aromatic, with suggestion of pear-drops. More complex and less developed than the standard blend. Definitely a *vin de garde.*
1984. Light golden. Nice, delicate fruit on nose. Light, but well made. More finesse and elegance than one might expect from a difficult year like '84.
1983. Slightly deeper colour than '84. Clean bouquet with good ripe fruit. In the mouth the ripe fruit is there, and some complexity of flavours. Good length, will keep and improve.
1982. Good light golden colour. Nose rich and powerful. Well-knit, concentrated flavour with a nice degree of acidity. Excellent with blue cheese.
1979. Colour very light gold. Nose very different to previous wines; could be a touch of *pourriture,* but *grise* instead of *noble.* Much better in the mouth than promised by the bouquet. Some richness, concentration and length, but with a little after-taste of the 'bad rot' found on the nose. This lessened with some aeration.
1976. Nice medium gold – comparable with '85, even after nine years. On the nose an astonishing concentration of honey, flowers and fruits – apricot and pear? A beautiful complex mouthful of richness and ripe fruit and the right kind of *pourriture.* A classic that will stay and stay.
1971. Colour still very light golden. Rich, slightly sulphurous nose. Good taste of ripe fruit with a little 'noble rot'. (M. Bretault told me that this wine had been over-sulphured, but it had recovered well.)

BEAULIEU-SUR-LAYON

M. & MME MORGAT, Château du Breuil, Beaulieu-sur-Layon. The Château du Breuil, situated on the road between Beaulieu-sur-Layon and Rochefort-sur-Loire, commands a splendid view over the Layon Valley. In general appearance, the nineteenth-century château looks as if it would be more at home in the Médoc or St Emilion than in this rustic corner of Anjou.

The house was, until 1960, the centrepiece of an estate of some 400 hectares which had belonged to a wealthy family by the name of Hamon. M. Hamon died a couple of decades before, and left a widow to live and battle on alone; the estate was sold off bit by bit until only the vineyard was left. Mme Hamon was a religious lady, and, during the 1950s, entrusted the running of the vineyards to the Jesuits, to whom she also gave the château for use as a school. The good fathers, feeling perhaps that the traditions of their order fitted them more for education than viticulture, allowed the vineyards to be used by the École Supérieure d'Agriculture et Viticulture for experimental purposes. The property was already making good white dessert wines, but trials with various encépagements soon determined the suitability of the plateau and slopes of the vineyard to the Cabernet Franc and the Grolleau, as well as the Chenin Blanc.

The house, vineyard and vinification buildings were acquired by Marc Morgat's father in 1960. Noting the increasing demand for dry wine, he replanted parts of the estate with varieties such as Sauvignon and Chardonnay; Marc still makes quite a lot of dry white from these varieties which is sold under the recently created Vin de Table label Jardin de la France. He also makes red Anjou from Cabernet and Gamay, two rosés, Cabernet d'Anjou and Rosé d'Anjou, sweet and dry respectively, and some Blanc de Blancs sparkling, but his pride and joy is his Coteaux du Layon. Like so many of the growers in the Layon Valley, Morgat gives one the impression that he would like to make nothing else but traditional Coteaux du Layon, and that all the other varieties are just boring necessities that have to be made in order to finance the real thing.

His Coteaux du Layon is certainly of an exceptionally high standard; he told me that the Chenins Blancs are picked by hand, and that the pickers will go through the vineyard as many as four times, selecting only the ripest and botrytis-affected grapes. Any grapes left on the vine after these tris are used in the dry white wine. I tasted the 1985 Coteaux du Layon, which was palest gold in colour and had a still-shy but very promising nose; it was beautifully clean, with a light, flowery sweetness and a long aftertaste – a very pretty little girl who will one day become a beautiful woman. Marc also gave me a bottle of his 1971 to try; although not a great year in this part of the world, the Chenin Blanc can yield some very nice surprises after a few years in bottle, and this was certainly such a wine. The colour was still very pale, and the wine had a rich, Christmas-pudding sort of nose. A beautiful complex and a lovely long aftertaste. It could easily keep another ten years and more.

Output, due to the large proportion of less strictly controlled wines produced, is relatively high at the Château du Breuil; in 1985 some 2,800 hectolitres were made from 50 hectares of vines. Twenty-five per cent of the Morgats' production goes abroad to the United Kingdom, Germany, Belgium and the United States. They also have a lively 'private sector' business, and receive visitors cordially in their attractive tasting-room, where they are pleased to show customers any wine from their wide range. I joined a French couple from the Rhône Valley who were on holiday in the area, and were looking for some good rosé for their cellar at home. Mme Morgat showed us the Château du Breuil Rosé de Loire, which was light, dry and an appealing thirst-quencher with no pretensions; we also tasted the Cabernet d'Anjou Rosé, which had a pale pink colour, a nice fruity nose, and had good fruit and sweetness in the mouth; the Cabernet d'Anjou Rosé is always vinified as a moelleux wine at the Château du Breuil.

CLAUDE PAPIN, Domaine de Pierre-Bise, Beaulieu-sur-Layon. Claude Papin is an enthusiast, one might even say a fanatic, about his wines. On the day of my visit to his 28-hectare property he was harvesting his Gamay crop; he appeared to be doing this manually and alone; he was stained red from head to foot and his hair was all awry, and would have had no trouble being cast as a Bacchant for a Roman orgy scene.

The Domaine de Pierre-Bise vines are in the communes of Beaulieu-sur-Layon and Rochefort-sur-Loire, and production embraces a whole range of Anjou appellations. As one might expect from such a devotee of the vine, Claude Papin's pride is in his

Coteaux du Layon, of which he makes a little Chaume as well as straightforward Beaulieu, and for which he has been awarded medals at various Concours for every vintage since 1977. Other wines made on the estate include Anjou Rouge from both Gamay and Cabernet, Anjou Blanc Sec from Chenin Blanc, plus a little Sauvignon and/or Chardonnay, Rosé de Loire Sec, Cabernet d'Anjou Rosé, Demi-Sec or Moelleux, and three *méthode champenoise* wines – *brut*, *demi-sec* and red.

Claude and his wife are both from a long line of wine-makers, and share an abiding passion for their way of life. Claude's original plan was to have been involved in more general agriculture, and all his studies were in that direction; when his father retired at the Domaine de Pierre-Bise, Claude came to look at the place and to see what had best be done and has never left the property since.

Papin is very traditional in his approach to wine-making, but is quick to apply his considerable oenological expertise to any aspect of the process. For example, the champagnisation of his sparkling wines used to be undertaken by a firm in Saumur; he was less than satisfied with the standard of the end product, and now the whole operation is carried out here at Pierre-Bise. Claude also believes very strongly in the importance of micro-climate and the influence of different soils. In the Beaulieu vineyard, for instance, there are two sections a mere 200 metres apart, which give Chenins Blancs imparting totally different flavours to the wine. We tasted the 1985 vintage from both parts, for Papin vinifies and sells them completely separately. The first wine was from a section of the vineyard called Les Soucheries, and had a very distinctive smell and taste of wild mint, whilst the second, Le Chêne Galant, had a richer, dried-fruit taste and was much stronger in alcohol – a totally different wine, vinified and bottled in exactly the same way by the same person, from the wine of Les Soucheries only a stone's throw away.

After the tour of the vineyard and the lovely countryside of the Layon Valley, with which the Papins are obviously totally in love, we retired to their kitchen and tasted their 1985 Coteaux du Layon Chaume; this was a beautiful, pale golden wine with a bouquet that was as yet unopened; it had a lovely honeyed, complex taste, fine and with a great deal of class and length. We talked long and widely as the shadows lengthened, of wine, men, history, the quality of life and the importance of friends. I felt very much at ease with this delightful

pair, and I trust that I didn't overstay my welcome.

There is a note in my tasting book between the 1985 Chaume and the last bottle, which reads 'Phoned M. Tijou, changed appointment to 11.00 tomorrow.' I remember making this call for two reasons: firstly, I was unwilling to break the spell of that evening, and secondly Claude Papin had brought forth a bottle of 1952 Chaume from Mme Papin's family property in nearby St Aubin-de-Luigné. This was an interesting treat; it had a dark golden-syrup colour, and a superb nose in which I distinctly picked out quince, honey and tobacco; the quince and tobacco came out in the taste, and the wine, though delicious, was probably approaching the autumn of its life.

All in all a most enjoyable visit. The Papins sell around 70% of their varied production to private customers, and a little to a *cave spécialiste* in Rennes. Luckily for us British, and also for the Belgians and the Dutch, the rest is exported.

PIERRE-YVES TIJOU, Domaine de la Soucherie, Beaulieu-sur-Layon. Pierre-Yves Tijou of the Domaine de la Soucherie in the commune of Beaulieu-sur-Layon has one of the neatest, most well-ordered properties in the valley. His lovely old Virginia creeper clad house, the immaculately tended vines, the grassy terrace overlooking the valley bottom, where the Layon winds its sleepy course, the spotless vat-house and the cool, newly built ageing cellar – all combine to give an impression of peace, care and order.

Tijou is of pure Layon stock, though his father only bought the Domaine de la Soucherie from the Duc de Brissac as recently as 1952. We talked of the difficulties inherent in making and selling fine Coteaux du Layon; Pierre-Yves Tijou feels that the taste for sweet wines is now on the ascendant once more, and reminded me that before the First World War the Layon wines were more fashionable, and more expensive, than Sauternes. It is surely an indication of some kind of renaissance for *vins moelleux*, when a major quality food chain like Sainsbury's in England ship Coteaux du Layon, which they buy from Tijou, to include in their Vintage Selection promotion.

Even with prestige importers like this it is difficult, if not impossible, to live by Coteaux du Layon alone. Tijou grows the usual gamut of varieties on his 35 hectares, from which he makes the whole range of Anjou wines, red, rosé, white and *méthode champenoise.* He makes three grades of Coteaux du Layon – standard, Chaume and Vieilles Vignes; for the standard blend, the grapes are not always picked in a succession of *tris,* but for the Chaume and the Vieilles Vignes wines the pickers will go through the vineyard three and sometimes four times, selecting only the ripest fruit and the bunches touched by the *pourriture noble.* All the wines are bottled on the premises, and the Coteaux du Layon is stored in the new underground cellar to age for a period in bottle before it is released. M. Tijou took me down into this cellar, where he also has a tasting-room for his private clientèle. We tasted an Anjou Blanc Sec and a Cabernet d'Anjou Rosé, both of which were clean, well made wines of unexceptionable quality.

We then looked at three Coteaux du Layon wines. The first was a Chaume 1985, a vintage which Tijou is particularly excited about. He showed me several newspaper cuttings of a visit by officials of the INAO, who recorded an incredible 20° in the must, a degree which is not seen more than once in a decade or more. The last time such a high degree was recorded at La Soucherie, Pierre-Yves' father registered an even more amazing 23° in 1959. The '85 had a light gold colour and a rich, ripe nose; in the mouth there was an extraordinary concentration of dried-fruit flavours, a good level of acidity and tremendous length. Next I tasted a straight Coteaux du Layon 1966, which was a nice rich golden colour, and had a

pleasing nose with some richness, but quite understated. A lightish wine, but well made, with some quince and lime-flower there; a little short, but by no means finished.

The Chaume 1971 had a colour similar to the '66, but the nose was more honeyed and pronounced. It was strong in alcohol and rich in ripe fruit flavours with excellent length; it will keep a few years yet.

CHAMP-SUR-LAYON

JACQUES & VINCENT LECOINTRE, Caves de la Pierre Blanche, Champ-sur-Layon. Jacques Lecointre and his son Vincent live in an old *maison noble,* which used to be called Roche-Maillet, on the edge of the village of Champ-sur-Layon. Their vines, which cover nearly 40 hectares, are spread out over the three communes of Champ-sur-Layon, Rablay-sur-Layon and Faye d'Anjou.

Some two-thirds of their total vineyard area is planted with red varieties, and, although some Rosé de Loire and Cabernet d'Anjou Rosé are produced, they are currently making major efforts with red wines both from the two Cabernets and the Gamay. Like almost every grower I met in the *appellation,* however, the Lecointres, father and son, are most proud of their Coteaux du Layon, which represents in

Domaine de la Soucherie

an average year about one-third of their production. Vincent told me that they have four hectares of Chenin Blanc in Rablay-sur-Layon, where he reckons the best conditions for Coteaux du Layon prevail. Here the grapes are hand-picked by successive *tris*.

The quality of the Rablay wine as opposed to a standard *non-tri* Coteaux du Layon was immediately apparent when we tasted one against the other. The *ordinaire* had very nice fruit on the nose, and was agreeable but fairly simple on the palate, with a nice balance of acidity; the Rablay wine, on the other hand, was far more closed and reserved on nose and palate, but had tremendous complexity and concentration of under-developed fruit and aromas which will evolve in to a great bottle of *vin liquoreux* with the passage of years.

Vincent Lecointre is a very keen and able young wine-maker, and a great enthusiast. He is a member of the Club des Layon Villages, which has its offices in the Mairie at Beaulieu; to qualify for membership a grower must have made at least ten *déclarations de récolte* in one or more of the seven villages, and the aim of the club is to exchange ideas and promote the wines of the Coteaux du Layon Villages. Their official guide to the characteristics of each commune's wine is helpful, but in parts waxes almost too poetic; if you are ever offered a glass of Coteaux du Layon said to have 'a nose that opens up like a peacock's tail', you can astound your friends by immediately indentifying its birthplace as St Aubin-de-Luigné; if another wine appears to be 'as sound as 100-year-old oak trees', then it must be from Rablay. Could it be that a Lecointre had a hand in the compilation of these notes?

ROCHEFORT-SUR-LOIRE

HENRI ROCHAIS, Château de Plaisance, Rochefort-sur-Loire. The Château de Plaisance occupies a commanding position on the high ground above Rochefort-sur-Loire, just off the by-road that leads down to the Quarts de Chaume vineyards. Henri Rochais and his son make very fine Coteaux du Layon Chaume from their 18-hectare estate. They also produce some nice Anjou Blanc Sec, a little red and rosé and some *méthode champenoise*, which is made for them in the cellars of Langlois-Chateau in St Hilaire-St Florent. But this is Coteaux du Layon country, and it is by

these wines that Plaisance should be and is judged. The Château Plaisance, Coteaux du Layon Chaume is exported throughout Europe and to the United States; it is to be found on the wine lists of the better restaurants, both locally and in the capital, and is sold in Paris by Stephen Spurrier at the Caves de la Madeleine. Rochais also sells some wine in bulk to *négociants*, as well as operating a thriving business with private customers who buy his wines in bottle and in cubitainer. Proof of the quality is also shown by the many medals that Rochais wines have won, mostly at the Concours Général Agricole de Paris, in an almost unbroken line going back to 1909.

We sat in Rochais' office on a very hot October afternoon, and tasted half-a-dozen vintages of his Chaume.

Tasted: 1985. Pale greeny gold. Rich quincy-mincy nose. Lots of fresh, ripe fruit with good acid balance. Long aftertaste. Will be superb.
1980. Good light gold. Bouquet clean, good and fruity, but not very assertive or exciting. A bit dull and short, with not much fruit or character. Rochais said it was going through an awkward adolescence, and would be better in a year or two.

Vineyards in Coteaux du Layon

1984. Fruit and beeswax on the nose, and a normal greeny-gold young colour. Less richness, fruit and complexity than the 1985, but Rochais said it was just starting the downhill path to its resting period, before emerging in full glory.

1975. Colour beginning to go a deeper gold. Quincy, dried fruits and apricots really showing powerfully on the nose. All these flavours very evident and aromatic in the mouth, with tremendous length.

1969. Quite a syrupy colour. Beeswax and honey bouquet. Very rich and concentrated Christmas pudding in the mouth. Perfect now.

1976. Rich, deep gold. Really rich, aromatic and spicy on the nose. A beautiful explosion of flavour, with quince, apricots and honey. Complex and long. The best yet.

I thank Henri Rochais and his son for their time, trouble and a really interesting tasting; this showed me clearly something I had been noticing wherever I tasted good wines from the Chenin Blanc, especially *demi-secs* or *moelleux*. They can be most appealing and fresh in extreme youth, and then, after a year in bottle, they go through an adolescent period of dumb insolence, giving nothing, until they emerge after a varying number of years to show their true colours.

APPELLATION: QUARTS DE CHAUME

'Small is beautiful' goes the saying, and Quarts de Chaume is both. This is one of two *super-appellations* of the Coteaux du Layon, the other and larger one being Bonnezeaux. A total of only 45 hectares may be planted with Chenin Blanc to produce this rare and highly prized *vin liquoreux*. The designated area is on four ridges that extend southwards from Chaume down into the Layon Valley, rather like the four fingers of a curved hand. The plateau that encircles these ridges gives them a special micro-climate, protected from all but the gentle south wind and giving maximum exposure to the sun's rays. This ensures the best ripening conditions; the soil, with its higher-than-average hard schist content, gives the wine that special 'green spine' that seems to run through the taste and bouquet, giving it a very slight bitterness in spite of its incredible rich sweet splendour.

The permitted yield of 22 hectolitres per hectare is smaller than for the rest of Coteaux du Layon, smaller, in fact, than that prescribed for Sauternes. All Quarts de Chaume is made from hand-picked grapes, and the pickers will usually make three *tris*, and sometimes four; only the very ripest grapes are used, and, whenever the conditions are right for its development, the noble rot is keenly sought after. It is not unusual for the harvest to continue well into November, and it is hardly surprising that the end product is rather expensive, though not, in my opinion, overpriced by a single *sou*! When I visited the vineyards with Jean Baumard on the 9th October 1986, the first *tri* was being made, the weather was perfect, and the incidence of *pourriture noble* was high and well-advanced; 1986 could well be a special year for Quarts de Chaume, though this would be against the law of averages; here, as with the rest of the *appellations* where the Chenin Blanc is turned into great dessert wines, they are lucky to have one great vintage in ten, and 1985 was one such year.

Only nine growers have the right to the Quarts de Chaume *appellation*, though in times past they would probably have preferred to have vines on less favoured ground; the name Quarts de Chaume relates to a mediaeval tax imposed by the local landlord, the Seigneur de la Guerche, whereby he took a quarter of the wine made in the parish of Chaume each year – and curiously enough he always chose the wine from this particular quarter!

Of the total 45 hectares, 17 belong to Jacques Lalanne of Château Belle Rive, 17 to the Laffourcades of Château de l'Echarderie and Château de Suronde, and 6 to Jean Baumard, the remaining 5 hectares being split between six growers.

JEAN BAUMARD, Logis de la Giraudière, Rochefort-sur-Loire. I paid a visit to the delightful Jean Baumard at his lovely house, the Logis de la Giraudière in Rochefort-sur-Loire. As I have said before, if a grower makes a multitude of different sorts of wine and amongst those wines is a *vin doux*, it is always the favourite child of his vinous family. If that *vin doux* happens to be Quarts de Chaume, then this is doubly true, and the owner positively beams with paternal pride. Such is the case with Jean Baumard, for he has 32 hectares in production, of which only 6 are in Quarts de Chaume.

The major part of his vines are across the Loire in Savennières, where he has a total of 15 hectares, of which 11 are currently in production. Savennières also tends to become the owner's lover, for different reasons, but I do not propose to dwell here on this *appellation*, for it has a corner of its own in this book. Baumard also grows 5 hectares of Cabernet for red wine and sparkling rosé, which he makes extremely well; he grows about 3 hectares of Chardonnay, some of which are used in the make-up of his Crémant de Loire, a new venture in 1986. The rest of his vines are Chenin Blanc in the Coteaux du Layon *appellation*.

In the hallway of the elegant eighteenth-century *logis* are some beautiful and recently uncovered murals of fruit-picking and vintage scenes that must date from the construction of the house. It was here that Jean Baumard gave me a tasting of four vintages of his Savennières – 1985, 1984, 1982 and 1981 – from the two vineyards of Clos du Papillon and Clos St Yves. All were extremely fine examples of this most beautiful of dry Chenin Blanc wines; the '85 was still very closed up, the '84 beginning to show very well, the '82 the roundest, fattest and readiest of the four, and the '81 was just beginning to show what a good Savenniers is all about once it has had a few years in bottle. We then proceeded to the treat I had been waiting for – my first taste of Quarts de Chaume. First Jean Baumard opened a bottle of the 1984 – it had a very pale, golden colour, and the nose was almost entirely closed, giving only a hint of the bounty that was to follow; in the mouth there was an enormous concentration of nobly-rotten fruit, with great length and huge potential.

Then he kindly opened a bottle of his 1967 – not a great year, as he modestly pointed out, but it was interesting to see how once more these Chenin Blancs, even from average vintages, blossom and flower after a few years in the cellar. The colour of this one was of wheat-straw, and it had a real 'peacock's tail' of a nose, with ripe fruit, flowers, beeswax and honey; the multiple flavours released in the mouth were so varied and complex that I could only identify a few – apricot, vanilla, quince, raisin and sultana were all there, and the aftertaste went on forever. A really excellent wine.

APPELLATION: BONNEZEAUX

Larger than its fellow *super-appellation*, Quarts de Chaume, Bonnezeaux is quite undeservedly less well-known. The area entitled to the name lies on three high, south-south-west facing plateaux to the north-east of the small town of Thouarcé. The soil is similar to that of the Quarts de Chaume, Chenin Blanc is also the only permitted grape and the exposure of the vineyards and the vinification are the same; the only significant difference is that the Bonnezeaux vineyards are less sheltered, making a perfect *arrière-saison* even more imperative for the production of Bonnezeaux. In the all-too-frequent vintages when Bonnezeaux cannot be made, the wine is either vinified as straight Coteaux du Layon, or as Anjou Blanc Sec. Due to this dependence on the rare years like 1985, 1976, 1964 and 1959, Bonnezeaux is almost always made along with other Anjou wines, white, rosé and red, still and sparkling.

The existence of Bonnezeaux as an *appellation* pre-dates Quarts de Chaume by three years, the former being created in 1951, the latter in 1954. Fine sweet wines from the Chenin Blanc have been made in the area for far longer, regardless of what they may have been called. Superb bottles from last century still exist in the cellars of growers like Jacques Boivin. The archives of his Château de Fesles contain a reference to the *vin exquis* of the Cru Bonnezeaux as early as 1070, though neither the type nor the colour are specified. A further reference to Bonnezeaux, giving clear proof of its quality in past centuries, is to be found in a letter dated 1789 from the Abbé de Bonneval to his merchant. He orders three hundred bottles of the 1788 Bonnezeaux, stating that he has heard that it was an excellent vintage in this canton. As a post-script, he suggests that a second barrel be despatched, since the wine is so good that the waggoner may drink the first one on the way. I do not see the logic; if one barrel is too good to resist, surely the second will go the same way?

JACQUES BOIVIN, Château de Fesles.
Jacques Boivin at Château de Fesles is certainly one of the major producers of Bonnezeaux, and 50% of his wines are exported all over the world. He has some 33 hectares of vines which are divided into two distinct sections: the south-facing slopes, or *coteaux*, are planted with the white varieties, mainly Chenin Blanc, plus a little Chardonnay for inclusion in the Anjou Blanc Sec, and for making Vin de Pays du Jardin de la France, and the plateau, where the clay-silex soil is better suited to the red varieties, Cabernets, Gamay and Grolleau.

M Boivin in his tasting-room at Château de Fesles

Yield at the Château de Fesles is low, especially for the Bonnezeaux, resulting from severe pruning and very strict selection, both at vintage time and in the cellar. Picking is still done by hand, even for the red varieties; for the grapes destined for the Bonnezeaux, the *vendangeurs* will pass through the vines three or even four times, picking only the grapes that are super-ripe or affected by *pourriture noble*. Even in good years, Boivin only declares part of his Chenin Blanc crop as Bonnezeaux, since yield is so low and the wine so expensive to make that economic pressures demand that he vinify a portion as the more abundant Coteaux du Layon or Anjou Blanc Sec.

Château de Fesles is a masterpiece of adaptation. Boivin is a great respecter of tradition and style; he has installed all the latest equipment for efficient vinification of his 'bread and butter' wines, but equipment has been altered to fit into the original buildings rather than the other way round. The result is an unchanged, harmonious exterior, with an up-to-date vinification plant hidden inside. If the balance sheet did not demand the making of reds, whites and rosés, little alteration of any kind would be necessary at Château de Fesles, since vinification for the Bonnezeaux wine has not basically changed for a hundred years. Fermentation is still carried out in oak casks, a long process that often lasts into January. Bottling is done soon after the fermentation process is finished, and all ageing takes place in bottle.

Jacques and his wife live in a creeper-clad cottage attached to the wine-making buildings, the main château being still occupied by his parents. It was in the comfortable living-room of their cottage that they gave me a tasting of four of their wines.

The first wine was their 1985 Anjou Blanc Sec, which was the best example of the genre that I tasted in my entire travels; light, bright golden in colour, it had a fresh but restrained bouquet. In the mouth, the wine was pleasingly fruity with a high level of acidity, made supple and charming by the Chardonnay influence.

We looked next at a 1983 Anjou Rouge, made from a 50/50 mixture of Cabernet Franc and Cabernet Sauvignon; a lovely deep red colour, with a typical Cabernet *cassis* bouquet – a nice, well-balanced wine, very agreeable to drink now, with a good long aftertaste.

Now to business! The 1985 Château de Fesles Bonnezeaux was produced; the lovely medium gold colour was a shade darker than any of the straight Coteaux du Layons of this vintage I had seen. The bouquet was quite muted, but Boivin said that it had been more open, and that the wine was starting its 'hibernation' period. Ripe fruits, honey and quince were present in the mouth, but all in a concentrated and undeveloped form. This will be a real stunner in the mid-1990s and way beyond.

Then Jacques magnanimously brought forth a bottle of his fabled 1947, perhaps the greatest vintage of this century for old Chenin Blanc wines. Although at the time of making this would only have been allowed the name Anjou Blanc, this was unquestionably Bonnezeaux, and served to give one some idea how the marvellous dessert wines of the *appellation* can age and evolve over almost unbelievably long periods. The colour was a deep, treacly gold, the nose rich and ripe, with an almost roasted concentration of spicy, peppery dried fruits; multiple rich flavours opened up in the mouth – raisins, sultanas, apricots and honey. Astoundingly long aftertaste – a great, even a classic *vin liquoreux*.

RENÉ RENOU, Thouarcé. I also paid a very brief visit to the premises of René Renou in Thouarcé. Renou, President of the Syndicat des Vins de Bonnezeaux, is very much involved in the vinous affairs of the Coteaux du Layon, and runs his wine business, as well as a thriving estate agency, from offices and cellars in the rather grandly named Place du Champ de Foire in Thouarcé. In spite of numerous attempts, both in person and over the telephone, I never managed to meet up with him, though I did meet his charming and hard-working wife as she was preparing supper for the grape-pickers.

She kindly gave me a taste of the Bonnezeaux, Domaine de la Croix Mission 1985; this wine won a gold medal at the Concours organised by CIVAS. It was extremely well made, and will undoubtedly make a superb bottle in years to come, though I thought it lacked the complexity and class of the Château de Fesles wine.

As a gastronomic footnote, I would add that the natives of the Coteaux du Layon like to drink their sweet wines either as an aperitif, which in this part of the world can be taken at any time of the day when friends meet, or with *foie gras*, blue-veined cheese, or with fish, veal or poultry in a cream sauce. Like their colleagues in Sauternes, they are almost universal in their condemnation of the barbarous custom of drinking them with very rich desserts.

APPELLATION: SAVENNIÈRES

It would be fair to say that Savennières hides its light under a bushel. In this tiny *appellation* are made dry white wines from the Chenin Blanc which have more class and certainly more ageing potential than any other dry wine in the Loire Valley. One could go further than that if one is talking of the wine of Coulée de Serrant, for more than one pundit has put this extraordinary wine amongst the top half-dozen white wines of the world.

The life of a grower in Savennières is not easy, and it is not entirely coincidental that there appears to be an unusually high proportion of lady owners in the *appellation*; the making of Savennières from the tricky Chenin Blanc in this dangerously frost-prone corner is too uncertain a game for a family to rely totally upon, so frequently the man of the family has an entirely separate occupation while the wife runs the wine business. It is not merely a question of the caprice of the Chenin and the unpredictable micro-climate that makes this such a difficult wine; in times past, before the *appellation* was created, the wines here were vinified as sweet wines, resulting in an extremely low maximum permitted yield being stipulated by the INAO. Until very recently, only 25 hectolitres per hectare were allowed, though this has been raised to a still-too-low 30.

As happens with the difficult and frequently non-viable sweet wines like the Coteaux du Layon, Moelleux Vouvray, Quarts de Chaume and Bonnezeaux, the superb dry Savennières are often subsidised by the production of less-demanding *appellations*; the fine Clos de Papillon and Clos de St Yves of Jean Baumard's property form only a small part of his vinous activities, the Soulez brothers at the Château de Chamboreau make red wine as well as their fabulous Savennières, and even Madame Joly and her son Nicolas are producing a Cabernet Anjou red to help bolster the economy of the Château de la Roche-aux-Moines and the fabled Clos de la Coulée de Serrant.

Situated on the north bank of the Loire in the most northerly of the wine-making regions of Anjou, the 60 hectares of AC Savennières vineyards are to be found on the south-facing slopes behind and to the east of the village. The soil is for the most part a volcanic schist, which accounts for the very special *goût de terroir* which characterises Savennières; the terrain is in places so steep that tractors cannot be used, yet another reason for only 60 of the total 240 permitted hectares of the *appellation* being planted.

Within the Savennières *appellation*, there are three separate AC wines entitled to the name – Savennières, Savennières La Roche aux Moines and Savennières Coulée de Serrant. The last two are the Bentley and Rolls Royce of Savennières, and are made on slopes to the north-east of the village on the river road that leads through Bouchemaine to Angers, a dozen miles away.

The wines of Savennières are a delight, and will be a revelation to most people, as they were to me; bone dry, they are delicious when drunk within the first twelve months after the vintage, but when they are well made they are best left for four or five years, when they will have developed the most extraordinary aromatic finesse. They are best with fish, and one of the most sublime marriages of food and wine I can remember was solemnised at the Auberge Jeanne de Lavalle in Les Rosiers-sur-Loire; the late M. Augereau, brilliant chef and kindly host, officiated, the bride was a blushing pink Loire Salmon dressed in a Sauce Beurre Blanc, and the handsome groom was a bottle of Savennières, Coulée de Serrant 1976.

A C SAVENNIÈRES, COULÉE DE SERRANT

MME DENISE JOLY & M. NICOLAS JOLY, Château de la Roche aux Moines, Savennières. The history of the Coulée de Serrant and Roche-aux-Moines are inextricably bound together. In the thirteenth century a fortified castle was built, rather against the wishes of the peace-loving monks of St Nicolas d'Angers who had lived there since about 1063. It later withstood several hard sieges, including one mounted in 1214 by King John of England; his defeat here by Louis, son of Philippe-Auguste, king of France, and then a few days later at Bouvines marked the end of the Plantagenet ownership of Anjou. To this day, the long walk from the present house to the terrace overlooking the vineyards is known as the Cimetière des Anglais.

The original fortress was dismantled in the late sixteenth century, victim of the religious wars of the time, and now only a few ruins remain in the section of the vineyard called Le Clos du Château. There have been several changes of ownership this century and the present proprietor, Madame Joly, bought the property in 1960; since then she has done tremendous work for both her own vineyard's quality and reputation and for the good of the Savennières *appellation* as a whole. Her son Nicolas, an MBA alumnus of Columbia University Business School, is now very actively involved with the running of the estate.

Since 1985 the vineyard has been managed under the 'biodynamic' system evolved by Rudolph Steiner in Germany and Switzerland. This ensures that no undue strain is placed upon the soil or the vines by the use of chemical fertilisers, weedkillers or systemic fungicides or insecticides. Three different treatments are used, three times a year – one to improve the nutrition and function of the soil, one to carry this nutrition to the vines and the third to reinforce the benefits of the sun's rays to the vines and the fruit. All three treatments are homeopathic, and are used in minute quantities of only a few grammes in 25 or 30 litres of water per hectare. 'Biodynamism' also demands that the soil only be ploughed or hoed when the phases of the moon and the constellations are in certain specified juxtapositions. When these principles are followed, the soil continues year after year to support and nourish healthy vines, which in turn bring forth healthy fruit. If modern viticulture is

Coulée de Serrant in Savennières

employed, with almost indiscriminate use of artificial fertilisers and chemical treatments, the soil becomes totally exhausted, and the structure of plants and fruit impaired and even poisoned. This, at any rate, is the Steiner theory, and it does not seem altogether unreasonable.

Apart from a passionate belief in the merits of 'biodynamics', Nicolas Joly ensures that the vinification of his wines also follows the most natural course possible. Fermentation of Coulée de Serrant and Château de la Roche-aux-Moines takes place in small wooden barrels, no added yeasts are used, no cold treatment, no fining by bentonite and no harsh filtration.

Biodynamics and natural vinification, allied to the extreme difficulty of working the slopes of a vineyard where only man and horse can tread, severe pruning and ultra-strict selection at every stage make for tiny yields from a small property; La Coulée de Serrant can never be a cheap wine. The Jolys have one great plus when it comes to pricing their wine, however; they own the entire *appellation* of Coulée de Serrant, which allows them to fix a fair and proper price for one of the world's most sought-after wines without fear of undercutting.

The wine of Coulée de Serrant has a place in history, and in the literature of wine and gastronomy.

It was drunk and admired by Louis XIV and was later a great favourite of Napoleon's Empress Josephine, to whom the Comtesse de Serrant just happened to be Lady-in-Waiting. The great gastronomist, Curnonsky, placed it firmly with Château Grillet, Château Chalon, Château d'Yquem and Le Montrachet as among the five best white wines of France. Dumas has d'Artagnan demanding if an innkeeper has a few bottles of it tucked away in his cellar, and J.-F. Bodin sums up its quality and rarity, writing in 1823, 'Parfum exquis de fleurs, de fruits murs ou de miel, chair, sève, ampleur, tout est harmonie et perfection. La Coulée de Serrant est si renommée et le clos qui le produit est si petit qu'il est bien difficile de s'en procurer.'

Nicolas Joly kindly opened a bottle of the 1976, which was quite naturally unlike anything in my tasting experience. It had a lovely deep golden colour, and a superb nose of ripe fruit, heady and honeyed. All the fruit, honey and flowers were released in the mouth, yet the wine was completely dry, with tremendous delicacy and length. On looking back to the last paragraph, Monsieur Bodin expressed the sensations engendered by La Coulée de Serrant far better than I, and every word he used 160-odd years ago holds good today.

AC SAVENNIÈRES, LA ROCHE AUX MOINES

MME J.-F. LAROCHE, Domaine aux Moines, Savennières. Just up the road from the gates of the Château de la Roche aux Moines lies the lovely eighteenth-century Domaine aux Moines, built in 1766 as a residence for the abbot of the Abbaye de St Nicolas d'Angers. There have in all likelihood been vines grown here as long as at the neighbouring Château, since both were monastic properties since the eleventh century, and the good monks were never slow to recognise the viticultural potential of a piece of land; wine was needed for sacramental purposes, and weary travellers and pilgrims needed refreshment, to say nothing of the good brothers themselves.

Mme Laroche, gentle, kindly, yet evidently extremely capable, runs the wine-making with the same attention to detail that she clearly gives to the house and grounds. Her husband, Maître J.-F. Laroche, is a *notaire* in Angers, and the day-to-day running of the vineyard, as well as vinification and

sales, are all in her hands. She has been at the Domaine aux Moines for five years, but is a native of Savennières. There are currently 5 productive hectares, but the total area will eventually be increased to 10. She is a passionate believer in the quality and individuality of Savennières wines; recent moves among local growers to be allowed a percentage of Chardonnay and Sauvignon to tone down the awkward nature of Savennières in youth meet with her total disapproval. Vinification is very traditional; there is one press, and only four pressings are done per day during the vintage; the wine goes into a large vat for 12 hours, and then into wooden *fûts* for fermentation. After a long, slow fermentation, the wine goes back into the large vats for blending, and is then returned to the wooden casks for a further month before bottling, which usually takes place between March and May following the vintage.

The resulting wine is Savennières, La Roche-aux-Moines of very high quality; the 1982 was chosen for sale by auction to celebrate the 30th anniversary of the creation of the *appellation*. Production is limited by size and circumstance to around 1,000 cases per year, and of this nearly half is exported to Canada which makes expansion difficult until the remaining 5 hectares come into production. When more wine is available, I shall certainly pay Mme Laroche a further visit, though I shall be wearing my wine-buyer's hat on that occasion.

I was given a taste of the 1985, which had a pale greeny-gold colour, and a very perfumed bouquet of ripe fruit; it was very long in the mouth with excellent fruit, still very green with quite high acidity. I should like to taste again in four or five years, when I should think it will be marvellous.

This wine was followed by the 1984, which had more gold and less green in the colour; the nose was less assertive, but had definite honey hints. The wine being one year older and perhaps a faster developing vintage, was considerably more forthcoming in the mouth, with good fruit and suggestions of the quincy character of the Chenin Blanc; excellent now, and will get even better.

AC SAVENNIERES

MME DE JESSEY, Domaine du Closel, Savennières. Madame de Jessey is a large and cheerful lady, yet one more of the able band of distaff wine-makers of Savennières. The Domaine du Closel is an old family property, nicely situated in a park full of what the estate agents often call 'mature specimen trees', hidden by a high wall from the village green.

The house was bought by Madame de Jessey's great-great-grandfather, the Marquis de Las Cases, who accompanied Napoleon into exile on St Helena in order to write his biography; it was with the proceeds from this work, entitled *Memorial*, that the Domaine du Closel was acquired. This was my second encounter with the Marquis; our paths crossed when I was writing the history of Château Léoville-Las-Cases for my book on Bordeaux.

I spent the afternoon with M. de Jessey, a successful civil engineer who has now retired and devotes much of his time to helping his wife run the wine business. They currently have 12 hectares planted with Chenin Blanc, with the possibility of planting a further three or four; they also have three hectares planted with Cabernet, which will be entitled to the new *appellation* for red wines, Anjou Villages; this is all aged in wood. Vinification of the white Savennières used to be done in wood, but the volume of production has expanded so much that there is no longer room for all the casks, so fermentation now takes place in horizontally placed cylindrical vats. There is no special secret in the vats being on their sides rather than in the more usual vertical position other than the extremely low ceilings of the vat-house. Like most producers of Savennières, the Jesseys have an extremely active export market, selling between 75% and 80% of their wines overseas; Belgium and Denmark are large importers, as are the United Kingdom and the United States of America.

YVES SOULEZ, Château de Chamboureau, Savennières.

Yves Soulez runs the family business at Château de Chamboureau; he took over the family vineyards in 1987, which comprise 10 hectares; 3.7 hectares are in the Savennières, La Roche-aux-Moines *appellation*, with a further 1.3 hectares recently planted. In 1982 Soulez also took over the important wine estate of the Domaine de la Bizolière; this added another 15 hectares to his vineyard, and there is also the possibility of extending the surface under vines at La Bizolière to a total 40 hectares; this is being carried out at the rate of 5 hectares per year. There are also a few hectares planted for red wine, of which half are

given over to Cabernet Franc and half to Cabernet Sauvignon.

Yves Soulez is an innovative oenologist, and has made several experiments with the vinification techniques for Savennières over the past few years. The formula which he finds best suited to the production of his kind of Savennières starts in the vineyard; contrary to most growers of the Chenin Blanc, he picks by machine, having found that with the speed of the mechanical harvester, he is able to pick individual plots of vines at exactly their optimum moment of maturity. The grapes are then rushed to the *pressoir* with the minimum of delay to avoid any risk of oxidation. Fermentation is in vat, contrary, once more, to local custom; he used to ferment in the traditional wooden *fûts*, but now finds that the best balance of *goût de terroir* and Chenin taste and aromas results from fermentation at between 22° and 24°C in a large volume and a maceration period of about 10 days. He has also found that if all his wine goes through the malo-lactic fermentation, this lowers the acidity and consequently impairs the keeping quality of the wine. His solution is to allow only part of the crop to undergo the 'malo', and blend both parts together at the *assemblage*.

Commercialisation of the Soulez wines is nicely balanced; 40% is sold to the restaurant trade in France, mostly locally, in Paris and in Brittany, 20% goes to private customers and the rest is exported. By far the biggest importers are Great Britain, with 50% of his export sales, where the quality of his wines can be judged by the list of importing companies such as Robin Yapp, The Wine Society, Adnams of Suffolk and Lay & Wheeler of Colchester. Other importing countries include Japan, Belgium, Germany, Canada and, depending on the strength of the dollar, the United States of America.

Tasted: Domaine de la Bizolière 1985. Greeny gold colour; the bouquet was fresh with some greenness about it, and a hint of pear-drops. Clean and fresh in the mouth, with high acidity and good length, with lots of fruit. *Château de Chamboureau 1985.* Same greeny gold colour, softer on the nose. Much softer and finer in the mouth, lower acidity. A more fleshy wine with long aftertaste. Chenin! *Roche-Aux Moines 1985.* Slightly darker colour than the preceding wines. Nose rich and inviting, with some quince. A fatter wine with more structure and class; great length and tremendous ageing potential. *Roche-aux Moines 1984*. Medium gold; nose quite astonishingly assertive for a young Chenin wine, with rich, quincy fruit. Right

for current drinking – a little short. *Roche-aux-Moines 1983*. Medium gold, brilliant; nose still quite closed. High acidity, but all fruit and richness present to make a superb bottle. Will go 10 to 20 years!

ANJOU & SAUMUR:
GUIDE TO HOTELS & RESTAURANTS

As I spent my months of research staying at the Hôtel Château de Rochecotte at St Patrice in Touraine, I did not have the occasion to try so many places in Anjou and Saumur.

In the town of Saumur itself, the Restaurant Gambetta in the street of that name (tel: 41.67.66.66) is really excellent. Just 8 km out of Saumur on the D751, you can stay in great comfort in beautiful surroundings at Le Prieuré in Chênehutte-les-Tuffeaux. The extensive wine list contains not only a complete range of the wines of the Loire, but a fine selection of Bordeaux and Burgundies as well. The cuisine is a judicious mixture of 'nouvelle' and traditional, and well worth the *Michelin* star that it carries (tel: 41.67.90.14.). The Prieuré is a member of the Relais et Châteaux, and is also featured in the chapter on that organisation.

Travelling towards Angers on the river road from Saumur, you will pass through Les Rosiers-sur-Loire; my advice is not to pass through, but to time your journey carefully so that you can either lunch or dine at the Auberge Jeanne de Lavalle (tel: 41. 51. 80. 17). I have not been there since M. Claude Augereau died, but I am assured that his talents have been

learned and inherited by his son, who is now in charge in the kitchen. A number of *spécialités de la maison* are listed in *Michelin*, but for my choice the laurels go to Poissons de Loire au Beurre Blanc, accompanied by a good bottle of Savennières, an *appellation* in which the restaurant specialises. There are a number of comfortable rooms in the Auberge, which are infinitely preferable to those in the annexe, Ducs d'Anjou, a building some 200 metres away, somewhat close to the main road.

On my visit to Savennières, Mme Laroche of the Domaine aux Moines kindly recommended me to the small and recently-opened restaurant on the river island of Behuard. I do not recall its name, and it is too new to be in the guide-books; it is, however, the only restaurant in the centre of the tiny village, and offers a simple, well-cooked menu which in warm weather may be eaten in the courtyard in the shade of trellised grape-vines; there is a brief but well-chosen list of local wines.

I was also recommended to the Vert d'Eau, a small restaurant in Angers in the Boulevard G. Dumesnil (tel: 41.48.52.86). I did not have the occasion to sample its wares, but hope to on my next visit.

THE PAYS NANTAIS
CONTENTS

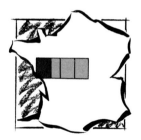

THE PAYS NANTAIS

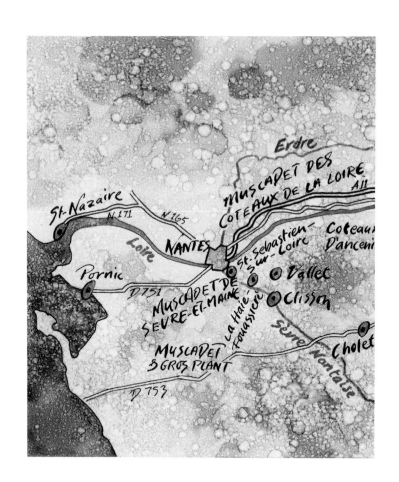

Château de Cassemichère, reputedly the home of Muscadet

The end of our long journey down the Loire brings us to the Pays Nantais, whose vineyards range along the river from Ingrandes in the east to Le Pellerin in the west. The latter is about 20 kilometres from St Nazaire, where the Loire meets the ocean. In this vast vineyard there are three *appellations* and two VDQS wines. The three AC wines are the three forms of Muscadet: Muscadet des Coteaux de la Loire, plain Muscadet and Muscadet de Sèvre et Maine. The two VDQS wines are the Gros Plant du Pays Nantais and the wines of the Coteaux d'Ancenis. The vineyards are on the south bank of the Loire, apart from a small area of the Coteaux d'Ancenis north of the town of Ancenis, part of which is also planted with Gros Plant.

In terms of volume, by far the greatest production is of Muscadet and Gros Plant; between five and eight million cases of Muscadet alone are produced annually, making this the second largest *appellation* in France after Bordeaux Rouge. The Gros Plant production has averaged around two and a half million cases, though indications are that growers are gradually converting to production of Muscadet where their geographic situation allows.

There is much confusion over the meaning and application of the term 'sur Lie' as applied to the wines of the Pays Nantais. The first thing to realise is that it is not an *appellation*, but a vinification process, applied to both the wines of Muscadet and the Gros Plant. To bottle *sur lie* means that the wine must rest on its lees, either in vat or wooden *fût* during the winter following vinification, and that it must be bottled without racking before the 30th June of the next year.

The basic idea behind bottling *sur lie* is to preserve the freshness of the wine as well as a slight 'prickle' of natural CO_2, which is soon lost if the wine is pumped about from vat to vat during the racking process, or if it is too vigorously filtered. The problems arise with the very large volume of Muscadets that are sold through the *négociants*, and do not come from the property of those *négociants*, but are vinified by the grower in a different and sometimes

142

distant part of the *appellation*. The *négociant* will wish to sell the wine with a *sur lie* label, since it will command a higher price. There are now three courses he can adopt. Firstly, he can take a mobile bottling unit to the premises of the grower, in which case a perfectly correct *sur lie* bottling can be effected; secondly he can stipulate bottling by the grower when he buys the wine, thus also ensuring the authenticity of the process; thirdly – and this is when abuses occur – he can have the wine collected from the grower in bulk for bottling on his own premises, which neither conforms to the accepted understanding of *sur lie* bottling, nor does it do any good to the wine, which may lose its freshness and 'prickle', the latter all too often being replaced by pumping CO_2 into the wine in vat.

This is perhaps an over-simplification of the difficulties arising from the *sur lie* process, but I am happy to report that there is a rising tide of protective feeling, particularly among the younger generation of both growers and *négociants*, towards the standards and practices of the *appellation*. Questionable practices in the Pays Nantais, which I am sure nobody would deny have occurred in the past, are definitely on the wane, and the quality of Muscadet in general is on the upswing.

VDQS Coteaux d'Ancenis

The Coteaux d'Ancenis wines are principally red and rosé from the Gamay grape, though a little Chenin Blanc is grown and vinified as a bone dry white; there is also a following for the Malvoisie grape, a white variety not dissimilar to the Tokay d'Alsace, from which a highly perfumed wine is made that may be anything from dry to very sweet. Some of the small production of Coteaux d'Ancenis is channelled through the many *négociant* houses of the locality, but the vast majority is consumed in the area; in common with most of the wines of the Pays Nantais, Coteaux d'Ancenis is fresh, fruity and uncomplicated, a wine to drink and enjoy without too much ceremony.

VDQS Gros Plant du Pays Nantais

Gros Plant is an underrated wine of VDQS quality that may be made almost anywhere that Muscadet is made. I find that it suffers from the 'poor relation' syndrome, at least outside France, in that people tend to think of Gros Plant as an inferior form of Muscadet at nearly the same price. This is to do the wine an injustice, since it is made from an entirely different and unrelated grape variety, and has its own distinctive taste and place in the vinous and gastronomic tapestry of France. Made from the Folle Blanche, a large greenish grape that often resembles a greengage rather than a grape, and which has been rechristened the Gros Plant by the Nantais, who never seem content to leave names as they are. The wine is uncompromisingly dry, and goes particularly well with all kinds of shellfish and crustaceans, a tendency which ensures its continued popularity in this fishy corner of France.

There are some 2,800 hectares of Folle Blanche planted, often alongside the Melon de Bourgogne, from which about 2,000,000 cases are made, most of which is destined to be consumed in north-western France.

Melon de Bourgogne

Decoration in the Château de Cassemichère

MUSCADET: EXPLANATION AND HISTORY OF THE APPELLATION

Perhaps one of the best known wine names – at least for dry whites – in the world, Muscadet can be found on the wine lists of almost every restaurant and wine merchant in the civilised world. Although the dry white wine from the Melon de Bourgogne has been made here since the eighteenth century, it was only known as a good regional wine and most of it was drunk locally until relatively recent times. The first growth period for Muscadet was between the wars, when the Breton coast started to become fashionable for holiday-makers. The crisp, clean, fresh-air-and-sunshine wine was gulped with enjoyment by tourists from all over France with the delicious Breton *fruits de mer*, and its popularity soon spread to the capital and other parts of the country. In the post-war years the tourist industry and the related growth of wine-drinking in the Anglo-Saxon countries has ensured a continuation of this boom, and export now represents a substantial and growing slice of the Muscadet market. In 1984–85 approximately 37% of all sales of Muscadet went abroad, and over half of this mini-lake was imported by the United Kingdom – around 10,000,000 bottles, and still growing!

The early history of wine-making in the Pays Nantais follows pretty much the same pattern as the rest of the Loire Valley, starting with the introduction of the vine by the Romans, continuing with the activities of the monastic foundations and coming under Dutch influence in the seventeenth century; the Dutch were largely responsible for converting the Pays Nantais from a red wine producing area to white, since the wine they were looking for was for distillation purposes. It was in the winter of 1709 that the region's vineyards were all but wiped out by frosts of indescribable severity, and it was from this point that the story of Muscadet really began. Following this disastrous year, the entire *vignoble* was replanted with the Melon de Bourgogne, a white variety from, as the name implies, the Burgundy district. The Melon had already been tried here and found suitable, but it was only now that its cultivation became so widespread. For reasons that are not entirely clear to me, nor to anyone I asked, the good folk of Nantes christened this grape the *muscadet*, and thus the name was born.

The *appellation* dates from 1936, when Muscadet de Sèvre et Maine and Muscadet des Coteaux de Loire were first defined. The more general *appellation* Muscadet followed a year later, in 1937.

APPELLATION: MUSCADET, DES COTEAUX DE LOIRE

As the name implies, this *appellation* covers an area on both banks of the Loire; it is to the north-east of Nantes, and includes the communes of Champtoceaux, Ligné, Ancenis and St Florent-le-Vieil. Its overall dimensions are about the same size as the area covered by the Sèvre et Maine *appellation*, but only 450 hectares are planted with AC vines. The soil here has a higher chalk content, and the wines lack the freshness and finesse of the Sèvre et Maine Muscadets.

APPELLATION: MUSCADET

Created a year after the other two *appellations*, rather as an afterthought, the simple AC Muscadet is applied to wines from a large area, mostly to the south-west of Nantes. The area under AC vines is only about 850 hectares, around a tenth of that of the neighbouring and superior *appellation* of Sèvre et Maine. Permitted yield is higher, and the wine tends to lack the essential *joie-de-vivre* that typifies good Muscadet.

APPELLATION: MUSCADET DE SÈVRE ET MAINE

There are close on 10,000 hectares entitled to the Muscadet *appellation*, and 80% of these are in the premier division of Muscadet de Sèvre et Maine. Some 8,000 hectares, planted mainly with the Melon de Bourgogne, lie in an area south-east of Nantes on either side of the Rivers Sèvre and Maine. The *appellation* is bounded by the communes of Vertou, Le Loroux-Bottereau, Vallet, Clisson and Aigrefeuille-sur-Maine, with La Haie-Fouassière and Saint Fiacre in the centre.

The Sèvre et Maine wines are not only the most important from a volume point of view, they are also the best of the Muscadets. The soil is of two types, both on a subsoil of ancient volcanic origin; the major part is sandy, but there is also some alluvial sandy clay. The whole of the Muscadet vineyard is almost entirely devoid of chalk or limestone, and it is the lightness and acidity of the soil that gives the wines their fresh and appealing character.

This part of the Muscadet *appellation*, and indeed the Pays Nantais in general, is an area of small growers, and the majority of commercialisation, as well as a good part of the vinification, is undertaken by the numerous *négociant* businesses, a number of which are based in and around the small town of Vallet.

LA CHAPELLE-HEULIN

DONATIEN-BAHUAUD, La Chapelle-Heulin. I have started the record of my visits in the Pays Nantais with the large *négociant* company of Donatien-Bahuaud in the village of La Chapelle-Heulin because they lay claims to being in a sense the cradle of Muscadet. This stems from the ownership by the Bahuaud family – my first attempt at pronunciation of this tricky name came out as 'bow-wow' – of the Château de la Cassemichère, where the first Melon de Bourgogne grapes are purported to have been planted in 1740. This may or may not be true – there are certainly other claimants, such as the village called Bourguignon – but there is a tragic little vignette of history associated with the Château de la Cassemichère.

At the time of the French revolution the château was occupied by a noble family called Leloup de la Billais; the father went to the guillotine in January 1794 and his wife and two beautiful daughters suffered the same fate only two months later. The daughters could have been saved, for they were both

In the cellars of Château de Cassemichère

made offers of marriage that would have exempted them. The suitors were not of the blood, however; their proposals were turned down and the two young ladies marched proudly up the scaffold steps. The scene was depicted by the artist Auguste de Bay, and can be seen in the Musée des Beaux Arts in Nantes to this day.

The wine of Château Cassemichère is Muscadet de Sèvre et Maine of the very highest quality. Vinification is carried out at the château rather than at the firm's large winery in the village; wooden *fûts* are used for fermentation, in which the wine rests on its lees pending an unimpeachable *sur lie* bottling in the spring or early summer following the vintage. I tasted the 1985, which was truly delicious, and exactly what one expects of a good Muscadet. More surprising was the bottle of 1980 which their export manager, Jean-Luc Blanchard, opened for me; it was, contrary to my expectations, still fresh and attractive with no hint of fatigue after five years in bottle.

Donatien-Bahuaud is one of the largest *négociant* firms in Muscadet, and, in addition to its own Château de la Cassemichère and other properties, buys in wine from the rest of the Pays Nantais and all the major *appellations* of the Loire Valley. They enjoy a wide distribution of their wines throughout France, and have a healthy share of the export market as well.

They have recently launched a special Cuvée of Muscadet de Sèvre et Maine Sur Lie, which they have christened Le Master de Donatien. This is an extremely well thought-out and professional marketing exercise, and, in addition, the product is excellent, and can do nothing but benefit the *appellation* as a whole. Samples are invited each year from selected growers – for the 1985 blend there were 57 wines chosen from 10 *courtiers*. Each sample submitted must have a guaranteed minimum back-up stock of 100 hectolitres, and from these wines are chosen 17 that will eventually become Le Master. Selection is carried out by a jury of experts, which for the 1985 included four restaurateurs, Jacques Puisais, premier oenologist of France, Jean-Luc Poteau, reputedly the world's most knowledgeable *sommelier*, journalists from the French and English wine press, M. Meyer, President of the Muscadet branch of the INAO, and Charles Eve, an English Master of Wine. The chosen wines are not blended, but are bottled in succession at their optimum moment of maturity; this does mean that purchasers of Le Master will note slight variations in style from time to time, but it also ensures that the wine has always been bottled at the correct moment. Presentation is excellent, and the distinctive silk-screen printed bottles – à la Perrier-Jouet Belle Époque – look very elegant. There has been an extensive PR and advertising campaign to back up this promotion, and it should help the growers of quality Muscadet to take the slice of the dry white wine market that is being opened up by the ever-rising prices of white burgundy, Sancerre and Pouilly Fumé, and which they could so easily and rightfully capture.

Donatien-Bahuaud are very PR-conscious; they have made an audio-visual to show to visitors, with a sound-track in various languages. The visual part is excellent, but it was a pity that the word 'expensive' was used in referring to their comprehensive range of products, rather than the desired 'extensive'.

LA HAIE-FOUASSIÈRE

PIERRE ET JOSEPH LANDRON, Domaine de la Louvetrie, La Haie-Fouassière. Pierre and Joseph Landron are a father and son team whose difference in age and approach combine to make the perfect philosophy for wine-making. Pierre, the father, is a twinkling charmer; he is also a traditionalist and a professional, against all that is for quick profit and corner-cutting. A clear illustration is his opposition to machine harvesting; although their own 22 hectares would more than justify the capital expenditure, he resolutely continues picking by hand, even though it may on paper be 50% more expensive. There are many hidden losses and disadvantages to machine-picking, such as damaged vine-stocks, impurities like twigs, leaves and even snails that find their way into the hopper, and burst grapes which lead to oxidation. Although he admits that there are many gold-medallists who have progressed to the machine, he points out that the majority of the fairs and *concours* are held too early in the year following the vintage for the problems of oxidation to have become evident.

Most of the Landrons' vines are on schistous rock on an excellent slope called the Coteaux du Breil; this soil gives his wines a special character. They make four different Muscadets, all *sur lie*, all de Sèvre et Maine. The basic wine is the Domaine de la Louvetrie, which is from grapes grown on the more sandy soil of the plateau, and lends itself to drinking very young and fresh. They also produce two wines

which depend on outside judgment each year; the Cuvée Concours label is only used when they receive a medal for a particular cuvée, and the Hermine d'Or label is awarded on sample by a committee of growers for each year – samples are tasted blind and marked out of a maximum of 20, and those wines given 16 and above may use the label. Their fourth wine is called Cuvée Prestige, and comes from only a very special section of the Coteaux vineyard, and is bottled in a special 'satinised' bottle.

The Landrons gave me a good cross-section of their wines to taste. We started with the Hermine d'Or 1984; not an easy year in which to obtain any distinction, but this was a very well-made wine; it had a lovely fresh bouquet, unusually perfumed for Muscadet, excellent length and good fruit/acid balance. A very distinct but hard-to-pin-down flavour, which Joseph Landron described as *sauvage*. This was followed by the 1984 Cuvée Prestige, which had a more open nose. In the mouth the wine had more prickle, fruit and richness than the Hermine d'Or, and just a touch of sweetness.

The 1985 Hermine d'Or had a definite pear-drops nose beginning to open out, and the same *bon-bon anglais* taste came out in the mouth. Quite a rich wine for Muscadet, with a very distinct *terroir* that the Landrons say is typical of the Domaine de la Louvetrie wines. Needs a few more months in bottle.

I was most impressed by the quality and elegance of the Landron wines, and by their courtesy and obvious integrity.

LOUIS METAIREAU ET SES VIGNERONS D'ART, Maisdon-sur-Sèvre, La Haie-Fouassière. Metaireau is a rebel, a voice crying in the wilderness. He is a passionate and bellicose defender of the quality and integrity of the wines of Muscadet, and is not afraid to air his views to the press or indeed anyone who will lend an ear. The crusade which provides his main motivation is waged against malpractice on the part of *négociants* regarding the use of the term *sur lie* on their labels. He is right to wage war, and I have no doubt that there are a large number of *sur lie* Muscadets that are less than correct. However, I have visited a number of *négociant* houses who take meticulous care over the use of the term, and only employ it on wines that have either been bottled by the grower, or by themselves in a mobile bottling unit on the grower's premises. My impression of Louis Metaireau is that he is a rugged individualist, a fine wine-maker and a natural-born crusader, and if it wasn't *négociants*, he would be waging war against something or somebody else.

It was his belief in the *appellation* and this very individualism that led him to start some thirty years ago his group of talented and like-minded *vignerons*, with the object of combining as an economic force and by-passing the hated *négociant* system. At the beginning there were only three of them, but they are now nine in number with 100 hectares of vines between them. Each year the nine meet to taste all their wines blind on three separate occasions and at different stages of vinification. In the early tastings they identify and if possible correct errors in vinification, and at the final judgment all the wines are marked, and all those failing to reach a certain level are eliminated, and will not be marketed under the Metaireau label. Thus it is perfectly possible, and not infrequently happens, that a grower will eliminate his own wine.

The proof of the Metaireau pudding was then offered in the form of a blind tasting of five wines. Two were 1984s and the other three 1985s, and two were his own Domaine du Grand Mouton. The point of the exercise was to see if I could pick out the two wines of the lesser year of 1984, which I was totally unable to do. The quality of all the wines was exceptional, and Metaireau was not a little pleased when I placed his own Domaine du Grand Mouton 1984 with supreme confidence as the best wine, and undoubtedly from the 1985 vintage!

With 100 hectares producing Muscadet of this quality, Louis Metaireau and his band of merry men are a force to be reckoned with on the market. Their influence must work to the good of the *appellation* as a whole, and his wines have their ardent supporters in many countries all over the world.

The dry white wine market is wide open for producers of top-quality wine from the Pays Nantais; there is a yawning gap being created by the ever-rising prices of white Burgundy and even Loire *appellations* like Sancerre and Pouilly Fumé, and it is men like Louis Metaireau and Jean-Ernest Sauvion who deserve to fill it.

LE PALLET

M. LUSSEAUD, Château de la Gallissonnière, Le Pallet. Monsieur Lusseaud has 38 hectares of vines grouped around the Château de la Gallissonnière in the village of Le Pallet. His production is almost entirely of Muscadet de Sèvre et Maine, though he also makes good Gros Plant *sur lie* which is sold under the label Cuvée Valerie. M. Lusseaud's wines have long been familiar to me, since he has for many years been a major supplier of International Distillers and Vintners, and I have bought them through the medium of Morgan Furze and the retail chain of Peter Dominic.

He allowed me to taste two or three *cuves* of the 1986, some of which were still fermenting; I was given the opportunity to taste the 1986 in this nascent state by more than one grower, and I did find it extremely difficult to form any kind of judgment. I also tasted a 1986 which had been vinified to be sold as Muscadet Primeur, which had a fresh, amusing fruitiness and was well up to the standard of the half-dozen samples of *primeur* that I looked at the following day at the offices of the CIVOPN.

We then looked at a couple of vat samples of the 1985, which were fruity and easy to taste, but a little short on acidity. Lusseaud then led the way into his tasting room, which is decorated with a veritable museum of old cooperage tools and vineyard equipment, including an incredibly primitive miniature crawler tractor. I tasted the Cuvée Philippe 1985 in bottle, which was much more fine and elegant than the vat sample of '85; another 1985, Cuvée Anne, was less fine than the Philippe, but it was nonetheless fresh and charming. Finally we looked at a red Vin de Pays made from the Cabernet grape, the first red wine that I had tasted in the Muscadet *appellation*; it had a nice nose, which was somewhat reminiscent of raspberries, and in the mouth it was easy and fruity.

Over 80% of the Château de la Gallissonnière wines are exported, and of this by far the largest customer is the United Kingdom. M. Lusseaud also sells to Belgium and Holland, as well as a little in Japan and, more surprisingly, Australia. The name of the château derives from the Admiral of the same name who built the house in 1737; he was eventually killed in a naval battle against the English Admiral Byng. His distinguished service career also included a spell as the garrison commander of Fort Mahon; history tells us that his cook was so frightened one day whilst performing his duties under gunfire that he did something unplanned with a sauce he was making, and thus was born the now ubiquitous Sauce Ma(h)yonnaise. The admiral was an ardent botanist, and planted the wood beside the vineyard with many exotic specimens culled on his long sea voyages, including Japanese walnuts and various species of magnolia. M. Lusseaud's grandparents bought the property in 1912, and had to completely replant the vineyard with grafted Melon de Bourgogne, following its virtual destruction by the phylloxera beetle.

M. LE COMTE DE MALESTROIT, Château la Noë, Vallet.

The Comte de Malestroit is the chatelain at la Noë; erudite and courteous, like all authors, he has had several novels published as well as a book about the region. He is intensely proud of his château, which, he says, is the only real castle in the area. It is certainly an imposing edifice, with its elegant colonnaded facade and lovely orangery. The original château was built in 1660, but was destroyed during the Revolution, and the present house dates from 1836. The estate has a total of 65 hectares of vines, of which de Malestroit runs 32, the rest being en métayage, an ancient system of sharecropping under which the growers pay their rent with a proportion of their harvest. When the present Comte took over from his father 30 years ago, all the wine was sold to the négociants; now all wine-making, bottling and commercialisation is under the direct supervision of the Comte.

Eight-five per cent of the Château la Noë wine is exported, the biggest importers being the firm of J.R. Parkington in England. The Comte also sells some to Japan, Germany and the United States. A little is sold in France through a Parisian distributor, and there is also a small volume of private business.

We took a most enjoyable walk in the grounds of the château, which boasts an English-style garden and ornamental lake, and also commands a magnificent and very un-English view across the Muscadet vineyards. The Comte and Comtesse, who had now joined us, then took me on a brief tour of the vinification buildings, where all was very orderly, traditional rather than hi-tech, though I did notice that the Comte has gone over to picking by machine. He said that he was totally satisfied, and that all that mattered was to have a capable driver, and to keep the machines immaculately clean after each day's work. Fermentation is still in wood, and they do not subscribe to the theory of cold fermentation.

We looked at a cask sample of the 1986, which had just finished fermenting; despite the presence of sulphur, the wine was obviously clean and well-made, good fruit was evident, and the desired amount of CO_2 was there.

Back in the house de Malestroit kindly opened a bottle of his 1985 while we finished our discussions. The wine had a nice pale, greeny gold colour, and the nose was fresh and clean. I found it fat and full-bodied for Muscadet, but this is the style of La Noë; it had enough richness to go well with all fish, even in quite heavy sauces, as well as white meats like chicken and veal.

ANDRÉ VINET, Vallet and Château la Touche.

The négociant firm of André Vinet deals principally in the wines of the Pays Nantais, though they also sell all the other appellations of the Loire, which they buy in bottle; this, they say, is their best guarantee of authenticity. Although 70% of their turnover is represented by sales of Muscadet, they only have one small three-hectare plot of vines themselves; this has been in the family for five generations and is now only made for consumption by family, friends and a few very favoured customers. The Muscadets and Gros Plants that they sell are mostly bought on a regular contract basis from growers whom they have dealt with for years, and in this way they can control quality and vinification from vine to bottle. The flagship of the Domaines that they sell is the Château la Touche, the property of the Boullault family, whom we went to visit.

Monsieur Boullault runs this property with the help of his two sons, one of whom, Frédéric, was there when we arrived. Frédéric is the specialist in vinification. Sole distribution is given to André Vinet, except for a small amount of wine which is commercialised by the Boullault family under the name Domaine des Dorices. At La Touche they make a special Cuvée Grande Garde, which spends eighteen months on its lees; I tasted the '85, the '82 and, incredibly, the 1973. All were exceptionally fine, with considerably more weight than the normal wine; the '73 was particularly interesting in that it had not lost freshness but was beginning to take on the character of an oldish Chardonnay; in addition to their really fine Muscadets, the Boullaults also make good Gros Plant, and a little méthode champenoise is made from the free-run juice, but this is made for them in Saumur. Although it is more of a curiosity than anything else, this Folle de Perle, as it is called, is sold in one restaurant in Belgium and one in Denmark.

After a very enjoyable hour at Château la Touche, Vinet drove back with me to Vallet and he told me a little more about the family business en route. They only export 20% of their wines, of which a little goes to the United Kingdom. Talking of the wines which they buy in bottle from other *appellations*, Vinet told me that one of the major problems of a *négociant* trying to play the honest broker by buying only in bottle, as they did, was the tiny size of most vineyards in the Loire; this meant that they would frequently have to change suppliers for, say, Saumur-Champigny or Chinon in mid-price list, which does not make for easy relations with restaurant customers.

I left Vinet with a bottle of the La Touche sparkling Gros Plant and one of the family Muscadet Sur Lie, Le Perthuis-Fouques, both of which I very much enjoyed back in England, and which brought back memories of a broker who really tries to get things right.

GUILBAUD FRÈRES, Mouzillon, Vallet.

My visit to Guilbaud Frères in Mouzillon was yet another in a chain of similar meetings; I have shipped Guilbaud's Muscadet de Sèvre et Maine Sur Lie, through my friend Geoffrey Vale in England, for more years than I care to remember, and it was a real pleasure to meet at last with the owners of the Domaine de la Moutonnière.

Pascal Guilbaud turned out to be as good as his wines, which is saying something, and proved of invaluable help to me in my researches. He not only gave me a tasting of all his own firm's wines, but went with me himself to visit several of his regular suppliers, and also gave me an introduction to the *courtier* André Luneau. Both Luneau and Guilbaud were real friends to me, and I would like to thank them both once more.

Guilbaud Frères are substantial growers and *négociants*. Aside from buying in wines on a more or less regular basis from growers all over the Pays Nantais, the Guilbauds' own vineyards include the Domaine de la Moutonnière and the Domaine de la Pingossière, from both of which they produce fine Muscadet de Sèvre et Maine Sur Lie. They also own the 1½ hectare Clos du Pont, where the grapes are always harvested last, and the wine spends one whole year in wood. I tasted a couple of vintages of this wine, and found it had little to do with Muscadet; its character was much nearer to that of white Burgundy, with a great deal of class. I hope it sells as well as it deserves. This similarity to the white wines of Burgundy was demonstrated to me in another

Guilbaud wine; Pascal opened a bottle of their 1976 Domaine de la Moutonnière, and it was in no way tired but had acquired definite Chardonnay features. The best-known Guilbaud wine is probably the black-labelled, gold-wired Muscadet de Sèvre et Maine Sur Lie, Le Soleil Nantais, a very skilfully blended *assemblage* which can be relied upon to give consistently good quality vintage after vintage.

André Luneau, Guilbaud's *courtier*, took me to visit several of the Guilbauds' regular suppliers. The most memorable of these was the Domaine des Laudières, owned by Messrs Fonteneau and Richard, who married two sisters of the Bahuaud family. The 10-hectare vineyard in the commune of Vertou has a high clay content, and the wine has a very marked *goût de terroir*. The wine is all commercialised by Guilbaud Frères, and is correctly sold as all the bottling is done on the premises. One-third of the wine is fermented and vinified in wooden *fûts*, and very impressive and well-kept the cellar looks. We tasted several wines of the 1985 vintage both in *fût* and in vat, and the overall quality was extremely high; one particular *fût* had the most extraordinary perfumed and aromatic character, more like a Gewürztraminer or Tokay from Alsace than a Muscadet. This is pure *goût de terroir*; the wine comes from a certain corner of the vineyard, and, year after year, it has this same highly specialised nose and taste.

The work is all carried out by one working manager; vinification owes more to tradition than modern technology, and cold fermentation might not even have been invented as far as the Domaine des Laudières is concerned. We tasted the 1986 before we left, and the general impression was that the vintage was of more than adequate quality, but not quite up to the standard of 1985.

With Pascal Guilbaud I visited another of his regular suppliers, Marcel Bertin at the Domaine de la Tour Gasselin, halfway between Vallet and Le Loroux-Bottereau. A very old property, with vinification buildings built of flint, La Tour Gasselin makes very traditional wines. Our tasting was all of the new 1986 vintage, some in underground cement vats, some in wooden *fûts*. One vat of Gros Plant was in a garage, and the cars had to be removed before we could get at the wine. The wines were all of fine quality, even the Gros Plant, and all were marked with varying degrees of *goût de terroir*.

ANTOINE SUBILEAU, Vallet. My last visit in
the town of Vallet was to the house of Antoine

Subileau, a large and friendly *négociant*, from whom I used to ship quantities of reliable Muscadet through the firm of David Baillie Vintners in Exeter. This old Vallet family have some vines of their own, but most of the wine they sell is bought in from local growers, whom they visit in March to taste the fermented wine. Their selections are then either bottled at the property with a mobile bottling unit, if they are to be *sur lie* wines, or, if they are to be sold as plain Muscadet de Sèvre et Maine, they can be brought back to the winery in the Rue St Vincent for treatment, blending and bottling. There are certain properties whose wines they commercialise on a regular basis from year to year, and which are sold under the property's own name, always bottled *sur lie*. These are the Domaine de l'Epinay, Domaine de Montys, Château de Fromenteau, Château de la Ferté and Château du Poyet. They also sell a range of Gros Plant wines, a Blanc de Blancs Vin de Table as well as red and rosé from the Coteaux d'Ancenis and a good selection of all the major Loire *appellations*. They also deal a little in other *appellations* such as Bordeaux and Burgundy, but their business is first and foremost with the wines of the Pays Nantais and the Loire Valley.

On my first visit to his offices, Antoine gave me a tasting of three of his best Muscadets, the Domaine des Montys, Château du Poyet and Domaine de l'Epinay. All were good wines, but interestingly different in style, the nuances being explained in part by different soils and in part by varying methods of vinification. All were bottled *sur lie* at the properties. My own preference was for the style of the Château du Poyet, which had the most finesse and feminine charm of the three; the Domaine des Montys was also very light in character, with a marked presence of CO_2 – always a feature of this wine, explained Antoine, partly due to cold fermentation. The Domaine de l'Epinay had the heaviest style of the three, with more fatness and body, and would be better for drinking with white meats and fish in heavier sauces, and would probably keep better than the other two.

On his kind introduction, I went to visit two of Antoine's regular 'labels'. The first was the Domaine des Montys, run by the very able and helpful young wine-maker Bernard Petiteau, the third generation of his family to make wine on this property, which is a few kilometres out of Vallet, to the left of the road to La Chapelle Heulin.

Hillside vineyards in the Pays Nantais

From 13 hectares, 10 of which are planted with Melon de Bourgogne, 2 with Folle Blanche and 1 with Cabernet Franc and Cabernet Sauvignon for making red Vin de Pays, Petiteau sells about 65% of his wines to *négociants* like Subileau, and the balance to private customers, with a little going to local cafés and restaurants.

Bernard's passion is making wine, and I found his enthusiasm infectious. He gave up a lot of his time, showing me round the vineyard and *cuverie*, and patiently explaining what he did and why he did it. If only every expert would communicate in this friendly way, how much easier would the job of research become. The soil at the Domaine des Montys is fairly typical for Muscadet de Sèvre et Maine – sand and pebbles on a base of schistous rock, with a little clay. Pruning is severe, and follows the local system, which is basically the Guyot Simple – one long branch with from 10 to 12 buds being kept, plus two short spurs with two buds, from which the branch for the following year will be chosen.

Picking is by machine here, and like most serious young wine-makers Petiteau is satisfied that as good, if not better, results can be obtained, with the usual caution about careful driving and meticulous cleanliness. Inevitably some bunches are left on the older vines because they are too near to the ground, but all the Montys vines are now being trained just a little higher to avoid this.

Fermentation is mainly in glass-lined cement vats, most of which are underground, and he also has two of stainless-steel and a range of oak casks. The wine fermented in vat is temperature-controlled to around 18° – if the must needs heating, this is done by inserting a serpentine coil into the vats, which is heated by the domestic heating boiler. He finds that this cool fermentation is most beneficial for conserving the freshness and aromas of the wine. His red Vin de Pays is always fermented in the stainless-steel vats, and when the alcoholic fermentation is over he warms the wine to around 20° to encourage the malo-lactic fermentation.

We tasted two samples of '86 Gros Plant from the *cuves*; the acidity level was 4.5°, the same as last year, and Bernard thought that the quality would also be equal to 1985. We also looked at several Muscadet samples from various *cuves*, with which he was also well pleased; one or two samples were tasted from the oak casks, and the vat samples were noticeably finer, all having that distinctive pear-drop hint on the nose which denotes cold fermentation.

Finally we looked at two vintages of his red Vin de Pays; the 1985 was really dark in colour, with rich *cassis* on nose and in the mouth, whilst the 1982 was also very blackcurranty, more rounded and drinkable than the younger wine – both were surprisingly good and full.

My second introduction from Antoine Subileau was to Henri and Christian Brault of the Château de Fromenteau just outside Vallet. Here again the soil is pebbly and sandy on a schistous sub-soil. Christian told me that they have 14 hectares under vines, as well as keeping a few cattle and growing the necessary hay and feed crops to support them. Eleven hectares are given over to the Melon de Bourgogne, 2.5 to the Folle Blanche for Gros Plant and half a hectare is planted with Cabernet Franc for making red Vin de Pays. The château is a pretty, old house, built on the foundations of an earlier castle. The cellars give a clue to the original importance of Fromenteau, for they are extensive and vaulted, and certainly date from pre-Revolutionary days.

Christian and his father sell almost all their wine through Subileau, and the mobile bottling unit ensures correct application of the *sur lie* description on their labels. In the long, low, stone-built vat-house, which certainly predates the present house, the 1986 wines were gently and audibly working away at their alcoholic fermentation; some were in underground cement tanks, lined with glass, and some in traditional Muscadet oak *foudres*, which are roughly rectangular with rounded corners. We tasted a sample or two from vat and oak, and here I definitely preferred the wine from the wood, though Christian told me that style and quality are more even from the cement tanks. We also looked at a bottle of the 1984 Muscadet de Sèvre et Maine; the colour was beginning to darken a little, but on the nose and in the mouth the wine was still fresh and clean, with quite a bit of body and fatness for a Muscadet.

SAUVION ET FILS, Château du Cléray, Vallet.

The fine eighteenth-century Château du Cléray enjoys a commanding position on wooded hills a few kilometres from Vallet, to the right of the road to Beaupreau. It is the centre of one of the most original and exciting *négociant* businesses in the Pays Nantais, the family firm of Sauvion & Fils. It is indeed a family firm, for there are three brothers and a father involved, and various children and nephews and nieces get involved in the business from time to time. It is the large, affable and bearded son, Jean-Ernest, who represents the spirit of this enterprise, and who carries its name and message across the Atlantic and to other far-flung corners of the wine-drinking world.

Although they are a *négociant* business dealing in all the wines of the Loire Valley, it is Muscadet that they are promoting, and promoting to very good effect. Apart from their own 30-hectare vineyard at Château du Cléray, Sauvion buy wine from the best growers all over the Muscadet *appellation*. It is in their buying and sales policy that Sauvion & Fils differ from the other *négociant* houses of the region. There are no regular contracts with growers, but every year they look at samples from hundreds of growers from which they select a varying number of wines that will bear their Découvertes or 'Discoveries' label. This is a standard label, bearing the words Muscadet de Sèvre et Maine Sur Lie and stating that the wine is Estate Bottled, with gaps left for the name of the Domaine and the grower who made the wine. In the 1985 vintage there were 16 of these Découvertes, but in less easy vintages there can be considerably fewer, as selection is rigorous.

Sauvion & Fils also produce a 'top of the range' Muscadet de Sèvre et Maine which they market under the name of Cardinal Richard, after a papal legate who once owned the Château du Cléray. In addition to this they sell a further prestige wine under the Lauréat label, which consists only of wines that have won either gold or silver medals, and a blended wine that may come from several different properties that is sold as Muscadet de Sèvre et Maine Carte d'Or.

In order to get these top-quality wines, Jean-Ernest believes in rewarding the growers; not only are they recompensed by being paid higher-than-average prices for their wines, there are also annual tasting competitions for all the Sauvion suppliers, and growers who produce the best wines are rewarded with handsome cash prizes. It is small wonder that wine-makers fall over themselves to become Découvertes or to supply wine for the Cardinal Richard or Lauréat labels; it is equally no surprise to learn that Jean-Ernest is not always the most popular man amongst his fellow *négociants*.

The proliferation of labels may be confusing, but Jean-Ernest Sauvion believes strongly in the integrity and in the future of good Muscadet, and he is fighting for those two causes in the only way he knows – by selling quality and paying a just price for it. This must work for the good of the *appellation*, as it surely works for Sauvion & Fils.

THE PAYS NANTAIS:
GUIDE TO HOTELS & RESTAURANTS

For the major part of my stay in the Pays Nantais I was adequately lodged in the Hôtel de la Gare in Clisson (tel: 40.36.16.55), where there are well cooked and reasonably priced set menus, supported by a good selection of local wines.

La Bonne Auberge (tel: 40.54.01.90), also in Clisson, enjoys an excellent reputation – so good, in fact, that it was fully booked on every occasion that I tried to eat there. *Michelin* lists as its *spécialités* Sandre Rôti au Fumet de Vin Rouge, Canette de Vendée aux Fruits and Millefeuille Tiède aux Pommes.

There is very little to divert the palate in Vallet, but you can eat fairly well in Le Muscadet.

The best restaurant I tried in the whole region was undoubtedly Mon Rêve at Basse-Goulaine (tel: 40.03.55.50), about 8 km out of Nantes on the D751. The menu is heavily fish-orientated, as you might expect, but there are some good meat dishes as well. The wine list is extremely comprehensive, with a particularly fine range of Bordeaux. The décor is restful, and the service discreet and friendly – altogether a good watering-hole.

There are two Relais & Châteaux hotels in the area, the Hostellerie le Domaine d'Orvault in the northern suburbs of Nantes, and the Abbaye de Villeneuve in Les Sorinières to the south; these are described in more detail in the chapter on the Relais & Châteaux.

TAILPIECE

I was told recently by a literary agent, who should know, that a book which starts at the beginning and follows a logical sequence through to the end is uncommercial, unfashionable, even unpublishable. This surprised me not at all, since my first foray into authorship left me convinced of one thing – that the world of books and publishing has little to do with logic.

Serious thought, however, was given to the words of the sage, and I have as a result decided to make a small bow of obeisance to the gods of success and commercialism by ending at the beginning.

My voyage along the Loire has been from east to west, for no better reason than that the Dutch writer, Hubrecht Duijker, went from west to east, and one must be different. The 'end' of my book proper, therefore, may be considered to be in the Pays Nantais, where I found myself in mid-November with an exhausted liver, several kilos of excess stomach, a suitcase full of notes and a longing for English ale, bacon and eggs, and home.

Whilst checking through my early notes before packing up, I had come across a hitherto unnoticed list of all the growers in Reuilly, some 300 kilometres away at the eastern end of the Loire vineyards; quickly glancing down the names of the proprietors before filing the list away, my eye was caught by the striking and unlikely name of Olivier Cromwel. How I had missed him on my visit to Reuilly six months before I cannot say, but there it was. An Englishman writing a book about the wines of the Loire was duty-bound to seek out this Parliamentarian throwback. I would also be killing two birds with one stone, as I would be ending at the beginning, thereby assuring the success of the book.

With a light heart I drove my battered old Lancia, faithful warhorse, back up the long and lovely river. It was perfect autumn weather, and vineyards and forests were in the full glory of their gold and russet plumage as I passed the now familiar places – Angers, Saumur, Bourgueil and Chinon, Tours, Vouvray and Montlouis. Crossing the Loire at Amboise, I cut across country to Montrichard and took the N76, following the River Cher to Vierzon. I was pondering one more unfulfilled, and, strictly speaking, unnecessary piece of research, a visit to the source of

the Loire, when coincidence or the muse struck again. A huge sign on the roadside proclaimed 'IGN, ici Vente des Cartes'. It was the printing works of the Institut Géographique National, and here, if anywhere, I could discover the exact whereabouts of the headwaters of the Loire; it was a sign not to be ignored.

A gnome-like figure greeted me at the sales counter, and, on hearing my request, reached unhesitatingly for Carte Topographique No. 2836 (est) as if 50 mad Englishmen asked him the whereabouts of the source of the Loire every day. These maps, drawn on a scale of 4cm to the kilometre, cover the whole of France and are, I suppose, the equivalent of the English Ordnance Survey maps. With the feverish excitement that Livingstone must have felt as he heard the Niagara Falls, I scanned the precious map. The profusion of green shading and Rip van Winkle wrinkles of contour lines showed this to be wild and mountainous terrain; my explorer's blood began to race. This was my quest, my pilgrimage, the Holy Grail of a true writer and lover of the Loire. As my eyes scanned the map from north to south, I took in the names of the peaks with increasing excitement – Mt Signon, very biblical, Mt d'Alambre, Mt Mézenc, 1450, 1691, and 1753 metres – no hills these, but real mountains, 5,000 feet and more. Finally, near the bottom of the map, not far from a wooded hill called Partridge Song, I found it; there they were, clearly marked, Les Sources de la Loire, four of them, little streams springing from the flanks of a mountain called Le Gerbier de Jonc, the Stack of Rushes, over 5,000 feet above sea-level.

The highest of the four streams rose quite close to the road. My enthusiasm was only slightly dampened by the fact that I was not to be the actual discoverer of the source of the mighty Loire, and I determined to make short work of M. Cromwel, drive on southward, lodge at a nearby hostelry and rise with the lark to ascend the glorious sunlit slopes of the Gerbier de Jonc.

Having at last run the redoubtable Cromwel to earth in the late afternoon, of which more in the appropriate chapter, I climbed into my car and consulted the map. To my slight horror, for it was now dark, I realised that I had not related my Carte Topographique to the rest of France, and that I was now faced with a 200-mile drive on not very good roads. Montluçon, Clermont-Ferrand, Le Puy – and then some. My pilgrimage was taking me nearly to the South of France, but I would not be like the 90-year-old chaplain of my prep school, who was reputed to have attempted to swim the Channel, got tired when only a mile from the French coast, turned round and swam back; no, I was made of sterner stuff, and set off without a backward glance.

Le Puy is a town I have passed through and above on several occasions, and it has always intrigued me. It lies in the bottom of a bowl, surrounded by mountains, and from the bottom of that bowl volcanic pressures in prehistoric times pushed up several excrescences or hills, like boils on a teenager's face. On the top of two of these pustules, the good citizens of Le Puy have seen fit to erect a church and a huge statue of Christ, and very dramatic they look too. Fascinating though it may appear, Le Puy is not, as I discovered, a place in which to linger. Whilst still some fifty miles away, I had, with unusual prudence, telephoned ahead and booked a room in the best hotel in the Michelin – well, it was my last night in France after all. It was called, strangely, the Christel. The night had by now turned cold and it was raining; I congratulated myself smugly as I switch-backed my way through the mountains, comforted by visions of a log fire and something delicious to eat and drink, served by merry mountain folk; afterwards there would probably be a four-poster bed and a blissful night's rest in preparation for the dawn assault on Le Gerbier de Jonc.

As so often happens in this life, reality fell somewhat short of the dream. I had a puncture on the top of a mountain road; after a half-hour search, I found the wheel brace under the front seat. Suffering from cold, thoroughly drenched by gale-borne horizontal rain and dizzy from altitude sickness, I finally changed the wheel. Filthy in appearance and temper, I descended the last fifteen miles into Le Puy. It was by now a quarter to ten and Le Puy had evidently been the victim of a recent nuclear strike or maybe a mild dose of bubonic plague. It was dark, empty of people, raining and infinitely depressing. I found a strange, mutant survivor, picking among some rubbish bags, who mumbled directions to my hotel.

I wish he hadn't. The hotel was closed, it was also very modern, aluminium and glass, with no possibility of log fires, food, wine, buxom serving wenches or any other comforts of the flesh. The hour was late and I must make do. After much banging and ringing of bells, I was at last admitted, if not exactly welcomed. Dinner? Certainly not, not even désolé! Coffee? Désolé, this time, but the machines have been turned off for the night. Monsieur would perhaps like some tea? Monsieur would not really, but it would be better than nothing.

My room, predictably, was on the seventh floor. Again the concierge was désolé, but the lift was not working. I comforted myself with the thought that those seven flights of stairs, carrying my half-ton suitcase, would be good training for tomorrow's climb. The room was also predictable – no heating, nylon sheets, one thin blanket, black hairs on the pillow and no hot water in the grandiosely termed salle de bain and, of course, no soap. Five minutes later, a tap on the door signified the arrival of my tea, borne by a curious midget lady, clad, surprisingly, in a gold lurex ball-gown. I had been wrong; the tea was not better than nothing. One solitary tea-bag dangled pathetically in two litres of lukewarm water. I dined less than regally off a bar of chocolate, and a cup of this unappetising beverage, and so to bed.

After a fitful sleep, I rose at seven, and gladly shook the dust of Le Puy from my feet. Dawn found me in the mountains of the Ardèche, though nothing else could have. I was in heavy cloud, a gale was blowing and the rain bombarded the car with the force of a fire-hose. Luckily, visibility was down to about three feet, for had I been able to see the precipitous gorges falling away from the miles of one-track hairpin bends, my courage would probably have failed me. By dint of dogged persistence and skilled map-reading, I eventually arrived at the point on the map nearest to my goal – though for all I could see through the impenetrable cloud, I could just as well have been in the centre of Birmingham. After stumbling for several kilometres in what I deemed to be the right direction, I literally ran into a rough wooden sign on the side of the road. Peering through the fog, I made out the words 'La Source de la Loire, Ici le Meilleur Accueil', above an arrow pointing away into the void. Visions of precipices, bottomless bogs of sucking mud and even savage wolves or wild boar lying in wait for the intrepid explorer were pushed aside, and I set off down a slippery path in the direction indicated.

After some twenty yards I came upon my objective, a small circle of stones in the midst of which was a blackish puddle of water. Another rude, hand-painted sign announced grandly: 'From here I commence my long journey to the ocean.' I dutifully photographed the scene, and then cast around for 'Le Meilleur Accueil'.

A tumbledown shack loomed out of the mist, bearing the magic words 'Bar-Café' above the door. It was clearly unoccupied, and I was just wondering what the second-best welcome would be like, when a large Dobermann-Pinscher rushed out from behind the shed, fangs bared and slavering. I took to my heels with prudent haste, reaching the car in the nick of time and, like a Sunday tabloid reporter, 'made my excuses and left'.

My discovery of the source of the Loire lacked something in dramatic impact, apart from my narrow escape from the jaws of Cerberus, but I had achieved my objective. Though my voyage of discovery was perhaps of less historic significance, I felt a certain empathy with my fellow explorer Captain Scott's words on arrival at the South Pole: 'Dear God, this is an awful place.'

RELAIS & CHÂTEAUX

Thanks to a fortuitous meeting with Patrice Ponsard, managing director of the Château de Marçay near Chinon and Regional Delegate of the Relais & Châteaux organisation, I have received a considerable degree of help and sponsorship from this august body of hoteliers and restaurateurs.

In return, it has been my very great pleasure, and a privilege, to visit all the Relais & Châteaux members in the Loire Valley, and to write the following chapter of appreciation. At Patrice's suggestion, I have also included those members whose establishments are in Britanny, and for two good reasons; firstly, as an Englishman, travelling as I did from east to west down the Loire, it seemed an excellent idea to return home by way of the incomparable Breton coast, and, secondly, there seemed to be sound logic involved, since the wines of the Loire go perfectly with the amazing cornucopia of fish and shellfish that largely make up *la cuisine bretonne*.

Apart from feelings of gratitude for their generous hospitality, I am full of admiration for the professionalism, dedication and genuine hospitality shown in every hotel and restaurant that we visited. The standards of comfort, décor, service and cuisine are universally high, and the Relais & Châteaux organisation is to be commended for the great contribution it is making to the hotel and restaurant profession worldwide.

I have tried to arrange the hotels and restaurants in some kind of logical geographical order, though I would not for a moment suggest that you try to visit them all in eight, days as we did!

NAME AND LOCATION

Domaine des Hauts de Loire, Onzain
Château de Chissay, Chissay-en-Touraine
Hotel d'Espagne, Valençay
Château d'Artigny, Montbazon
Domaine de Beauvois, Luynes
Château de Marçay, Chinon
Laurent, Loué
Château de Teildras, Cheffes-sur-Sarthe
Le Prieuré, Chenehutte-les-Tuffeaux
Restaurant Richard Coutenceau, La Rochelle
Abbaye de Villeneuve, Les Sorinières
Hostellerie Le Domaine d'Orvault, Orvault, Nantes
Castel Marie-Louise, La Baule
Le Bretagne, Questembert
Castel Clara, Goulphar, Belle Ile en Mer
Les Moulins du Duc, Moelan-sur-Mer
Château de Locguénolé, Hennebont
Hôtel de la Plage, Plonevez-Porzay
Manoir de Lan-Kerellec, Trebeurden
Château Hôtel de Coatguelen, Pléhédel

DOMAINE DES HAUTS DE LOIRE,
Onzain
Tel: 54.20.72.57

On the north bank of the Loire, between Blois and Tours, you will find the little town of Onzain, and the Domaine des Hauts de Loire is about 2 kilometres north of the town.

This lovely hotel, converted from an old hunting lodge of the Comte de Rostaing, is situated in secluded woodland, surounded by the vineyards of Touraine. The gardens, lake and exterior of the house are a delight to the eye, and the décor in the public rooms, bedrooms and apartments has been carried out with taste and care. Pierre-Alain Bonnigal and his wife are at the same time professional and thoroughly charming hosts. The bedrooms are elegant and comfortable, and the bathrooms exceptionally good. Service in all parts of the hotel is an impeccable blend of friendliness and professionalism – difficult to achieve and all too rarely found.

The cooking is very good, with well-balanced menus that delight but do not overwhelm, and the wine list boasts a good selection from all the best vineyards of France, especially those of the Loire Valley. The Savennières was particularly good with the main course, a mousseline of pike with freshwater shrimps. The lovely dining-room enhances the enjoyment of every meal, with its creamy-yellow walls, curtains edged with a border of flowers, nice tableware and glass, fresh flowers on every table, and, praise be, perfect lighting.

This is an idyllic place to stay, perfect for exploring the châteaux, vineyards and lovely countryside of the Eastern Loire.

CHÂTEAU DE CHISSAY,
Chissay-en-Touraine
Tel: 54.32.32.01

Historic Château de Chissay is situated on the north bank of the River Cher, between Montrichard and Chenonceaux. Partly twelfth-century, but mainly sixteenth, the château passed from one noble family to another, until the St Genix de Beauregards gave it up in 1952.

It was at Chissay in 1940 that Paul Reynaud, head of the government, established his headquarters, and it was from Chissay that de Gaulle left for London, having failed to dissuade Reynaud from moving the entire government to Bordeaux. It was converted into a luxury hotel in 1986 by Philippe Savry, the present owner, who has four other hotels. Of the five, Château de Chissay, the Abbaye de Villeneuve near Nantes and the Château de Brécourt in Normandy are members of the Relais & Châteaux organisation.

The hotel is beautifully situated on a hillside in the village of Chissay, overlooking its own gardens and swimming-pool, with views across open country to the River Cher. It is an excellent centre for visiting many of the famous châteaux in the locality.

The reception area was the original kitchen of the château, and the huge stone fireplace and bread-oven are still there. A cloistered courtyard divides the chateâu in two, and provides a good setting for drinks and meals in the open air. The bedrooms are all different, with mosaic decorations in the bathrooms. One room has a jacuzzi, and the round bedroom at the top of the twelfth-century keep has a bathroom above with a glass floor, perhaps more suited to younger couples.

I did not, alas, have time to sample the cuisine, but the menu looked mouthwatering, and the chef enjoys an excellent reputation. The young manager, Patrice Longet, is charming and anxious to please.

HÔTEL D'ESPAGNE,
Valençay
Tel: 54.00.00.02

Situated just outside the gates of the lovely château in Valençay, the Hôtel d'Espagne offers an excellent cuisine and comfortable, modern bedrooms.

A typical menu at the time of our visit comprised a Salade aux Magrets de Canard, Escalope of Salmon with Basil, stuffed Saddle of Lamb with Vegetables, Cheese, and a Strawberry Mousse. The cooking, presentation and service were excellent, and the price not unreasonable at F180.00. A delicately tinted Valençay rosé made a perfect accompaniment for every course on a hot August day.

Approached through an old-fashioned coach entrance, the restaurant and hotel are grouped around a very attractive courtyard, with tables and chairs where guests can take their aperitifs or coffee.

CHÂTEAU D'ARTIGNY,
Montbazon
Tel: 47.26.24.24

Built high on a bluff commanding wonderful views over the valley of the River Indre, the *grand-luxe* hotel Château d'Artigny is some 10 kilometres south of Tours on the N10. Surprisingly, this stately pile is almost brand-new, for one feels immediately transported to an earlier and more graceful age. In fact d'Artigny was built as a private residence by the fabulously wealthy *parfumier*, M. Coty, and was only completed in 1948.

At Château d'Artigny luxury, comfort and service are paramount, and the cuisine, which rates a rosette in *Michelin*, frequently surpasses that accolade; the wine list is of particular interest, since it carries a treasure-house of old wines of the Loire Valley, especially the reds of Chinon and Bourgueil. The dining-room is a delightful and gracious setting in which to enjoy both food and wine, with lovely views on to the terrace and the Indre Valley below. All the public rooms have the same air of grace and space, and antique furniture blends happily with beautiful and carefully chosen fabrics of today.

There are 46 rooms and 7 suites at d'Artigny; all have their own individual character, and are both luxurious and comfortable with superb bathrooms.

Château d'Artigny stands in its own grounds of 25 hectares, with immaculately tended gardens, two private tennis courts, a heated swimming-pool, a practice golf range and, of course, a heli-pad.

Close to the commercial centre of Tours, yet at the same time set in peaceful countryside, this is a marvellous centre for a holiday exploring the châteaux of the Loire, the vineyards of Touraine and the lovely surrounding country, or for doing nothing at all, and being very spoilt whilst so doing.

DOMAINE DE BEAUVOIS,
Luynes
Tel: 47.55.50.11

The Domaine de Beauvois, some 15 kilometres west of Tours off the road to Langeais, is a seigneurial manor-house, parts of which date back to the fifteenth century. It was in the hands of the same family for over 250 years, the last of whom, Henri de

la Béraudière, sold the estate to the Blanchard family in 1887. The property then passed through a number of private owners until it was bought by René Traversac for his hotel chain, Les Grandes Étapes Françaises, in 1966.

Beautifully situated in wooded parkland, the hotel commands lovely views over sloping gardens to the lake beyond. There is a splendid swimming-pool, where meals and drinks are served at lunch-time in fine weather, and a tennis court.

The décor has been well thought out and executed, blending the best of modern design in curtains and other fabrics with antique furniture and Persian rugs. Both the bedrooms and the public rooms are extremely comfortable, and the large dining-room is especially elegant, overlooking the terrace and the former swimming-pool – now a goldfish pond.

As one might expect, the cooking at Beauvois is sublime, and the wine list full of treasures; as well as a really fine selection of Bordeaux and Burgundy, the wines of the Loire are represented in force. We were offered a quite stunning dry Vouvray from Audebert of the 1962 vintage, proof of the astonishing keeping-powers of well-made wines from the Chenin Blanc grape. After a really fine dinner, we were taken on a privileged tour of the Beauvois cellar, delved out of the rock beneath the house. I was amazed and impressed by the breadth and length of the range of wines, even down to vintage port, a rare bird in a French cellar! Gerard Bonnin, who is responsible for the wines, is a charming and knowledgeable man, and is to be congratulated on this splendid cellar.

All the staff at Beauvois are courteous and efficient, and service is prompt and impeccable. The whole establishment runs like a well-oiled machine under the very capable direction of the general manager, Jean-Claude Taupin. Altogether I rate the Domaine de Beauvois as a privileged and luxurious base for a holiday in Touraine.

CHÂTEAU DE MARÇAY,
Chinon
Tel: 47.93.03.47

Château de Marçay is about 5 kilometres south of Chinon in the heart of the country. This is a genuine fifteenth-century castle, and when you see the thickness of the walls you realise at once that life in those days was not as peaceful and secure as it is today. Despite the mediaeval exterior, all is comfort and luxury within. The château has 34 rooms and 4 superb suites; all are comfortable, well-decorated and have excellent bathrooms.

The grounds at Château de Marçay are beautiful; there is a fine swimming-pool and tennis court, and golf and riding can be arranged in the vicinity. Every time I have lunched at Marçay, I have been lucky with the weather; there is a fine terrace, sheltered by the two wings of the castle, where lunch is served on fine days. There can be few more enjoyable gastronomic experiences than taking lunch here on such a day. The view across the rolling 'Rabelaisian' countryside is breathtaking, the cooking superb and there is a wine list to please even that great swigger of a poet. An interesting feature of Château de Marçay is that they have their own vineyard; the wine produced does not come under the Chinon *appellation*, but is a well-made red from almost entirely Cabernet-Sauvignon.

The managing director at Château de Marçay is Patrice Ponsard, formerly of the Domaine de Beauvois. He is a most charming and able man, and I owe him a personal thank-you for all the help he has given me. If you are looking for a perfect base from which to visit Chinon and other nearby places of interest, especially the many vineyards of Chinon and Bourgueil, Marçay and Patrice Ponsard between them will ensure your comfort and well-being.

LAURENT,
Loué
Tel: 43.88.40.03

The minute you enter the Restaurant/Hôtel Laurent in Loué, you know that you are in for something very special. The welcome is warm, and the dining-room one of the prettiest I have seen anywhere, with its creamy stone floor, painted ceilings and long wall made entirely of French windows overlooking the terrace, garden and swimming-pool. The china – different with every course – and the glassware are beautifully chosen, and there are fresh flowers on every table.

On our visit we left the choice of menu and wine to the chef/owner, Gilbert Laurent, and it proved to

be a very wise move. From 'amuse-bouches' through to dessert, the entire meal was a never-to-be-forgotten delight, balanced and tuned with all the art of a great orchestral work. With a refreshing mosaic of vegetables in two sauces, and with the turbot in lobster sauce that followed, we drank a lovely Sancerre, Clos du Chêne Marchand 1987; then, with a superb fillet of beef in a wine sauce, served with onions, carrots cooked with bacon and fresh pasta, we drank a fruity red Anjou, Clos Ste Anne 1986, which also went well with the delicious selection of cheeses. To finish, we were given delicate ice-cream, served on grey marble-pattern plates, surrounded by wild strawberries, loganberries and blackberries in a raspberry *coulis*. The mignardises served with the coffee were imaginative and excellent – tiny raspberry tartlets, chocolate cups with walnuts and miniature lemon curd tarts.

The rooms are extremely comfortable, with tastefully chosen fabrics, and original paintings on the walls. Gilbert Laurent is himself an artist, and in fact painted part of the floral ceiling in the dining-room. This is a special place.

CHÂTEAU DE TEILDRAS,
Cheffes-sur-Sarthe
Tel: 41.42.61.08

In the heart of the Anjou countryside, the Hôtel Château de Teildras lies to the north of Angers near the village of Cheffes-sur-Sarthe. One of the nicest of the many French hotels I have stayed in, this small sixteenth-century manor-house welcomes its guests with a warm informality more akin to that of a private house belonging to friends you have known for a long time.

It is, in fact, the country house of the Comte and Comtesse de Bernard du Breil, and is run by two of their pretty and very charming daughters. Quite small for a château-hotel, there are only 11 bedrooms, which are very comfortable and nicely decorated, with excellent bathrooms; here especially you feel that you are in the guest bedroom of a private house rather than in a hotel.

Sheltered by the two wings of the house, the hotel has a lovely terrace where roses abound, and moss-covered steps lead down to the parkland, which in turn stretches away to a lake in the distance. The whole place has a feeling of timeless tranquillity, and is a perfect haven away from the pressures of modern life.

The dining-room is cosy and well-lit, with beige wall coverings and pink tablecloths. The food is excellent, and beautifully presented on blue Limoges china, and the wine list, though not enormous, is most exciting; there are very few wine lists in France, or anywhere else for that matter, on which you can find either old or rare vintages of Bordeaux or Burgundy, but this has the lot. Treasures like Château Latour 1949, and Domaine de la Romanée-Conti wines of 1971 and even earlier are there to tempt, and the prices, though obviously not inexpensive, are by no means greedy.

All in all, Château de Teildras is a gem to which I hope very much to return.

LE PRIEURÉ,
Chênehutte-les-Tuffeaux
Tel: 41.67.90.14

Saumur is a splendid centre from which to explore the region, and the city itself has much to offer the tourist. There is the splendid Château de Saumur itself, the Musée de Cheval in the castle, the Musée de la Cavalerie and the famous Cadre Noir dressage riding-school. Le Prieuré is undoubtedly the best hotel from which to make your expeditions; it is some 8 kilometres north-west of the town on the little D751 which runs along the south bank of the Loire.

On your way out of the town, you pass through the suburb of St Hilaire-St Florent, where most of the great Saumur sparkling wine houses have their bottling plants and cellars. Most of them welcome visitors, and their cellars in the rock are most impressive; some of them go on for miles, like those of their colleagues in Champagne, and the *dégustation* of delicious cool sparkling wine comes as a welcome refreshment at the end of such a tour.

Le Prieuré is a Renaissance manor-house, set on a magnificent wooded bluff overlooking the Loire at Chênehutte-les-Tuffeaux. There are 35 rooms and 2 suites. The standards of décor, comfort and service are of the highest, and the restaurant is superb. They have a well-deserved rosette in *Michelin*, and I would not be a bit surprised to see another in the near future. The wine list is very well chosen, with the accent obviously on the wines of the Loire Valley; there are some very good Saumur-Champignys, and the lovely dry white Chenins Blancs of Savennières are also well represented.

The hotel has a swimming-pool and a tennis court, and riding and fishing can easily be arranged. The Prieuré is a delightful place to stay, and the Manager, Philippe Doumerc, will do everything to ensure your comfort and enjoyment.

RESTAURANT RICHARD COUTENCEAU,
La Rochelle
Tel: 46.41.48.19

Sadly we did not have time to go as far south as La Rochelle, for Richard Coutenceau enjoys a formidable reputation for seafood. Restaurant Richard Coutenceau is a Relais Gourmand, and does not offer any accommodation, but by all accounts this 'merits a big detour', to coin a phrase from the *Guide Michelin*.

The restaurant is situated on the Plage de la Concurrence looking out towards the Iles d'Oléron and de Ré. The restaurant is closed Monday evening and all day Sunday, and for the rest of the week it is advisable to book.

Specialities include Suprême de Turbots aux Artichauts and Homard Rôti aux Légumes Croquants, and the wine list features not only the wines of the Loire and all the other main vineyard areas of France, but also actively promotes the wines of nearby Haut Poitou; the excellent Sauvignon which they make there, as well as the Chardonnay, make interesting and delicious alternative accompaniments to fish and shellfish.

I look forward very much to a future visit.

ABBAYE DE VILLENEUVE,
les Sorinierès
Tel: 40.04.40.25

The Abbaye is one of Les Hôtels Particuliers, the group that belongs to Philippe Savry. It lies about 10 kilometres to the north of Nantes; this hotel appears to be particularly well-suited to and geared for the needs of the businessman as well as for the discerning traveller. There are large rooms especially for seminars and receptions, and special menus for such occasions. The grounds are extensive, and there is a beautiful circular swimming-pool. As you enter the hotel reception area, a long glazed cloister leads you to the great stone staircase, with the public rooms on your left, and a view of the garden and pool to your right.

There are 17 bedrooms and 3 suites, all immaculate and equipped with all the creature comforts, decorated in soft, muted tones. The bathrooms have the same mosaics found in the sister hotel at Chissay.

The food is as good as you might expect in an establishment of this calibre, and is served in the spacious, high-ceilinged dining-room. The wines have been well chosen, and a wide variety is offered. We drank a delicious Muscadet de Sèvre et Maine Sur Lie 1987 from Sauvion's flagship Château du Cléray, which went very well with a delicate roast salmon with basil.

If you have business in Nantes, or merely wish to discover the lovely Pays Nantais from a luxurious base, the Abbaye makes a fine starting point.

HOSTELLERIE LE DOMAINE D'ORVAULT,
Orvault, Nantes
Tel: 40.76.84.02

This hotel is modern, set in a pretty garden in the suburb of Orvault, just off the N137 on the outskirts of Nantes, as you drive north towards Rennes.

There are 29 rooms and one suite at the Domaine d'Orvault; all are clean and comfortable, but the restaurant is the *raison d'être* of this establishment. On the occasion of our visit, the dining-room was full of solid Nantais citizens enjoying the splendid variety of *fruits de mer* on offer, all of which was beautifully presented. House specialities include Poêlées de St Jacques or Langoustines, and Filets de Sole aux Cèpes, which were quite superb. The selection of wines obviously leans towards the wines of the Pays Nantais, with a good choice of Muscadets and Coteaux d'Ancenis, although the other wine regions of France also figure in abundance. Service is discreet and attentive, and the restaurant extremely comfortable.

The Domaine d'Orvault is owned and run by Jean-Yves Bernard and his wife Aline.

CASTEL MARIE-LOUISE,
La Baule
Tel: 40.60.20.60

The first of the Relais & Châteaux hotels in this chapter that is not, strictly speaking, on the 'wine circuit', Castel Marie-Louise does, however, form the first link in a chain of these fine hotels that will take the English traveller on a delightful journey back to the Channel ports and home. It seemed also to be a logical progression for the writer of this book, and, hopefully, for the reader too. What could be nicer, after a tour of discovery of the lovely and varied vineyards of the Loire, than to wend one's way gently home along the wild and rocky Brittany coast, staying in great comfort, sampling the varied and succulent cornucopia of fish and shellfish that abounds here. And what better way to test what you have learnt on your earlier travels, for the delicate wines of the Vallée de la Loire are the perfect accompaniment to all these fishy delights.

La Baule is a large, old-fashioned seaside resort, with a great deal to offer the holidaymaker. The Hotel Castel Marie-Louise belongs to the Lucien Barrière group, which also owns two more hotels in La Baule, l'Hermitage and the Hotel Royal, as well as the beautiful 18-hole golf course, 30 tennis courts, the Casino and a new Sea Water Treatment Centre. Guests at the smaller, but equally comfortable Castel Marie-Louise are welcome to use the heated sea-water swimming-pool at the neighbouring Hôtel l'Hermitage, and the many sporting facilities offered include, of course, golf and tennis, sailing, windsurfing and horse-riding.

The welcome and the service in this comfortable Edwardian marine residence are at the same time friendly and efficient. Much thought has been given to the décor in public and private rooms, and the atmosphere throughout is warm and cheerful. The bedrooms mostly have sea views, looking out over lush green lawns and well tended flowerbeds, where guests may sit and enjoy a drink, or just sit. The rooms are pretty and comfortable; all have colour television, and the bathrooms are exceptionally good.

The restaurant is bright and cheerful, with fresh flowers and nice silverware; a large fish tank with live lobsters, crabs and other fish gives promise of gastronomic delights to come. The maître d'hôtel is particularly pleasant and friendly, and gives that all-too-rare impression of wanting to please every customer equally. The accent is naturally very much on fish and shellfish, which are cooked and presented beautifully, and there is an excellent selection of wines on the *carte des vins* to complement any dish. We were very impressed by the wide variety of home-baked breads that were offered.

There is a comfortable and friendly bar, where light meals are served. Mention should also be made of the breakfasts, which are really good – freshly-squeezed orange juice, brioches and other tempting offerings from the hotel's talented baker, accompanied by good coffee or tea.

The young manager, Pascal Lambert, is professional and determined to please; he deserves success and I am sure he will achieve it.

LE BRETAGNE,
Questembert
Tel: 97.26.11.12

About an hour's drive north from La Baule is the village of Questembert, set back a few kilometres from the coast. Here you will find a creeper-clad Mecca for gastronomic pilgrims, the Restaurant-Hôtel Le Bretagne.

Georges and Michèle Paineau are a rare and wonderful couple. They clearly love each other and what they do, and they work together perfectly as a team. In addition to being one of the great chefs of France, Georges Paineau is also a painter of more than average talent; many of his bold, bright pictures adorn the walls, and he is shortly to hold his first exhibition in Paris. The décor throughout is lively and imaginative, and carved wood statues of elephants and oriental deities are a reminder of Paineau's four years as a restaurateur in Bangkok.

There are about six bedrooms, comfortable, luxurious, and sparkling clean. Madame Paineau is clearly as much of a perfectionist in her housekeeping as is her husband in the sanctum of his kitchen.

The restaurant is panelled in dark wood, with a lovely deep blue carpet. The glassware and the china

are quite beautiful, every item chosen with love and care to enhance the food or wine entrusted to it. The *menu de dégustation* which Georges Paineau prepared for us was without doubt the best meal I have enjoyed in my life. Throughout the whole lunch, we drank a superb Meursault 1985 from Yves Boyer-Martenot. Possibly due to the Oriental influence of his time in Thailand, I found no difficulty at all in coping with so many dishes; the portions were not tiny, but just enough, and everything so delicate, carefully balanced and lightly spiced – a harmonious and perfect experience. The meal was so memorable that I reproduce the menu below in full, without apology.

Crème de Choux Fleurs en Gelée
•
Tarte de Moules et Petits Coquillages
•
Crème d'Algues aux Huîtres
•
Crêpe de Pomme de Terre à la Peau
de Lait aux Quatre Epices
•
Ravioles de Cèpes et Ris de Veau
au Cerfeuil
•
Noisettes de Turbot au Jus Blanc
en Croustillant
•
Salade de Chèvre Fermier
•
Soufflé au Chocolat
•
Glace Vanille au Coulis d'Orange
•
Petits Fours
•
Truffes
•
Café

Before leaving we invited the Paineaus to come and visit us in England. I hope very much that they do, and I am glad that we have a superb Chinese restaurant nearby.

CASTEL CLARA,
Goulphar, Belle Ile en Mer
Tel: 97.31.84.21

Some 12 kilometres across the sea by ferry from Quiberon lies the aptly named Belle Ile. It is an island rich in history, and blessed with an extraordinary and varied natural beauty. Dramatic, rocky coastline alternates with long sandy beaches, and there is much to discover and enjoy in the main town and harbour of Le Palais, and in the little fishing villages like Sauzon in the west and Port Locmaria in the east. The beauty and tranquillity of Belle Ile have made it a refuge and home for many great artists and poets, and the actress Sarah Bernhardt spent every summer of her declining years in her converted military fort near Basse-Hiot at the north-western tip of the island.

Halfway along the southern coast lies a spectacular fjord-like inlet called Port Goulphar, at the head of which are situated the hotel Castel Clara and its sister hotel, the Manoir de Goulphar, whose lucky residents enjoy one of the most beautiful sea-views I have ever seen.

Castel Clara, member of the Relais & Châteaux organisation, is a modern hotel with 32 rooms and 11 suites. Public and private rooms alike are beautifully light and airy, decorated in shades of beige and pink, with much use of cane furniture, nice pictures and an abundance of fresh flowers everywhere. The disposition of the general manager, Jean-Louis Goumy, and his staff is as sunny, charming and totally welcoming as the hotel itself.

All the usual activities associated with a seaside holiday are on offer, and the hotel has its own swimming-pool and tennis courts, if your appetite needs any extra stimulus.

The restaurant is attractive, again in pink and beige; there are pink tablecloths, good glass and china, fresh flowers on the tables and a large and tempting tank full of fat and somnolent lobsters. At lunch-time there is a 'Déjeuner Léger des Relais et Châteaux' on offer, consisting of an Amuse-Bouche, Blanquette de Poisson du Marché, Dessert and Coffee. There is also a heavily fish orientated à la carte menu, with a truly impressive-looking Plateau de Fruits de Mer. In the evening there is a 'Dîner Gourmand du Castel Clara', comprising Foie Gras, a Pâté of Fish and Shellfish, a choice of Tournedos or Escalope of Sea-Bass, followed by a choice of Desserts. A well-balanced if limited wine list complements the menu; a good selection from the Loire, white Burgundies, Alsatian wines from Trimbach and most of the Grandes Marques Champagnes are there for the fish eater, whilst there is a good list of clarets, many from the fast-disappearing, good value 1980 vintage. The already

pleasurable experience of eating at Castel Clara is enhanced by the smiling charm of the young lady maître d'hôtel.

Castel Clara and Belle Ile are definitely on my list for future holidays.

LES MOULINS DU DUC,
Moelan-sur-Mer
Tel: 98.39.60.73

The Hôtel Moulins du Duc is, as the name implies, formed out of two mills. Only one of them actually belonged to the Duke of Brittany, but a little poetic licence is permissible. The mills, and the restaurant and bedrooms, converted from stables and other outbuildings, are grouped along the verdant banks of the rushing River Belon. The mill-pond is at the very door to the reception area, and the immediate impression on arrival is one of natural beauty and quiet.

Robert Quistrebert, who is ably assisted by his son in the running of the hotel, is a *bon viveur* with a great love of life and a passion for the outdoors. The creation of the Moulins du Duc has been a labour of love since he started 20 years ago. He has a particular love and feel for old stone, and has been personally responsible for all the building, rebuilding, conversion and restoration of the many buildings that make up the whole. All has been beautifully done, and the constant noise of rushing water and the tumbling flowers and trees that border the river combine to make this a very special place. Wildlife abounds; from the picture windows of the restaurant we could see wild duck everywhere, and a kingfisher darted downriver on his electric-blue path.

The cuisine is excellent and varied, with a choice of four menus, a children's menu and a wide selection of *à la carte* dishes, all heavily accented towards fish and shellfish. We had an Amuse-Bouche of pig's trotter in cream sauce, followed by home-made fresh Foie Gras de Canard, accompanied by a lovely bottle of old Sauternes, a Château de Malle of the 1962 vintage. For our main course, we were treated to one of the chef's new dishes, fillets of Sole, marinated in red Bourgueil, served with fresh pasta, with which we drank a red Bordeaux, Château Caronne Ste Gemme 1975, and with the cheese we drank the 1970 vintage from the same property. The pudding was another 'first' from the chef, a strawberry mousse served in a cocotte dish, surrounded by a gratin of summer fruits. With our coffee, M. Quistrebert gave us a *fine* from Mouton-Rothschild.

Another of mine host's passions is good wine, and he took us on a tour of his cellar. All is in perfect order, and his careful planning is evident from the bins of successive vintages from his favourite properties. Bordeaux is his first love, and he has a wide variety of well-chosen Crus Bourgeois and Crus Classés, as well as a few real collector's gems. I glimpsed a few bottles of Latour '49, and a dusty old magnum of Cheval Blanc.

An iron will or a cast-iron constitution would be a prerequisite for a stay of any length at the Moulins du Duc, for Robert Quistrebert is a persuasive host who loves his wine and loves to share his passion. He says that this is his *petit coin de paradis*; we tended to agree with him, and shall certainly return.

CHÂTEAU DE LOCGUÉNOLÉ,
Hennebont
Tel: 97.76.29.04

Château de Locguénolé is a large Victorian mansion, standing in its own wooded park with commanding views over the tidal waters of the River Blavet. It is the ancestral home of the proprietor, Madame Alyette de la Sablière, a charming and very correct lady of the old school, who runs this gracious château-hotel with the help of her sister, her son and her daughter-in-law.

This is a large establishment, very professionally run, with good staff who give excellent service. There are in total 32 bedrooms and 3 suites which are spread between the main house, the adjacent manor-house and a farmhouse some 3 kilometres distant. The house also has good facilities for receptions, business conferences and seminars.

The bedrooms are beautifully done, with antique furniture and well-chosen fabrics; the bathrooms are particularly impressive, with much use of marble, lovely thick peach-coloured towels and matching bathrobes. As in the rest of the house, every bedroom has fresh flowers, carefully chosen to go with the decor. The best rooms are on the first floor, and have breathtaking views over the park to the river.

The restaurant, which deservedly rates two

Michelin rosettes, is at basement level, again with the fabulous river view. It is an elegant but friendly room, with a stone-flagged floor, and the colour-scheme is cream, with much use of yellow silk; a huge Aubusson tapestry takes up the whole of one wall. The china is very attractive, and there are fresh flowers on every table.

The *suggestion du jour* menu consisted of highly original Amuse-bouches, tiny oval dishes of iced gaspacho and little plates of fried squid, followed by a fish mousse, with a main course of what seemed like a whole saddle of lamb, served with aubergines and artichoke hearts and the juices of the meat. This was followed by a delicious *gratin* of summer fruits, which was most attractively presented. The whole meal was a delight not only to the palate, but to the eye as well. The wine list was well put together, with a nice selection from all the important areas, and an especially good list of Loire wine. We drank a delicious Bourgueil, Le Grand Clos 1985 from Audebert, an excellent accompaniment to the lamb. The portions were nothing short of gargantuan, and the next time I go there I shall fast for a couple of days first.

Locguénolé is a spoiling and luxurious place to stay, with all the amenities you would expect – tennis court, swimming-pool, bicycles for hire, fishing and sailing. It is 5 kilometres from Hennebont, and about 20 from the sea.

HÔTEL DE LA PLAGE,
Plonevez-Porzay
Tel: 98.92.50.12

The Hôtel de la Plage is actually in the tiny seaside village of Ste Anne la Palud, about 10 kilometres up the coast from the port of Douarnenez.

It was still high season when we were in the region, and the Proprietor, M. Manick Le Coz, regretfully told us that he was absolutely full and unable to receive us. This we understood completely, and shall certainly return with a little more notice.

From photographs, this hotel, which looks to be literally on the beach, appears quite charming. There are 26 bedrooms and 4 suites, and, as well as all the normal facilities associated with seaside holidays, there is also a heated swimming-pool and a private tennis court.

The restaurant enjoys a very good reputation, and in 1988 there was a menu at F170 as well as one at F350, and a wide selection of *à la carte* dishes.

The Hôtel de la Plage looks an ideal base for a seaside holiday, or for exploring the western tip of Brittany with its countless bays, inlets, islands and beaches.

MANOIR DE LAN-KERELLEC, Trebeurden
Tel: 96.23.50.09

The Manoir de Lan-Kerellec at Trebeurden on the north Brittany coast enjoys one of the most spectacular sea views I have seen from a hotel. The manoir sits high on a wooded slope, overlooking the harbour and a beautiful bay studded with rocky islets, on the largest of which the hotel stages beach picnics in fine weather.

The house was originally the home of the present owner, Gilles Daubé's grandfather, and Gilles remembers huge family gatherings there in his youth. The dining-room is lovely, an almost circular room, panelled in warm timber, with a ceiling like an inverted ship's hull, and, indeed, a large model of a sailing-ship hangs suspended from the centre of the roof-beams. Large windows give stunning views over the bay. The floral chintz curtains, the warm rusty-pink carpet, the tablecloths and chair-coverings, as well as the lovely flower arrangements all blend together perfectly. The décor and the flowers are the province of Luce Daubé, the proprietor's wife, and we were sad to miss her, as we were sure from her taste that she must be a delightful person.

M. Daubé is full of smiling Breton charm, and proposed a light menu that would not overwhelm us. It was wonderful, presented with the same artistry and flair that imbues the whole place. The now ubiquitous Amuse-bouches were delicate and original – tiny spinach tarts, mussels wrapped in aubergine in an olive-oil dressing, and tiny pots of vegetables in a light herb sauce. The serious business began with light-as-a-feather raviolis in a delicate Sauce d'Homard, with whole chunks of lobster in the sauce; this was followed by Saint Pierre, which is I think a fish called John Dory in English, served in a light sauce of white wine and cream, on a bed of spring onions, the whole garnished with winkles – a

triumph. We then had hot goat's cheese with lettuce and walnut salad, and finished off with a succulent nougatine in a strawberry coulis.

Before we left, M. Daubé showed us the light and comfortable salon, decorated in white, with a white carpet and Persian rugs. There is a great stone fireplace, and clever use has been made of large gilt looking-glasses – again a mass of flowers, and Madame's perfect sense of colour.

There are 14 bedrooms and 1 suite, and every one is different. All are lovely, light and airy, with the same professional use of colour and fabrics. It is hard to imagine a more delightful place to spend a seaside holiday.

CHÂTEAU HÔTEL DE COATGUELEN, Pléhédel
Tel: 96.22.31.24

Situated on the north coast of Brittany, the Château Hôtel de Coatguelen is on the inland road from Paimpol to Saint Brieuc, about 5 kilometres south of Paimpol and within easy reach of one of the most beautiful coastlines in France, or anywhere for that matter.

Coatguelen is a rose-pink eighteenth-century château, with a large round tower, and steeply pitched slate roofs. The former home of the Marquis de Boisgelin, who now lives in the nearby manor-house, the château sits in a 100-hectare park, much of which is taken up by an 18-hole golf course; other sporting facilities include riding, tennis, swimming, ping-pong – and a sandpit for smaller athletes.

The welcome from Mme Le Roy, wife of the chef/manager Louis, is warm and full of enthusiasm. Throughout, the decoration has been carried out with care and taste, and good use has been made of colour and fabrics in public and private rooms alike. Coatguelen is another in the Relais & Château organisation whose bedrooms feel more like guest rooms in a private country house than hotel rooms. There are the most lovely flower arrangements everywhere, a daily task of Madame Le Roy, which takes her a solid two hours every morning.

Downstairs there is a comfortable bar in the round, stone-flagged base of the tower. The walls are covered in a warm, rust-coloured, corduroy-type material which, on the occasion of our visit, were hung with an exhibition of paintings of the 'naive' school; they were bright and colourful, and I would have been very happy to have owned several of them.

The very pretty dining-room leads off the bar, and occupies the entire ground floor of one wing of the castle, commanding beautiful views of the park and golf-course on one side, and of the terrace and swimming-pool on the other. Fresh flowers, good glass and monogrammed white Limoges china look elegant on the pale green tablecloths. M. Le Roy is a master-chef, with two books to his credit, *La Cuisine Bretonne d'Aujourd'hui* and *La Cuisine Tonique*. His food is stunning. We left the choice of menu to him; this started with an Amuse-bouche of a fresh sardine, nestling in a puff-pastry case shaped to the fish. This was followed by one of his specialities, sea-bass in a light, creamy sauce with fresh Girolles – wild mushrooms. A second fish-course came next, Emince d'Homard – lobster in a lightly curry-flavoured sauce, served with spinach and carrots. The meat course was breast of duck with sesame seed, surrounded by a colourful and delicious variety of fresh fruit slices –

kiwi, orange, watermelon, strawberry and pineapple – an unusually good marriage of colours, tastes and flavours; the duck-legs were then served as a separate course, plain roast and nicely crisp, with a green salad. The cheese selection was quite limited, but very good and mostly local, served on a flat basket, and nestling on vine leaves. Finally we reached the dessert, which consisted of a number of tiny helpings of different things like kiwi-fruit mousse, nougatine and miniature chocolate mousses, each with its own individual sauce. To complement this mini-banquet we drank a good Sancerre, Clos du Chêne Marchand 1987 with the fish and followed with a Bourgueil, Grand Clos 1985 from the house of Audebert.

Monsieur Le Roy took coffee and digestifs with us afterwards, and told us of the cooking courses he plans to offer in the low-season months. He will accept a minimum of four people, and the cost of F1,000 per day includes tuition, breakfast, lunch, dinner and wine as well as accommodation; each day starts with a trip to the market to learn how to buy the basic ingredients. It sounds like very good value.

GLOSSARY

FRENCH WORDS AND TECHNICAL TERMS

AC, AOC Appellation Contrôlée, Appellation d'Origine Contrôlée – the French legislative system by which the naming and production of wine is controlled.

adhérent member (of a co-operative).

ampelology the study of the vine.

andouillette a kind of sausage, rather like an English faggot.

appellation the name of a wine, the area in which it is grown, as defined by the INAO (q.v.).

arrière-saison late summer, early autumn.

assemblage the blending of different vats of wine.

auberge an inn.

bentonite a colloidal substance, used for clarifying or fining a wine.

bibliothèque library

boisé woody.

bonbon anglais literally 'English sweet', refers to the smell of acid drops.

boîte a kiosk.

bon rapport qualité prix good value for money.

Botrytis cyneria Latin name of the 'noble rot', essential for the making of really fine sweet white wine.

bottle-sick a condition affecting wine adversely just after bottling, from which it soon recovers.

bouchet another name for the Cabernet Franc grape variety.

brut very dry (of sparkling wine).

Cabernet Franc black grape variety, widely used in the Loire for quality red wine.

Cabernet Sauvignon black grape variety, less common in the Loire, but the classic grape of the Médoc.

cailloté pebbly.

canton an old French word for *département* or administrative area.

cassis blackcurrant.

casse-croûte literally 'break-crust', a light meal or snack.

cave cellar.

caviste cellarman.

cépage grape variety.

chambre d'hôte bed and breakfast

chasse shooting.

Chasselas white grape variety, used in Pouilly-sur-Loire.

châtaigne chestnut, a wood used traditionally for casks on the Loire.

châtelain(e) proprietor, proprietress of a château.

Chardonnay white grape variety, classic of burgundy, gaining ground in the Loire.

Chenin Blanc white grape variety, used in Vouvray, Montlouis, Coteaux du Layon, Savennières, and all over the Loire in varying proportions.

clos a walled vineyard

commune parish

Cot black grape variety, elsewhere known as the Malbec.

coteaux slopes

coterie band or set (of people).

coulure failure of the infant berries due to bad weather at the time of the flowering.

crémant sparkling.

cuve vat.

cuvée a blend

cuverie vat-house.

cuvaison period of fermentation and skin contact in vat.

cubitainer, cubi container for buying wine in bulk, usually 5 or 10 litres capacity.

déclaration de recolte obligatory return of wine produced each vintage by the growers.

débourbage clarification of wine in vat by running it off the lees.

dégorgement expulsion of dead yeast-cells caused by second fermentation in bottle of sparkling wine.

dégustation tasting.

demi-muid wooden cask of 600 litres.

demi-sec medium dry.

département administrative area or county.

domaine estate.

donjon keep or tower of a castle.

dosage the addition of sugared wine to a sparkling wine at *dégorgement.*

doux sweet.

élevage the care of an adolescent wine.

en brosse hair in crew-cut.

en vrac in bulk.

encépagement the types of grape planted in a vineyard.

épicerie fine high-class grocery.

eutypiose a disease of the vine, particularly affecting the Sauvignon.

fête feast or party.

fine to clarify a wine by means of a colloidal agent, e.g. egg-whites for red wine, bentonite for white.

foire a fair.

Folle Blanche white grape variety, used for Gros Plant.

foudre large wooden cask.

friture a 'fry-up' of tiny river fish, not unlike whitebait.

fût large wooden cask.

Gamay black grape variety, widely used for young and fruity red wines and rosés, the native grape of the Beaujolais.

goût de terroir taste of the earth.

grande carotte practical joke.

graviers gravelly soil.

gris a light rosé wine.

Groslot, Grolleau black grape variety, much used for rosé in the Loire.

gueule de bois hangover

INAO Institut National des Appellations d'Origine, the government body controlling the naming and production of French wines.

jeune loup literally 'young wolf', one who runs outside the pack, a rebel.

Kieselguhr type of filter.

lieux-dit place name.
liquoreux sweet, rich.

macération carbonique vinification process involving fermentation under CO_2, suited to fruity young wines like Gamays.
maderised condition of wine, usually due to oxidation, when the colour turns brown, and the nose and taste cooked and tired.
malo-lactic fermentation fermentation following the alcoholic fermentation, in which malic acid converts to lactic acid and carbon dioxide; it is desirable for this to occur in vat or cask in a red wine, as it results in a reduction in acid strength.
magnum large bottle of 1.5 litre capacity.
Malbec black grape variety, known in the Loire as the Cot.
Malvoisie white grape variety, used in the Coteaux d'Ancenis.
Melon de Bourgogne white grape variety, the only one used for Muscadet.
méthode champenoise the Champagne method of making sparkling wine, involving second fermentation in bottle, *dégorgement* and *dosage*.
moelleux sweet wine.
mousse the bubbles in sparkling wine.
mosseux sparkling.
must unfermented grape juice.

négociant mechant.
noble rot *Botrytis cyneria* to give the Latin name, or *pourriture noble*, the rot that shrivels the grapes, concentrating sugars and flavour to such an extraordinary degree, and without which no really great *vin liquoreux* can be made.

oenologist a qualified wine chemist.
oenology the study of wine.
oxidation the action of oxygen on a wine.

Phylloxera vastatrix the Latin name of a root-eating beetle that ravaged the vineyards of Europe in the late nineteenth century; grafting on to resistant American root-stocks was found to be the only answer.
pastis aniseed-based apéritif.
pépiniériste seedsman or nurseryman.
pierre-à-fusil gunflint.
pétillant lightly sparkling.
pigeage, système de an automatic system for breaking the 'cap' of a wine in vat by hydraulic rams during the fermentation process, invented by the celebrated oenologist, Jacques Puisais.
Pineau d'Aunis black grape variety used much for making rosé.
Pineau de la Loire another name for the Chenin Blanc grape.
Pinot Noir the classic black grape of Burgundy, also used in Sancerre, and, to a lesser extent, throughout the Loire.
pompe à chaleur heat exchange pump, for cooling or heating the must during the fermentation process.
polyculteur a farmer who is engaged in many different forms of agriculture.

pourriture noble see 'noble rot'
pourriture grise rot caused by excessive moisture, harmful to the grape.
pressoir the press-house.
premier cru a 'first growth', the highest classification given in the 1855 Classification of Bordeaux wines.
pupitre the two-sided, hinged, sloping 'desk', in which there are holes for bottles of sparkling wine to undergo the *remuage* part of the *méthode champenoise*.
rack to transfer the wine off its lees to a clean cask.
régisseur manager, foreman.
remuage the process in the *méthode champenoise*, wherein the bottles are gradually twisted from the horizontal to the near-vertical, cork downwards position, causing the dead yeast cells to slide down and rest on the cork or crown-cap, until they are expelled by opening the bottle, the process known as the *dégorgement*.
rendement yield.
rillons chunks of cooked pork, a Loire speciality.
rillettes a sort of pâté made of shredded pork or goose.
Romorantin a white grape variety, said to have been introduced into eastern Touraine by King François I.

sables sandy soil.
Sancerrois belonging to Sancerre, a native of Sancerre.
Sauvignon white grape variety, used exclusively in Sancerre, Pouilly Fumé, and the eastern Loire, and to a lesser extent throughout the Loire.
sec dry.
SICA Société d'Intérêt Co-opérative Agricole, a co-operative farming group.
sur-plaques a filtration system.
sur lie on the lees, referring to a bottling and vinification process adopted in the Pays Nantais.

tartine a slice of bread, spread with butter, cheese, etc.
tastevin silver tasting cup, much used in Burgundy.
terres blanches literally 'white lands', clay, limestone soil on the hilltops, giving a wine a great finesse in the Sancerrois.
TGV Train à Grande Vitesse.
tonneau a cask of large capacity; in Bordeaux a measure of bulk wine equivalent to 100 cases of 12 x 75 cl bottles.
tri literally 'a sorting-out', refers to successive passes through the vineyard by the pickers to select only the super-ripe grapes necessary for making *vin liquoreux*.
troglodyte cave-dwelling.
tuff volcanic, chalky rock.

VDQS Vin Délimité de Qualité Supérieure, a category of wine just below Appellation Contrôlée.
vente directe a sign outside a wine-maker's premises, denoting that he sells direct to the public.
vendangeur a grape-picker
vigneron a winemaker, vineyard worker.
vignoble vineyard.
vin de base the base wine used for sparkling wine.
vin de mode a fashionable wine.
vin liquoreux sweet wine.
vin tranquille still wine.
vin de garde a wine to keep, or lay down for a long time.
viticulteur a cultivator of vines.

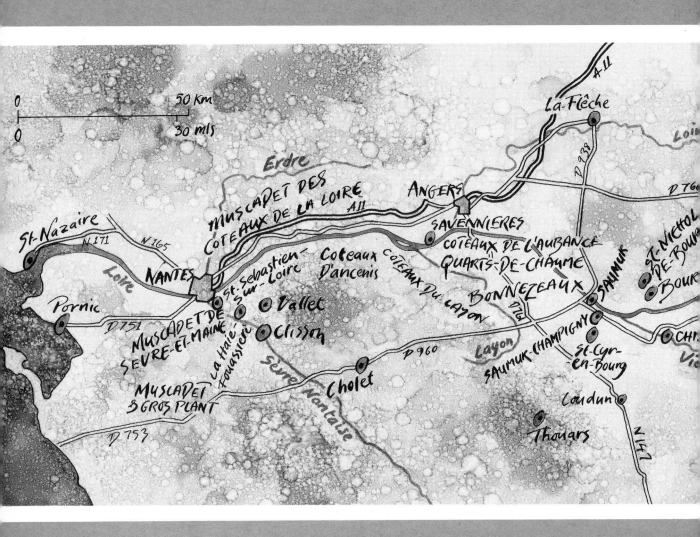